Studies in Regional and Local History

General Editor Nigel Goose

D1451901

Previous titles in this series

Volume 1: *A Hertfordshire Demesne of Westminster Abbey: Profits, productivity and weather* by Derek Vincent Stern (edited and with an introduction by Christopher Thornton)

Volume 2: *From Hellgill to Bridge End: Aspects of economic and social change in the Upper Eden Valley, 1840–95* by Margaret Shepherd

Volume 3: *Cambridge and its Economic Region, 1450–1560* by John S. Lee

Volume 4: *Cultural Transition in the Chilterns and Essex Region, 350 AD to 650 AD* by John T. Baker

Volume 5: *A Pleasing Prospect: Society and culture in eighteenth-century Colchester* by Shani D'Cruze

Volume 6: *Agriculture and Rural Society after the Black Death: Common themes and regional variations* by Ben Dodds and Richard Britnell

Volume 7: *A Lost Frontier Revealed: Regional separation in the East Midlands* by Alan Fox

Volume 8: *Land and Family: Trends and local variations in the peasant land market on the Winchester bishopric estates, 1263–1415* by John Mullan and Richard Britnell

Volume 9: *Out of the Hay and into the Hops: Hop cultivation in Wealden Kent and hop marketing in Southwark, 1744–2000* by Celia Cordle

Volume 10: *A Prospering Society: Wiltshire in the later Middle Ages* by John Hare

Volume 11: *Bread and Ale for the Brethren: The provisioning of Norwich Cathedral Priory, 1260–1536* by Philip Slavin

Poor Relief and Community in Hadleigh, Suffolk, 1547–1600

Marjorie Keniston McIntosh

University of Hertfordshire Press
Studies in Regional and Local History

Volume 12

First published in Great Britain in 2013 by
University of Hertfordshire Press
College Lane
Hatfield
Hertfordshire
AL10 9AB
UK

British Library Cataloguing in Publication Data
A catalogue record for this book is available from the British Library

ISBN 978-1-907396-91-5 hardback
ISBN 978-1-907396-92-2 paperback

Design by Mathew Lyons
Printed in Great Britain by Henry Ling Ltd

For J.R.M.
Ut in principio, sic in fine

Publication grant

Publication has been made possible by a generous grant from the Marc Fitch Fund

Contents

Figures

Tables

Appendices

Acknowledgements and conventions

In undertaking this project, which has spanned nearly 30 years, I have received generous assistance from Hadleigh's archivists and historians, people with an impressive knowledge of their own community and its records.[1] I am deeply indebted to three Hadleigh town archivists for their assistance in working with the remarkable manuscripts in their care and for helping me to understand them. W.A.B. Jones gave me regular access to the documents in the spring of 1984 and the summer of 1990 and encouraged my interest in the town's history through his book, *Hadleigh through the ages*, and our many conversations over lunch in his kitchen.[2] He also gave me a copy of his fuller typescript for that book, called 'Hadleigh: a Viking royal town'. After Mr Jones' death, Cyril Cook kindly assisted my research in 1991. To Sue Andrews I owe particular thanks. Much of the background for this study is informed by the excellent chapters on the town's history that she wrote for her book with Tony Springall, *Hadleigh and the Alabaster family: the story of a Suffolk town during the Tudor and Stuart periods*.[3] Sue has also been unfailingly helpful in our conversations and correspondence, drawing upon her rich depth of knowledge to answer my questions. She modified a draft of Figure 1.1 and commented on a draft of Chapters 1 and 6, catching some errors and adding further information. Dr Springall kindly gave me permission to use the map of Hadleigh that he prepared for their volume (Appendix I, p. 331) as the basis for my Figures 1.2 and 6.1; he and Sue sent scans and photos of possible cover illustrations.[4] Hadleigh is indeed fortunate to have been served by such competent archivists, fine historians and generous colleagues.

I am grateful to others as well. As described more fully in Appendix Intro.3, much of the initial computer work was done in 1986–8 by two exceptionally able undergraduates, Carin Corbett Bentley and Elspeth McIntosh Dusinberre. In the early 1990s John Craig (now at Simon Fraser University) and I divided up the process of taking notes on wills from Elizabethan Hadleigh, using shared headings and definitions. The late Peter Northeast kindly gave me copies of his detailed notes on Hadleigh wills prior to 1540. Lyn Boothman, who is currently doing a PhD thesis at Cambridge University on Long Melford, 1560–1861, generously sent me copies of her

---

1. For my earlier essays on Hadleigh, see Marjorie K. McIntosh, 'Networks of care in Elizabethan English towns: the example of Hadleigh, Suffolk', in Horden and Smith (eds), *The locus of care*, pp. 71–89, and 'Poverty, charity, and coercion in Elizabethan England', *Journal of Interdisciplinary History*, 35 (2005), pp. 457–79.

2. Ipswich, 1977.

3. Privately published by Sue Andrews, Bildeston, 2005. The chapters that deal with Hadleigh's private benefactions stem from Andrews' MA thesis, 'The charitable response to poverty during the late medieval and early modern periods in the local context of Hadleigh, Suffolk' (University of Essex, 2000).

4. William Bredeman, a PhD student in Geography at the University of Colorado, did most of the map work.

notes on the Melford wills from 1530 to 1600 and commented on those sections of the book that deal with her area of expertise. Richard M. Smith, who has encouraged my interest in demography and social history for many years, offered valuable suggestions on the full text. Nigel Goose, the editor of this series, and Jane Housham of the University of Hertfordshire Press provided useful guidance along the way. My research and writing were supported by fellowships from the National Endowment for the Humanities and Newnham College, Cambridge, in 1983/4; a Faculty Fellowship from the University of Colorado at Boulder in 1990/91; and Distinguished Professor research grants from the University of Colorado in 2011–13. I greatly appreciate all of this assistance.

Several conventions are used below. All money is recorded in the form used at the time, in which 12 pence (d) = 1 shilling (s), and 20 shillings = 1 pound (£). Dates are given in accordance with the system used in England at the time, which differed from the one used on the continent, but I have converted entries for a given year to run from 1 January to 31 December, not from Lady Day (25 March) to Lady Day as was done at the time. Thus, a date shown in the records as 15 February 1579 is noted here as 15 February 1580. Tables and Appendices drawn from the poor relief accounts do not list their sources, which are described in detail in the References. Wills from The National Archives (Public Record Office) cited as PROB 11 followed by a single number were used through digitised copies and are identified further by the name of the testator and date. I have modernised the spellings of place names, personal first names and information from local manuscript sources, but kept the spellings of direct quotations from contemporary petitions and printed works. When a second reference is provided at the end of a footnote with the wording, 'For below, see ...,' it refers to the following sentence in the text.

Boulder, Colorado
August 2012

Studies in Regional and Local History

General Editor's preface

It gives me the greatest pleasure to introduce Marjorie Keniston McIntosh's *Poor Relief and Community in Hadleigh, Suffolk, 1547–1600* as Volume 12 of Studies in Regional and Local History. Professor McIntosh is without doubt one of the foremost social and cultural historians of her generation, and has done so much to advance the cause of later medieval and early modern English history. Her *Controlling Misbehavior in England, 1370–1600* (Cambridge University Press, 1998) was a truly pathbreaking study, and one that was honoured by the devotion of a special edition of the *Journal of British Studies* (Volume 37, 1998) to that book. She has also published extensively on women's work, both in late medieval and early modern England and in twentieth-century Africa. The present volume is a micro-history, and in that sense echoes Professor McIntosh's previous work on the Manor and Liberty of Havering, which produced two full-length studies: *Autonomy and Community: The Royal Manor of Havering, 1200–1500* (Cambridge University Press, 1986) and *A Community Transformed: The Manor and Liberty of Havering, 1500–1620* (Cambridge University Press, 1991). But Marjorie McIntosh is one of those rare historians who have the capacity to produce broad general studies as well as micro-histories, as witnessed by the recent publication of her *Poor Relief in England, 1350–1600* (Cambridge University Press, 2012).

The present study reflects Professor McIntosh's long-standing interest in the history of social welfare: indeed, the present project, she tells us, has been in progress for nearly 30 years. The book describes how Hadleigh, a small town in Suffolk of some 2,400–3,300 inhabitants, responded to the needs of its poor inhabitants in the second half of the sixteenth century, a period which saw significant population growth and inflation on a national scale, accompanied by increasingly acute poverty problems, punctuated by crises such as that ushered in by four consecutive poor harvests between 1594 and 1597. While it was the larger incorporated towns that introduced some of the earliest and most comprehensive poor relief schemes in England, often ahead of national legislation requiring them so to do, by the 1590s this small Suffolk cloth town was running the most sophisticated social welfare programme offered by any English community of its size. Hadleigh's social welfare officers, moved by Christian concerns as well as the need to impose order on the community, struggled to provide for the elderly, for children as well as for the labouring poor.

Despite the employment of both formal mechanisms of social welfare and private philanthropy, they were never entirely successful, notwithstanding the efficient operation of the complex networks of care they had established. The problem of poverty remained, while the changing economic context had a powerful influence too, for the town's staple textile industry went into severe decline around 1600, amplifying the need of those who were poorly paid or under-employed. By the end of the second decade of the seventeenth century this ancient clothing town was reportedly filled with 'an extraordinary abundance of poverty', while those on relief continued to constitute perhaps 15 per cent of the town's population at mid-century. While this was a society held together by a shared belief in the need for social welfare, which helped to validate the town's social and political structure, this was also a society severely divided in its distribution of wealth. A local sermon quoted by Professor McIntosh alleged that whereas some clothiers were worth £20,000 at the time of their death, a workman who had been employed by them for 20 years might die with nothing more than 20 groats (6s 8d). 'Social polarisation' is an epithet now commonly employed to describe the progress of early modern English society, and while it hardly tells the whole story, its general validity can be seen at national level, but much more sharply in the context of a detailed local study such as that so elegantly and persuasively provided here.

Nigel Goose
October 2012

Abbreviations

A&S, *Hadleigh*	Sue Andrews and Tony Springall, *Hadleigh and the Alabaster family: the story of a Suffolk town during the Tudor and Stuart periods* (privately printed, Bildeston, 2005)
APC	*Acts of the Privy Council of England, 1542–1604,* ed. J.R. Dasent, 32 vols (London, 1890–1907)
BRO	Bedfordshire Record Office
CCA	Canterbury Cathedral Archives
ERO	Essex Record Office, Chelmsford
HadlA	Hadleigh Archive, kept in the Guildhall–Town Hall complex
JP	Justice of the Peace
L&P	*Calendar of letters and papers, foreign and domestic, of the reign of Henry VIII,* 22 vols in 37 parts (London, 1864–1932)
LPL	Lambeth Palace Library
SR	*Statutes of the realm,* 12 vols (London, 1810–28)
SRO-BSE	Suffolk Record Office, Bury St Edmunds branch
SRO-I	Suffolk Record Office, Ipswich branch
TNA PRO	The National Archives, Public Record Office, Kew
Jones, *Hadleigh*	W.A.B. Jones, *Hadleigh through the ages* (Ipswich, 1977)
Jones, 'Hadleigh'	W.A.B. Jones, typescript of 'Hadleigh: A Viking royal town' (a longer but unpublished version of his *Hadleigh through the ages*)

Introduction

England faced severe problems with poverty during the middle and later years of the sixteenth century. Population growth that outpaced economic expansion left more people in need.[1] During the 1520s, 1530s and 1540s, bad harvests, heavy taxation, changes in the value of money and the closure of monasteries and many hospitals contributed to a growing number of the poor. Indigent people who left home seeking better opportunities elsewhere heightened fears of vagrancy and begging among local and national leaders. In the reign of Edward VI the central government set up a system of parish-based assistance. A statute of 1552 (modified slightly in 1563) required parishes to collect aid from their more prosperous members to provide help for those who could not support themselves. Although the concerns of civic humanism and early Protestantism promoted this approach, all Christian churches of whatever doctrinal position advocated charity to the poor both before and after the Reformation. During the second half of the sixteenth century some of England's towns and cities experimented with their own forms of relief. But local assistance found it increasingly difficult to keep up with demand, especially because rapid inflation was not matched by an equivalent rise in wages, squeezing those who worked for pay. The 1590s experienced crisis conditions due to a series of crop failures and resulting high food prices. In 1598 and 1601 Parliament – fearing desperation among the poor and serious unrest – passed omnibus sets of laws that intensified and extended the provisions for collecting and distributing poor rates within parishes and addressed a number of other problems with earlier forms of aid. Those statutes initiated the period commonly known as the Old Poor Law, which continued until 1834.

This book describes how Hadleigh, Suffolk, a small town lying nine miles west of Ipswich, responded to the needs of its poor residents between 1547 and 1600 (see Figure Intro.1). In that period, the leaders of this cloth-manufacturing centre developed and operated an exceptionally comprehensive and expensive system of poor relief for some of its 2,400–3,300 inhabitants. By the 1590s they were running the most complex array of help offered by any English town, one that we may still admire today.[2] Hadleigh's economy was dominated by its wealthy clothiers, middling-scale entrepreneurs who organised and financed the various steps necessary to the production of heavy woollen broadcloths. They hired and paid the carders, spinners, weavers and finishers and then sent many of their cloths to London or Ipswich for export to the continent. Clothiers also held political power within the town, serving as the Chief Inhabitants who made decisions about a wide array of urban matters. They also chose officers for the town and its market, the administration of poor relief and

---

1. For fuller discussion of these general developments, see Marjorie Keniston McIntosh, *Poor relief in England, 1350–1600* (Cambridge, 2012), pp. 15–25.

2. An assessment based upon my use of all surviving poor relief records from this period throughout England.

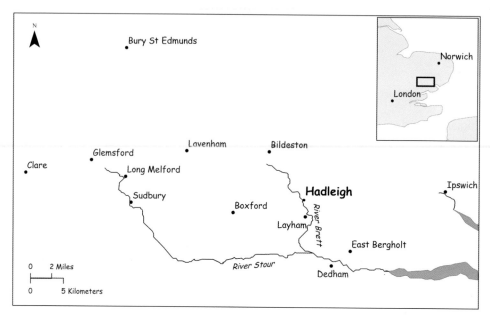

Figure Intro.1 Hadleigh and neighbouring communities.

even the parish. Attitudes towards charitable assistance in Hadleigh were influenced by the preaching of its early Protestant rector, who argued that a primary obligation of a Christian community was to attend to the needs of the poor. The prosperity of the clothiers coupled with the poverty of many of their workers, the authority and concerns of the Chief Inhabitants, and the Christian charitable message were among the factors that contributed to Hadleigh's willingness to offer aid to many needy people.[3]

Hadleigh's system of relief, providing individual assistance to at least 603 residents between 1579 and 1596, included multiple components. Most of the help was given to people living in their own homes. The largest group, people who were poor but could usually manage on their own earnings, received aid only occasionally, in the form of cloth, clothing, fuel or cash. Others were supported during periods of special need – such as an illness – or only after death, if their families could not pay for a decent burial. A smaller set of poor or disabled people received regular weekly payments at a level dependent upon their ability to earn part of what they needed to survive. Boarding formed a different type of aid, in which a person needing help would be cared for by another household, with expenses met by local officers. This approach was used especially for young orphans and children from troubled poor families, but also sometimes for adults temporarily unable to look after themselves owing to illness or injury. More than half of those who boarded others were themselves recipients of poor relief: the town's assistance thus filled two social needs at the same time. A third form of relief involved entering a residential institution. The town operated two sets of almshouses, endowed with land by charitable benefactors, in which 32 elderly poor

---

3.   See Chapter 6 below.

lived rent-free while receiving a weekly cash allowance plus firewood and occasional gifts of household goods. Certainly by 1589, and possibly as early as 1574, Hadleigh was running an institution that was sometimes termed a hospital but was more accurately labelled a workhouse. It provided residential care, a disciplined setting for labour, training in basic skills (preparing woollen thread and knitting stockings) and in some cases punishment for the 30 poor children and idle young people sent to it. The town also paid to have orphans placed with another family and arranged positions for slightly older children as servants or apprentices, as well as opening public employment to needy men and women.

Hadleigh assisted an unusually large percentage of its residents for an Elizabethan urban community. During three years between 1582 and 1594 for which we have complete accounts, 111 to 149 people received individual relief annually (see Table Intro.1). Four to five per cent of the town's estimated residents were thus helped directly, and many of them presumably shared their benefits with other family members.[4] Paul Slack has suggested that one should double the number of direct recipients to obtain an approximate figure for all the people being assisted. The resulting fraction of 8–10 per cent getting aid in Hadleigh was considerably higher than the adjusted values seen in five somewhat smaller Elizabethan towns and in the cities of Exeter and Norwich, though lower than the fraction relieved in a poverty-stricken parish in Warwick.[5] If we think in terms of households, at least one member of 91 to 110 domestic units was helped annually in Hadleigh between 1582 and 1594; those households constituted 14–15 per cent of the town's estimated 660–780 units.[6] Further, the average weekly payment of 3.6d per recipient in Hadleigh was well above the 2.2d awarded in the five comparable towns though below the 4.6d in seven cities. As well as administering residential institutions for the poor, Hadleigh's Chief Inhabitants were also helping a wider range of people than was true elsewhere. Most interesting was the town's willingness to assist illegitimate children, youngsters from dysfunctional families and some married adults of working age.

---

4. The fraction would be even higher if one added some of the young inmates of the workhouse, which provided a form of poor relief for some of its residents. Just over half of its roughly 30 inhabitants at any one time were needy children and teens who had not been awarded other forms of public assistance but were given temporary housing, food and clothing while receiving occupational training (see Chapter 4, 'Training and discipline in the workhouse', below). For below, see Paul Slack, *Poverty and policy in Tudor and Stuart England* (London, 1988), p. 174.

5. The combined average in the five smaller towns was 5.6 per cent (Marjorie K. McIntosh, 'Poor relief in Elizabethan communities', forthcoming, for Bishop's Stortford, Herts., Melton Mowbray, Leics., Framlingham, Suffolk, Wivenhoe, Essex, and Faversham, Kent, market centres or ports with estimated populations of 500 to 2,000 residents). Exeter's adjusted figure was 4.2 per cent in 1563 and Norwich's was 2.6 in 1578–9 (Slack, *Poverty and policy*, p. 177). St Mary's parish in Warwick assisted 7.4 per cent in 1582 (A.L. Beier, 'Poverty and progress in early modern England', in Beier, Cannadine, and Rosenheim (eds), *The first modern society*, pp. 201–39, esp. p. 207).

6. In St Mary's, Warwick, 11 per cent of the 373 families received relief in 1582, and another 18 per cent were "ready to decay into poverty" (A.L. Beier, 'The social problems of an Elizabethan country town: Warwick, 1580–90', in Clark (ed.), *Country towns in pre-industrial England*, pp. 46–85). Warwick had about 2,000 residents in 1563 and 2,500 in 1586. For below, see McIntosh, 'Poor relief in Elizabethan communities'.

Table Intro.1

Recipients of relief and payers of poor rates as percentage of the population for six years with full or nearly full accounts.

Year	Years with entirely full accounts^	Total estimated population of town*	Estimated no. of households#	Recipients (excluding inmates of the workhouse)				Rate payers		
				No. of individual recipients	% of total estimated population	No. of households containing recipients	% of all estimated households	No. of individual payers	% of total estimated population	% of all estimated household heads
1579		3,083	734	91	3	78	11	165	5	22
1582	X	3,279	781	149	5	110	14	157	5	20
1585		3,253	775	93	3	77	10	195	6	25
1590		2,778	661	101	4	85	13	128	5	19
1591	X	2,778	661	126	5	100	15	127	5	19
1594	X	2,778	661	111	4	91	14	122	4	18

Notes:
^ For the records that survive for each year, see App. Intro.2.
* For the total estimated population, calculated by quinquennia, see App. 1.1.
# The estimated number of households was derived by dividing the total estimated population by 4.2 for the number of people per household. That figure was used, not 4.5, because of the sizeable number of poor (and hence almost certainly smaller) households in Hadleigh. For discussion of household sizes and the impact of poverty in other small towns, with references, see McIntosh, *A community transformed*, p. 42.

This complex system was expensive to run. During the 1580s the average total disbursed annually to poor people and the almshouses was £94; between 1590 and 1596, when need intensified owing to high grain prices and when the workhouse was also in operation, the average rose to £140 per year.[7] To pay for the forms of aid Hadleigh's Chief Inhabitants were able to draw upon multiple sources of income: rents from endowed properties they held in effect as charitable trustees for the poor; current gifts and bequests, some distributed over a period of years or set up in perpetuity; and poor rates, compulsory local taxes. Rates were imposed each year on 122 to 195 people, the heads of the town's most economically comfortable households; some paid by the week, others by the quarter. The people assessed for rates formed 18–25 per cent of all household heads, and their payments supplied around a quarter of the total amount disbursed annually to poor people, the almshouses and the workhouse.[8] (In most English communities, the costs of whatever poor relief was undertaken had to depend far more heavily upon taxation, as they lacked the sizeable landed endowment expressly for the poor that Hadleigh enjoyed.) Poor relief officials did not insist that extended families assume sole responsibility for their own poorer members: a third of the recipients of relief had local relatives who were prosperous enough to be assessed for rates. The assistance provided by the town was supplemented by private gifts and bequests, and it reinforced the informal help provided by friends and neighbours.

While Hadleigh was thus unusually responsive to the needs of the poor, its Chief Inhabitants were also concerned about idleness, vagrancy and the cost of relief. From the mid 1570s they worked to maintain good order and prevent needy immigrants from settling in the community; they named responsible local residents to monitor their neighbourhoods, drawing to public attention any troublemakers and poor new arrivals. In the 1590s the town's workhouse had a dual function: not only did it take in children and teenagers for training but its master was required to accept people picked up on the street as idlers and vagrants. He was to force all the residents to work, punishing them if they did not; the town purchased locks and chains for a few recalcitrant inmates in their late teens and early 20s. The Chief Inhabitants were also prepared to spend money on expelling poor people from Hadleigh before they had lived there long enough to qualify for relief, and they demanded bonds to ensure that children born in the town or newcomers to it would not become a charge on poor relief funds. Similar practices are documented in other communities.[9]

An intriguing feature of Hadleigh's system of poor relief is that it lacked legal authority. The statute of 1552 that initiated appointment of Collectors for the Poor and distribution of aid to the needy and the statute of 1563 that renewed and slightly expanded that measure said that the new approach was to be implemented in every parish or in those cities, boroughs and towns that had been formally incorporated.[10] The statutes placed responsibility for developing and supervising poor relief upon the minister and churchwardens of parishes or upon the mayor, bailiffs or other heads of

---

7. See App. Intro.1.

8. For comparative figures, see Chapter 2, note 61 below.

9. McIntosh, *Poor relief in England*, pp. 245–50.

10. 5 & 6 Edward VI, c. 2, and 5 Elizabeth, c. 3 (*SR*, vol. iv, pp. 131–2 and 411–14).

those civic bodies with corporate status. Because Hadleigh did not receive its charter of incorporation until 1618, Elizabethan poor relief should have been handled within the parish. The self-appointed and self-perpetuating Chief Inhabitants had no legal standing as governors of the town, yet there is no indication that Hadleigh's residents questioned their authority, even when they appointed poor relief officers and levied poor rates. Their own personal status and willingness to devote time and energy to the community's wellbeing apparently led to acceptance of their orders.

Hadleigh's experience illustrates many of the challenges and solutions seen in other early modern English communities as they addressed the issues of poverty.[11] While it was generally accepted that some kind of poor relief was necessary, on grounds of both Christian charity and practical expediency, Hadleigh did not provide assistance to people other than its own established residents. Further, although those people who were physically unable to labour were supported and some temporarily unemployed clothworkers were evidently helped, the Chief Inhabitants stopped short of offering generic assistance to the families of men who could not find work. People were encouraged to remain in their own homes as long as possible and to be part of familiar community patterns even when living in an almshouse. For those who needed short-term care, boarding at the town's expense filled the gaps in an older network of informal assistance generated throughout the community; provision of longer-term boarding ensured that orphans and certain children would receive ongoing care. Moreover, tax-based relief was seen as a supplement to the many forms of voluntary charity: the beneficence of wealthier families served to lessen the burden of obligatory rates. Although Parliamentary legislation played an enabling role in the sixteenth-century history of poor relief, Hadleigh's Chief Inhabitants operated almost entirely on their own as they struggled with how to implement genuine religious and social concern for the poor, how to maintain order and discipline within their community and how to do all this without unsustainable expense.

Not only was Hadleigh's approach to poor relief exceptionally ambitious, to the good fortune of historians it is also exceptionally well documented.[12] Especially valuable is the town's own archive, including detailed accounts of income and expenditures for poor relief in many years between 1579 and 1596.[13] The evidence is not, however, perfect: we have entirely full accounts only for 1582, 1591 and 1594, plus most of the accounts for three other years and partial information for the

---

11. See, more generally, McIntosh, *Poor relief in England*, esp. ch. 8, for this paragraph.

12. The Hadleigh Archive began in the early 1960s with two collections. (I am grateful to Sue Andrews, Hadleigh's current Town Archivist, for this information.) The first set of documents was found in the office of a local solicitor's firm when it closed down. Because the firm had been the collector for the town's charitable properties it had records going back to the thirteenth century. The second collection, unearthed under an old staircase in the Town Hall, contained borough records, 1618–85, and some earlier pieces. The documents were catalogued by W.A.B. Jones, then the headmaster of a local primary school, and Cyril Cook, the head of history at a secondary school; in 1974 the Hadleigh Town Council became responsible for the archive. The materials are now stored in the Archive Room in the Guildhall–Town Hall complex.

13. HadlA 021/A/02–06, 021/B/05–09, 021/C/01–08 and 021/D/01–04. Most of the accounts give an annual total for each recipient of regular weekly payments, but some are laid out by week or month. For below, see App. Intro.2.

remainder. All figures provided in this study for the number of people helped and the amount of aid given must therefore be regarded as minimal values. We learn more about those who received and administered relief from a fairly complete parish register of baptisms, marriages and burials from the late 1550s onwards.[14] Poor relief records may be supplemented by a thick book of town records, 100 sixteenth-century wills, some court cases and other material from central government sources and scattered information from the Canterbury Cathedral Archives.[15] Foxe's *Actes and monuments* and a surprising sermon delivered around 1600 highlight religious concerns. Our knowledge of Hadleigh's past has also benefited from the fine research and writing of two of its town archivists. W.A.B. Jones published in 1977 a short history of the town from the early medieval period through the nineteenth century.[16] His work has recently been augmented by an impressive study of the Tudor and Stuart periods prepared by Sue Andrews, the current town archivist, and Tony Springall, a historian of Hadleigh's Alabaster family.

This book offers a unique analysis of poor relief within a community context during the second half of the sixteenth century. For no other town in England can we trace in such detail a network of care, looking not only at who received and provided assistance but also at patterns of aid across a span of years and at how help was given to household units. It thus forms a counterpoint to my general study of poor relief in England, which traces patterns throughout the country over several centuries.[17] Although poor relief has not been studied in similar detail in any other Elizabethan community, we can set some of the quantified measures of Hadleigh's activity against the experience of other villages, small towns, and cities. For reasons of brevity and focus, this discussion deals only with charitable assistance to the poor, not with education or such projects as a revolving loan fund for tradesmen.[18]

The study is methodologically important, furnishing an example of what may be termed 'the new demographic history'. Whereas the first generation of computer-based studies of population and related events provided important factual information

---

14. SRO-I FB 81/D1/1, copied by kind permission of the Rector of Hadleigh.

15. The town book is HadlA 004/A/01. The wills are scattered between TNA PRO PROB 11, ERO D/ABW, LPL and a few copies in HadlA. The court cases come primarily from TNA PRO C1, C2, C3 and REQ 2, plus material from *L&P, APC*, State Papers Domestic and miscellaneous central government records.

16. W.A.B. Jones, *Hadleigh through the ages* (Ipswich, 1977), and see also his 'Hadleigh, a Viking royal town', typescript published in reduced form as *Hadleigh through the ages*. For below, see Sue Andrews and Tony Springall, *Hadleigh and the Alabaster family: the story of a Suffolk town during the Tudor and Stuart periods* (privately printed, Bildeston, Suffolk, 2005). Sue Andrews wrote the chapters on Hadleigh, Tony Springall the ones on the Alabasters. Henceforth A&S, *Hadleigh*.

17. McIntosh, *Poor relief in England*.

18. Hadleigh's Grammar School was in existence by 1382 and apparently continued to function at least on a small scale into the eighteenth century (A&S, *Hadleigh*, pp. 193–7). The town also had various kinds of informal primary education, and a non-classical elementary school was endowed in 1637 (HadlA 004/A/01, p. 125, a payment of 40s in 1578 by the churchwardens to 'little John Torner's wife for teaching the children', and A&S, *Hadleigh*, pp. 264–6). For loan funds, see A&S, *Hadleigh*, pp. 99 and 105.

about general patterns in early modern England, they were sometimes criticised on two grounds: for failing to represent individual human experiences, and for their limited ability to identify the causes of the patterns they documented. An in-depth case study based upon rich and diverse records can address both of these issues. For Hadleigh we can integrate quantitative material from poor relief accounts and the parish register, analysed after entry into computer databases, with narrative sources to trace the lives of specific residents.[19] Particularly significant is that we can go beneath the surface to explore not only *what* happened but also *why* people acted as they did: most notably, the concerns that motivated the leaders of this community to provide help for their needier neighbours.

The book begins with a description of Hadleigh in the sixteenth century, looking at its physical setting and population, economic life, religion and town government. With that picture as background, we turn to the system of relief, the men who administered it and how it was financed. The next three chapters focus on the people who received aid. Chapter 3 provides an account of the individuals and households that were helped, with a close look at 1582 as a sample year. Chapter 4 examines the care and training of poor children and teens, while Chapter 5 considers special provisions for ill, disabled and elderly people. The final chapter discusses the factors that influenced the creation and maintenance of this network of assistance and control, showing how they interacted cumulatively within the specific context of this town.

---

19. See App. Intro.3 for the quantitative methodologies used and App. 5.1 for some biographical examples.

Chapter 1

The context of poor relief in Hadleigh

To make sense of Hadleigh's system for dealing with the poor, we need to understand the setting within which it developed and functioned. This little town had an unusually interesting history during the mid and later sixteenth century. As well as being a successful cloth-manufacturing centre, it gained an early exposure to Protestant beliefs during the latter part of Henry VIII's reign and under Edward VI; its reformist rector and his curate were then burned at the stake under Mary. The town was run by a self-appointed group of 20–25 men who termed themselves the Chief Inhabitants, though they held no formal authority at all.

Hadleigh's physical setting and neighbourhoods

The parish or, as it was occasionally called, the 'township' of Hadleigh lay near the Stour valley of south-west Suffolk, some nine miles west of Ipswich and eight miles south-south-east of Bury St Edmunds.[1] Its 4,288 acres included the urban community in the centre, along the river Brett, plus agricultural land and a few scattered sub-settlements. The rural areas were devoted to mixed farming, with small enclosed fields used for raising grain and other arable crops intermingled with pasturage for animals, especially cows and pigs.[2] As was common in this region of Suffolk, Hadleigh did not have a single, dominant manorial landlord but was instead divided between multiple estates: three larger manors and two lesser ones, most of which held land in other parishes as well. Beginning in AD 991, the main manor of Hadleigh was held by Canterbury Cathedral Priory and after the Reformation by the Dean and Chapter of Canterbury; Toppesfield manor was held by a series of private owners.[3] The primary residences of those two estates were located on either side of the parish church in the centre of the town, and they divided urban properties and the river's corn (or grain) mills between them. The manor of Lafham, later known as Pond Hall, lay on the eastern side of Hadleigh and was acquired by the D'Oyley (Doyle) family in the fifteenth century.[4] The smaller manor of

---

1. See Fig. Intro.1.

2. A&S, *Hadleigh*, pp. 4–7, and Jones, *Hadleigh*, pp. 12–14, for this and the various estates. For below, see Mark Bailey, *Medieval Suffolk: an economic and social history, 1200–1500* (Woodbridge, 2007), pp. 27–34.

3. In May 1991, the author was honoured to give a talk in Hadleigh as part of a celebration of the 1,000th anniversary of the community's connection with Canterbury. Since her country (USA) had recently celebrated with considerable patriotism the 200th anniversary of its founding and her state (Colorado) its 100th anniversary, the contrast did reinforce awareness that white settlement in North America is still in its infancy!

4. That manor was authorised to create a deer park in the fourteenth century, which probably explains why the town never expanded in an easterly direction.

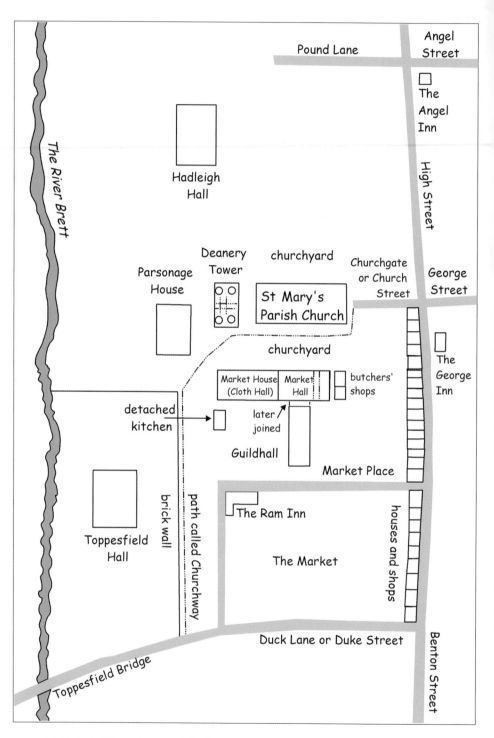

Figure 1.1 Major buildings in central Hadleigh, sixteenth century.

Cosford Hall, located to the north of Hadleigh, went with Pond Hall into the D'Oyley's hands, while the little manor of Mausers or Hadleighs was bought by the Timperleys of Hintlesham in the fifteenth century. Because lordship was so fragmented, manorial authority had relatively little impact and will receive scant mention in this study.

Hadleigh's urban core had evidently been laid out in the earlier medieval period as a regular gridwork of streets, though it did not develop fully.[5] Two primary bridges crossed the river on the edges of the town: Hadleigh Bridge to the north, and Toppesfield Bridge to the south. By the Elizabethan period the town's physical, religious, economic and social centre was situated in a cluster of buildings that lay to the west of what is now High Street, Hadleigh's main north–south thoroughfare, between Hadleigh Hall and Toppesfield Hall. As Figure 1.1 shows, that area contained the parish church (dedicated to St Mary) and cemetery, the parsonage house, the Deanery Tower and the marketplace with its associated buildings (the Market House, Market Hall and Guildhall).[6]

The religious buildings were the most impressive. Hadleigh's church had been enlarged in the Decorated architectural style during the fourteenth century, with only its tower remaining from the previous structure; at the peak of the town's prosperity in the fifteenth century parts of the church were rebuilt in the Perpendicular style, adding a clerestory and large stained glass windows.[7] The church's tower contained six medieval bells, and the clock on its eastern face had a fourteenth-century bell that rang the time. Thanks to the generosity of pious merchants and clerics, St Mary's was well provided with crosses, plate, vestments and some books prior to the Reformation.[8] Behind the church stood an imposing three-storey tower erected by William Pykenham in the 1480s or 1490s.[9] Pykenham, rector of Hadleigh and Archdeacon of Suffolk by 1471, apparently intended this grand building, made of brick with four crenellated corner towers, as a gatehouse that would lead from the church to a rectory dwelling nearer the river, which he probably intended to rebuild as well. His death in 1497 prevented the latter, leaving an old timber-frame structure as the parsonage house.

Hadleigh's marketplace and the buildings near to it have an atypical history because from the early fifteenth century they were held by feoffees (or trustees) on behalf of the town.[10] In 1252 the manor of Toppesfield was granted the right to hold a weekly market, and in

---

5. Anon., 'Hadleigh on the Map VII: medieval town planning', *The Hadleigh Historian*, 7 (2011–12), pp. 15–17.

6. For the earlier names of the streets shown here, see note 22 below.

7. Jones, *Hadleigh*, pp. 20–21, and A&S, *Hadleigh*, p. 9. Hadleigh also had two small chapels in the early sixteenth century. One was attached to Hadleigh Bridge, where travellers lit a candle to the Virgin Mary in hopes of a safe journey or in thanks for returning from one; the other, later known as 'the Row chapel', was dedicated to SS Mary Magdalen and Catherine and located to the east of the town centre where it served as the chapel for the row of almshouses that Pykenham built beside it (Jones, *Hadleigh*, pp. 25–6).

8. For the sale of church goods under Edward VI, see Chapter 2, 'Financing poor relief', below.

9. Roger Kennell, *Hadleigh Deanery Tower through six centuries* (Hadleigh, 2011), for this and below. For the almshouses that Pykenham founded, see Chapter 5, 'Help for old people', below. The passageway through the gatehouse was later enclosed.

10. For this paragraph, unless otherwise noted, see A&S, *Hadleigh*, pp. 7–9, and Anon., 'This is not the Guildhall!', *The Hadleigh Historian*, 5 (2011), pp. 4–7.

1417/18 the lords of Toppesfield granted to feoffees a piece of ground near the churchyard and an adjoining unit called 'Cherchecroft'. After Henry VI issued a confirmatory charter in 1432 for a weekly market to be held on Mondays and a three-day Michaelmas fair in late September, the property with market rights was conveyed to a new group of Hadleigh feoffees in 1438.[11] The section of Cherchecroft next to the cemetery now included 'one long house newly constructed called le markethows, with the chambers existing below the same called almessehouses'. The market and fair were held on the open space that extended eastward from Toppesfield Hall to what is now High Street and northward from what is now Duke Street to the churchyard. Around 1451 the market feoffees erected a three-storey building with two shops below it immediately next to the older Market House. By 1469, the building formerly termed the Market House was being called the Cloth Hall, suggesting that its large upper room was used primarily for the inspection and sale of textiles, while the recently built unit had not yet acquired its later name of the Market Hall. A grant to new feoffees in 1496 indicates that the Cherchecroft property was now called the Market Ground and contained three buildings: the Market House or Cloth Hall with the rooms beneath it; the Market Hall, including two butcher's shops, priests' chambers and a wool house; and a newly built Guildhall somewhat to the south.[12] The Guildhall was at first connected to the Market Hall by an external passageway but later was extended so that all three buildings joined.

Before the Reformation, the Guildhall was the meeting place of Hadleigh's five lay religious fraternities, to which many male household heads belonged, perhaps joined by their wives. In addition to supporting lights to their patron saints in St Mary's church, each guild hosted an annual feast and probably provided assistance to its members in times of need, using the funds required for admission and income from the land they had been given. Although we lack a listing of guild participants, we know that between 1542 and 1545 they were headed by some of the town's leading men; when guild money was loaned (with interest charged) to probable members, they were people of middling status within the local economy: two weavers, two cardmakers, a carpenter, a butcher, a plumber and a cobbler, as well as a clothmaker and a yeoman.[13]

In 1547, all guilds in England were terminated by the central government and their property declared subject to confiscation by the crown.[14] Although Hadleigh's guilds managed to sell their movable goods and probably their stocks of land, money and animals before they were seized, they lost the Guildhall. The Guildhall was later bought from the crown by several non-local gentlemen, who sold it in turn to Henry and Richard Wentworth. Hadleigh's Chief Inhabitants then decided to acquire it for the town. In 1569 Robert Rolfe, an important clothier acting on behalf of the Chief Inhabitants, presented a tun of wine [252 gallons] to 'my Lady Wentworth'; three years

---

11. HadlA 001/A/01 and 001/B/01, for this and below. For further enfeoffments of the property, see SRO-BSE E3/2/3–4 (from 1451) and SRO-I HD11/1/8.13 (from 1469). For almshouses, see Chapter 5, 'Help for old people', below.

12. The rooms for priests probably housed those who served the town's guilds. A royal charter of 1513 confirmed the right of the 'inhabitants of the town of Hadleigh' to hold a Monday market (*L&P*, vol. i, pt. 2, p. 840).

13. HadlA 026/C/06–08 and 026/D/04–05.

14. See Chapter 2, 'Financing poor relief', below.

later the town was apparently engaged in legal action with the Wentworths, for the Chief Inhabitants allowed £5 to Rolfe and £21 5d to Thomas Alabaster as reimbursement for their expenses 'about the town suit' or 'suits in law'.[15] In December 1573 the dispute between the Chief Inhabitants and the Wentworths was resolved by arbitration: representatives of the town were to pay 100 marks to obtain ownership of the Guildhall. The town book notes for 24 December 1574: 'We have bought of Mr. Henry Wentworth all his title in the town house otherwise called the gelde hall, for the which we have disbursed in ready money besides all other charges – £66 13s 4d.'[16]

During the rest of the Elizabethan period, the Guildhall and adjoining buildings were employed for a variety of purposes, including renting out certain rooms, using other areas for storage and – at least by 1589 – accommodating the town's workhouse. The Guildhall and the open area beside it were also the setting for stage plays. Hadleigh's players had already been performing by 1482; in the 1520s they travelled to Tendring Hall to entertain the Duke of Norfolk and in the 1530s to Canterbury.[17] Despite the Reformation, they continued to put on plays at least locally until the end of the sixteenth century, paying 5s to the town for use of a large room in the Guildhall or the space outside it. In 1597, the Privy Council wrote to the sheriff of Suffolk, William Forth of Hadleigh, and two esquires, reporting that it had been told of a plan in the town 'to make certaine stage playes at this time of the Whitson holydaies next ensuinge, and thether to draw a concourse of people out of the country thereaboutes, pretending heerein the benefit of the towne'.[18] The Council prohibited the idea, especially at a time of food scarcity, 'when disordred people of the comon sort wilbe apt to misdemeane themselves'. The recipients of the letter were to ensure that local officers did not go forward with the plan and that the stage prepared for the plays be 'plucked downe'. From then on, players apparently moved inside and were regulated more closely. In 1599, John Allen, Hadleigh's market bailiff and keeper of the workhouse located in one section of the Guildhall, was instructed not to permit any plays to be performed in that building without consent of six of the Chief Inhabitants; all plays or wedding festivities were to end before dark and to cause no damage to the building.[19]

The rest of central Hadleigh consisted of a mixture of residential housing, shops, inns and production units.[20] In the Elizabethan period neighbourhoods varied considerably in terms of the wealth and occupations of their household heads, but each contained people of diverse statuses. The people living and working within them must therefore have had some vertical as well as horizontal interactions with their

---

15. HadIA 021/B/01 and 004/A/01, 97. For below, see A&S, *Hadleigh*, p. 93, note 21.

16. HadIA 004/A/01, p. 104. Most of that amount came from cash loans from four clothiers, two of whom were starting to be called gentlemen: £35 from Robert Rolfe, £15 from Thomas Alabaster, £11 13s 4d from Thomas Parkins and £5 from John Turner. They were repaid over the next four years from a gift of £5 from William Veysey, from sale of wood and brush from a piece of town property and from general income (*ibid.*, pp. 104–5 and 123). For below, see *ibid.*, e.g., pp. 149, 235 and 259, and Chapter 4 below.

17. Jones, *Hadleigh*, pp. 16–19. For below, see A&S, *Hadleigh*, p. 72.

18. *APC*, vol. xxvii, p. 96.

19. HadIA 004/A/01, p. 264.

20. These buildings are suggested only for two segments on Figure 1.1.

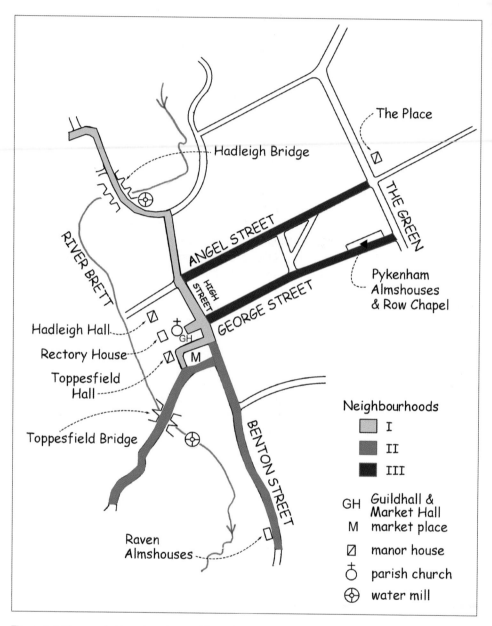

Figure 1.2 Three neighbourhoods used for collection of poor rates, 1579–85.

neighbours. Dealings across economic and social groupings may in turn have contributed to a sense that Hadleigh was a single community and had a shared identity.

Hadleigh's 660–780 households can be divided into four main economic groups, averaged over the years 1579–94, thanks to information about people who paid poor rates or received relief and other assorted sources.[21] Category A consisted of the wealthiest 6 per cent, those whose heads paid poor rates on a weekly basis, for a total of 4s 4d to £1 6s annually. Category B included another 15 per cent whose heads paid only quarterly, for a total of 4d to 4s annually. The third and by far the largest category, coming to 66 per cent, comprised those households that neither paid rates nor received assistance. The remaining 13 per cent, Category D, contained members who were relieved by town officials. Though we have no locational information for most people in categories C and D, several of the poor rate records list payers in Category B by street, and we know the residences of many people in Category A.

Figure 1.2 displays the three areas within which poor rates were collected, giving modern street names.[22] Neighbourhood I formed Hadleigh's wealthiest area. Of 133 households in Categories A and B (though they were not all there at the same time), 23 per cent were in Category A and the rest in Category B. That neighbourhood contained many clothiers, mercers or gentlemen, and most of the people in Category B were independent craftsmen or traders.[23] Angel Street and George Street acquired their names from the respectable inns that lay at the corners where they intersected High Street. Neighbourhood II was somewhat less prosperous. Of its 116 known households, 16 per cent were in Category A and were still generally headed by clothiers; more of its Category B residents were engaged in food and drink work.[24] In Neighbourhood III, the poorest area, only 8 per cent of its 92 households were headed by men in Category A. It functioned as a manufacturing and retailing area for foodstuffs and had the largest number of weavers.[25] Although the latter were sufficiently prosperous to be assessed for poor rates, it is likely that many other people of limited means – cloth workers among them – lived on those two streets and the smaller ones that connected them.

---

21. The information comes from lists of rate payers in 1579 and 1585, outlays by town officials for the poor and scattered other sources. For the average number of households and the average number of rate payers at the two levels, see Tables Intro.1 and 2.3.

22. Angel Street was originally called Biggen Street; the western end of George Street was Buck Street and the eastern end Hell or Mawdelyn Street; and the northern section of High Street was Hadleigh Bridge Street. The section of High Street south of the market was called Benton Street on its west side and Soddington Street on its east side (Anon., 'Changing Names in the High Street', *The Hadleigh Historian*, 4 (2011), p. 19).

23. Of the 31 people in Category A whose type of work is known, most were clothiers, plus two mercers and two gentlemen. People in Category B included four shermen, three lesser clothiers, two wringers, two millers, two weavers, one smith, one tailor, one cardmaker, one woodworker, one ironworker and one shopkeeper.

24. Of the 18 people in Category A, most were again clothiers, plus two yeomen and one mercer. Known occupations of people in Category B were weaver (five), baker (three), butcher (two), smith (two), lesser clothier (two), miller (one), haberdasher (one) and shopkeeper (one).

25. Most of the seven people with known occupations in Category A were clothiers, plus one yeoman. Of people in Category B, there were seven weavers, four butchers, two tallow chandlers, two smiths, two lesser clothiers, two shopkeepers, one baker, one sherman, one cobbler, one cardmaker and one carter.

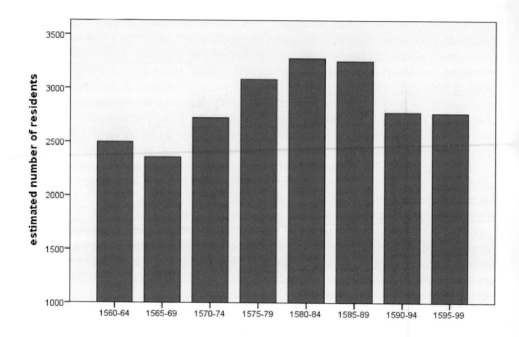

Figure 1.3 Estimated population of Hadleigh, 1560–99 (values derived from number of baptisms).

The estimated population and demographic information

The full parish of Hadleigh, including both urban and rural areas, contained around 2,400–3,300 people per quinquennium (5-year period) between 1560 and 1600. Figure 1.3 shows the estimated population based upon the number of baptisms recorded in the parish register.[26] The town was smaller in the 1560s, with some 2,350–2,500 people, owing probably to heavy mortality during the 1550s, but the population rose to an estimated 2,700 in the early 1570s and to 3,100–3,300 between 1575 and 1589 before dropping to 2,750–2,800 in the 1590s.[27] If the total population is estimated from the number of marriages rather than from baptisms, the numbers are much lower (only 68–89 per cent of the value per quinquennium). This discrepancy suggests that an unusually large number of people in Elizabethan Hadleigh did not wed in church, choosing instead to constitute their marriage in the more traditional manner by saying their vows – worded in the present tense – to each other in the presence of at least two witnesses.[28] That possibility is

---

26. See App. 1.1 for the actual numbers and the method used to obtain them.

27. For high mortality in the 1550s, see Chapter 6, 'The impact of Rowland Taylor and opposition to him, 1544–54', below. Between 1600 and 1619 the estimated population was between 2,600 and 3,000, but it declined quite consistently thereafter, reaching a low of perhaps 1,250 by the 1690s (A&S, *Hadleigh*, p. 303, calculated by multiplying the average number of baptisms per decade by 30). For below, see App. 1.1.

28. This possibility was suggested to me by Tony Wrigley. Private marriages were discouraged by the church but accepted as legally valid. For marriages of poor relief recipients, see Chapter 3, 'Recipient households and family relationships', and Chapter 5, 'Help for old people', below.

reinforced by the observation that many recipients of poor relief, for whom the cost of a church wedding would have been a deterrent, do not appear in the marriage section of the parish register although their children's baptisms were recorded. If one compares the ratios of baptisms to marriages and baptisms to burials for Hadleigh with those calculated in a large national study, some interesting contrasts emerge. Apart from the earliest quinquennium, Hadleigh's ratio of baptisms to marriages was higher than the national average, probably due again to private marriages although perhaps influenced also by outmigration of young people before marriage. The ratio of baptisms to burials was also above the national average in most quinquennia, another probable indicator of emigration.

While very few Hadleigh records shed light on the demographic events that shaped the size of the total population (birth, marriage, death and migration patterns), we gain a rare glimpse into some of those moments through the depositions given in 1576 concerning a legal dispute over lands in Hadleigh and East Bergholt, Suffolk.[29] One of the issues was in what year Augustine Sparrowe, a glover born in Hadleigh though now living in Woodbridge, had come of age. The responses of the six witnesses called from Hadleigh to speak about Augustine's birth remind us that in a semi-literate society that did not make regular use of calendars, establishing the date of something that occurred in the past would usually be done in relation to saints' days or memorable events. In this case, Queen Mary's move to Framlingham Castle, just 20 miles from Hadleigh, in order to gather her supporters after Lady Jane Grey seized the throne in July 1553 had obviously made a deep impression.[30] Alice Scoyle, a widow aged 86 years, deposed that Augustine was born between Michaelmas and Hallowmas 'next after Queen Mary did lie at Framlingham' (i.e., between 29 September and 1 November 1553); she knew that to be true because she 'was with his mother at the birth of the said Augustine'. Widow Marion Johnson, aged 66, said that she too had been present at the birth and used the same dating reference. She added that a baby named Thomas Blanchard, son of William Blanchard, was born the following Lady Day (25 March 1554) and 'sucked upon the milk' of Augustine's mother. William Blanchard, a 48-year-old weaver, said that he knew that the dates already reported for Augustine's birth were correct for he had married about a fortnight before that Michaelmas, and his wedding dinner was held in the house of Augustine's father.

Other deponents added further pieces of information, as well as confirming the basic dates. Margaret Browne, a 60-year-old widow, said that she had lived near Augustine's father and mother for nine years and was very well acquainted with them. At the Candlemas next after Augustine's birth (2 February 1554) her own son Edmond was born; Edmond had died, but if he had lived until the Candlemas after her deposition he would have been 25 years old. John Smyth, a weaver aged 46, said that Augustine's parents had moved from Hadleigh to East Bergholt 'the next Michaelmas twelve months after the said Queen Mary was at Framlingham', by which time Augustine was old enough 'to go alone', presumably having started to walk, and his mother had given birth to another baby.

---

29.   TNA PRO REQ 2/75/25 for the next three paragraphs.

30.   Andy Wood notes that although the Protestant gentry of Suffolk supported Jane, the 'common people' objected 'with murmurs of discontent and great indignation' (*Riot, rebellion and popular politics in early modern England* [Basingstoke, 2002], p. 71).

Tallowchandler Robert Kynge, aged 62, gave a charming – if chronologically imprecise – report, illustrating the kind of business-cum-social interactions that could occur between neighbours. In the final year of Edward VI's reign (1553) Kynge went to the house of William Sparrowe, who lived in what was later Angel Street, to buy pears for his wife, who was pregnant. Sparrowe told him that the only pears he had were hard and still on the tree behind his house, implying that this discussion took place in the late summer or autumn. Kynge, eager to please his wife, replied, 'Let me have them such as they be'. The men started outside, but a baby boy cried to go with his father, whereupon Sparrowe 'picked him up in his arms and bore him with him and gathered for this deponent two pennyworth of those pears'. Augustine Sparrowe 'was the same lad that cried after his father'.

A more somber tone emerges from examination of the register of burials in Hadleigh, which begins in 1560, and especially as regards the peaks of deaths in certain years. The listing indicates that 1572, 1582–3 and 1592 saw exceptionally high mortality, probably due to the plague. During the six months from September 1582 to February 1583 99 burials were recorded, 3.7 times higher than the average over the previous nine years of 53 burials per full year. During the calendar year 1592 118 people were buried, 97 per cent higher than the average of 60 for the seven previous years. Epidemics struck some families terribly heavily. During 24 days between 22 December 1582 and 14 January 1583 five members of the Red family were buried in Hadleigh's churchyard: first a 2-year-old girl, then the father, next a girl of 12 years and a boy of 6 years, and lastly the mother.[31] Similarly devastating was the experience of the Blanchard family, headed by the same William who had deposed in 1576. Between 20 November 1582 and 15 January 1583, a period of nine weeks, seven of its members were buried. Two children died before the end of 1582; during four awful days early in January, William and three more children were buried; and the last child died ten days later. Only the mother was left alive. High mortality may also have disrupted planned marriages, leaving some espoused women to give birth to illegitimate babies: the second half of 1592 and first nine months of 1593 saw an unusual cluster of seven illegitimate births.

A striking feature of Hadleigh's population is how few foreigners appear to have moved into the town during the later fifteenth and sixteenth centuries. This pattern was eventually to have a deleterious impact upon its woollen cloth industry, for many of the people from the Low Countries who came to East Anglia brought with them alternative techniques of weaving and finishing that produced the 'New Draperies'. In the Alien Subsidy Roll of 1485 308 foreigners were listed in Suffolk but only 4 in Hadleigh.[32] The subsidy returns of 1524 include six 'aliens' in Hadleigh, only two of whom worked in cloth manufacturing: three 'Dutchmen' (a cordwainer, beerbrewer and fuller), one Frenchman (a servant), one Scot (a sherman) and 'John, an Iceland man, servant to Robert Foorde, gentleman, taking no wages'. A John Jenybon, weaver, mentioned in 1545, may have been French, and in the 1568 tax listing we are told that four men were foreign (Malignus Freman, James Legas, John Lucas and James Ston) but not given their occupations or where they were born.[33]

---

31. SRO-I FB 81/D1/1. Neither the Reds nor the Blanchards (below) received poor relief or paid poor rates, suggesting that they lay somewhere in the middling economic range.

32. Jones, 'Hadleigh', p. 42. They were born in Cologne, Magdeburg, Scotland and 'beyond the seas'. For below, see *Suffolk in 1524: subsidy returns*, Suffolk Green Books 10 (Woodbridge, 1910), p. 157.

33. *Suffolk in 1568: subsidy returns*, Suffolk Green Books 12 (Bury St Edmunds, 1909), p. 110. For Legas, a surgeon, see Chapter 5, 'Care for people who were ill or disabled', below.

Economic life

For local purchasers and some small-scale traders, Hadleigh's weekly market, held on Mondays, provided both an economic and a social centre. Market activity was opened by the ringing of a bell at 10 or 11 in the morning; it remained in session until 4 or 5 in the afternoon, depending on the season.[34] Traders could hire wooden stalls for a penny per day, and no other booths were allowed. The market bailiffs also collected rents for the various buildings situated around the marketplace, including thirteen shops, six butchery stalls, six 'standings' and six houses. In 1571 stall rents yielded £5 6s 8d, shop rents £13 17s 3d and the standings £3 6s, while the Michaelmas fair produced £5 8s 8d. In 1589, in response to the issuance of a set of standard weights and measures by the Exchequer the previous year, Hadleigh reduced the size of its official market bushel to bring it into conformity with the national unit. But although the market was important for local trading it played relatively little part in the production and sale of woollen cloth, the overwhelmingly dominant component of the town's economy.

Cloth manufacturing and clothiers

Hadleigh was a major manufacturer of woollen broadcloths for domestic use and export to the continent from the development of that industry in England during the fourteenth century until at least the early seventeenth.[35] Records of the alnager, the royal official who inspected broadcloth for export, indicate that during the years between 1465/6 and 1468/9 Hadleigh produced between 1,000 and 2,000 cloths annually, each one around 75–90 feet long; that level was exceeded only by Bristol, Salisbury, York and two places in Somerset. In 1468/9 Suffolk was the most productive county in England, with 5,188 cloths for export, of which Hadleigh made 1,707; its output exceeded that of Lavenham and the larger centres of Colchester and Norwich in adjoining counties.[36]

Woollen cloth was manufactured in a series of separate stages, organised by capitalist entrepreneurs known in the earlier sixteenth century as clothmakers and later as clothiers. Between 1558 and 1640 Hadleigh had the largest number of broadcloth clothiers of any town in Suffolk, with 81 mentioned in the records.[37] Although information about occupations is incomplete, 14 to 17 clothiers are known from local records to have been at work in each decade between 1540 and 1600 except for the 1550s, when 19 were named. An Exchequer document from 1577 lists 21 clothiers in the town.[38] The output of such men during the Elizabethan years was substantial. In the 1570s four of Hadleigh's clothiers alone produced 680 broadcloths

---

34. For this paragraph, see A&S, *Hadleigh*, pp. 62–5 and 75, and Jones, 'Hadleigh', p. 76.
35. A&S, *Hadleigh*, pp. 143–8. For below, see Jones, 'Hadleigh', pp. 44–5, and a personal communication from Sue Andrews.
36. Gladys A. Thornton, *A history of Clare, Suffolk* (Cambridge, 1928), p. 153. Colchester produced 1,390 cloths, Lavenham made 1,001?, and Bury St Edmunds, Norwich, Dedham, Ipswich and Coggeshall made between 510 and 644 each.
37. John E. Pilgrim, 'The cloth industry in Essex and Suffolk, 1558–1640', MA thesis (University of London, 1940), pp. 228–9. Unfortunately, that study does not break down that number by shorter periods.
38. TNA PRO Exch. K. R. Mem. Rolls, 372, Easter 51, as cited by Pilgrim, 'Cloth industry', Notes, vii, p. 28.

called 'Spanish shorts', around 70–85 feet long, every year; their cloths were joined by the ones made by other local producers.[39] Most of the cloths were taken to London merchants for export, while a smaller number went through Ipswich.

The various processes through which cloth was made were usually carried out by specialised and independent workers in their own homes or workshops, who were paid when they delivered their product. After fleeces with the right kind of fibres had been selected and purchased, the wool had to be sorted and cleaned. It was then carded (rubbed between two wooden cards with short metal wires embedded in them) to align the fibres and spun into yarn using a spindle or wheel. All of these initial operations were normally performed as bye-employment – fitted in around domestic tasks – by women and children, who were paid by the amount of wool handled or yarn produced. A good deal of the yarn used by Hadleigh's weavers was probably prepared in smaller communities and rural areas outside the town. In west Suffolk, which was famous for its coloured cloths, much of the yarn was then dyed ('in the wool'), using madder to ready the yarn to accept the dye and a range of possible colours, especially the blues made from woad for which Suffolk was famous.[40]

The yarn was next taken to weavers, who generally worked at home using their own looms. John Smyth of Hadleigh, a witness in the case involving Augustine Sparrowe, testified that he had been 'aweaving' in his shop one day about a year before, when a friend came to his window to ask him a question.[41] Sitting at their large looms, usually assisted by a second worker who helped to throw the shuttle back and forth and by a boy who made quills, most weavers produced heavy, long cloths. Statutes of 1551/2 and 1557/8 had fixed the dimensions of Suffolk's coloured 'long cloths' at 28 to 30 yards (84–90 feet) when wet, and 'short cloths' at 23 to 25 yards (69–75 feet); both types had to be at least 1¾ yards (63 inches) wide.[42] A 'streit' was much smaller and lighter, measuring about 13 yards (39 feet) by 1 yard (36 inches). Weavers were usually paid a set amount per cloth, though some had an ongoing relationship with a particular clothier. In his will of 1577 Thomas Parkins, a clothier whose widow later endowed a charity in Hadleigh, left 6s 8d 'to every one of my weavers that are married and shall be my weaver at the time of my death'.[43]

The cloth was then ready for finishing. If the yarn had not been dyed before weaving, it was coloured at this stage. Next it went to a fuller, who soaked the fabric and pounded in a special clay to obtain a tighter, more unified surface, using a water-driven mill if possible. Because fulling tended to shrink the cloth, it would be stretched back to full size on a rack of tenterhooks and allowed to dry. The final stage consisted of removing any 'burls' or knobs from the cloth, roughing up its nap, and cutting it down to a uniform depth with large shears.

---

39. TNA PRO E 133/10/1622, undated, probl. 1570–77. For below, of 13,500 Suffolk cloths exported in 1565, 72 per cent were short cloths sent from London, a few were long cloths from London and 27 per cent were short cloths from Ipswich (Pilgrim, 'Cloth industry', pp. 198–9).

40. Pilgrim, 'Cloth industry', pp. 11–14, who describes 'blues', 'azures' and 'plunkets' (a greyish blue).

41. TNA PRO REQ 2/75/25.

42. 5 & 6 Edward VI, c. 6, and 4 & 5 Philip and Mary, c. 5 (*SR*, vol. iv, pp. 136 and 323). Broadcloths were to weigh 80 lbs when dry; shorts were to be 64 lbs (Pilgrim, 'Cloth industry', p. 19). For below, see Bailey, *Medieval Suffolk*, 270.

43. TNA PRO PROB 11/59/29.

In Hadleigh, as elsewhere in East Anglia, clothiers commonly encouraged their finishers to tenter or stretch the cloth more strenuously after fulling so as to produce an apparently larger but weaker and less durable product. Despite legislation of 1552 that stipulated that no cloth was to be strained beyond one yard in length or one-eighth of a yard in width and that prohibited use of 'any winch, rope, or ring ... or any other engine' while tentering, many producers arranged for their cloths to be stretched.[44] Sometime in the 1570s four of Hadleigh's leading clothiers (Robert Rolfe, Thomas Parkins, Thomas Alabaster and William Gale) were charged by the crown with 'deceitful stretching of cloth on the tenterhooks'. The questions administered to Harry Tottye, Richard Reason and unnamed other local clothiers asked how many 'short cloths' called 'Spanish or Dansk sorts' the men had made weekly over the past two years. The interrogatories requested confirmation that Rolfe and Parkins had each made at least 250 short cloths every year, Alabaster 100 and Gale 80. The witnesses were to say whether any of the cloths were longer than required by the statute: between 22 and 25 yards when 'well thicked' and wet. Was it true that the four clothiers 'commonly use to set the first end of every cloth upon teynter hockes which are knocked in the end of every teynter, and after ... draw out the other end of the cloth with a certain thing called a Heddynge, having a ring and a rope thereto fastened?' Was it not their usual practice to stretch cloths to a length of 3 or 4 yards beyond their size when wet and then attach a seal made of lead that certified their length at the extended dimension? Why did the clothiers not stretch their full-sized broadcloths but only their short cloths, and what were the names of the merchants who bought such cloths? The answers to these questions and the outcome of the charges are not recorded, but royal investigation may have led the clothiers to limit more egregious stretching. The case perhaps lay behind a petition sent by the clothmakers of Suffolk to the central government around 1577 arguing that the statute concerning cloth making should be revised; among other concerns, they asked that cloths be measured according to weight, not to size.[45]

Proper standards for broadcloth intended for export were supposed to be maintained by alnagers. From the late fourteenth century most cloths going to the continent were brought to a central depot in London, Blackwell Hall, for inspection.[46] Based upon the Ulnage Statute of 1353, which defined requirements for size and quality, a royally appointed official had to certify that the cloth had been properly made; after the required tax had been paid, he affixed his lead seal. The position of alnager could be farmed out to people in London and the clothmaking centres. In the sixteenth century several Hadleigh clothiers gained leases of fractions of the alnage, paying a set sum to the crown and keeping the fees received. In 1539 clothmaker Thomas Debnam appointed John Freeman, a merchant or clothier, as the supervisor of his will, asking him to assist his wife; in thanks, he gave Freeman 'my years of the

---

44. 5 & 6 Edward VI, c. 6, secs. 11–12 (*SR*, vol. iv, p. 139). Complaints of illegal stretching of cloth were so frequent that Pilgrim was able to base his list of the broadcloth makers working in Suffolk and Essex between 1558 and 1640 upon them ('Cloth industry', App. 7). For below, see TNA PRO E 133/10/1622.

45. TNA PRO SP 12/106/1, fol. 105.

46. Jones, *Hadleigh*, p. 16, for this and below.

lease of the alnage and sealing of woollen cloths'.[47] Freeman hoped to renew the lease in 1551: in his will of that year he left to his sons-in-law and executors 'the lease of the alnage which I shall have at Michaelmas or the money that I laid out for it'.

Being an alnager created opportunities for extortion. In the late 1590s the Attorney General brought charges against four 'alnagers and searchers of broad cloth in the city of London'.[48] Responding to a complaint from 37 clothiers of Suffolk, including 8 from Hadleigh, the accusation states that the alnagers, rather than inspecting cloths to maintain quality and then affixing their seal, had instead impounded such wares. After assaulting and beating some of the clothiers and carriers, they seized loads of cloth sent into London by horse or cart and demanded large sums of money before releasing the goods. Four of the Hadleigh clothiers had been made to pay £2–3 each, three others paid £4–7 and John Gale gave £22 to get his cloth back.

Various clothiers and carriers were deposed to present further evidence. Nicholas Strutt of Hadleigh said that in May 1597 he had hired a 'carman' of London to carry 24 cloths to the city, but before they reached their destination the alnagers used force to make the carrier take the goods to their private office.[49] Two months later he sent another eight cloths by a local carrier, which were also seized, and he had to pay £21 10s for the release of both loads. The cloths of another Hadleigh man had already reached Blackwell Hall when they were taken by the alnagers. Carrier Robert Colbrone reported that the alnagers used to appoint people to watch for cloth coming into London, giving them advance warning so they could seize the cloth:

> No carrier or clothier could come to the city by night or day but there were spies deputed by them lying continually in taverns or alehouses to watch them in coming, in so much that this deponent was enforced always to come very late in the night for fear of them, and many times at one of the clock at night to give the porter at the gate sometimes 3d, sometimes 4d to let him in.[50]

Jerome Burman, another Hadleigh carrier, referred to one impounded load that consisted of four cloths sent by one local clothier and two packs of four cloths each sent by another.

Whereas broadcloths had traditionally formed the basis of England's exports, during the second half of the sixteenth century changes started to appear.[51] Demand for the heavy older cloths began to lessen as the result of new fashions in clothing and the rise of new markets in warmer settings. Broadcloths were replaced in some settings by a range of lighter, more varied, and cheaper fabrics or 'stuffs' known as the New Draperies. These fabrics used long-stapled wool that was not carded but rather

---

47. TNA PRO PROB 11/27. For below, see PROB 11/34.
48. TNA PRO STAC 5/A25/27.
49. *Ibid.* At the statutory weight of 80 lbs for dry broadcloth and 64 lbs for shorts, this delivery would have weighed between 1,536 and 1,920 lbs.
50. *Ibid.*, for this and below.
51. A&S, *Hadleigh*, pp. 150–52.

'kembed' (oiled and aligned using heated combs or stockard frames, large spiked heads fastened to posts); after weaving, stuffs did not need fulling. The newer fabrics would eventually result in an increased demand for labour, but some weavers and clothiers failed to adopt the newer fabrics, sending their towns into a slow decline.[52] Hadleigh, however, like Sudbury and Nayland, prospered through the end of the sixteenth century. Some weavers still produced traditional broadcloths but others moved to woollen fabrics that were smaller and less heavy though made according to the familiar stages; more innovative workers wove certain kinds of 'stuffs' or linen. For women and children, knitting stockings became an option.[53]

Although clothiers were often able to reap great profit once a cloth was sold, they had to make a considerable investment of cash or have good access to credit that might extend over a period of years. They needed to buy appropriate wool and pay for the work done at each stage along the way. When the cloth was finished it went to London (or in some cases to Ipswich), where it was handed over to the merchants who would take it to the continent for sale. The clothier was generally paid only a fraction of the price at the time the cloth was delivered, receiving the full amount only after it had been sold abroad, which might take months or even years. Further, the amount of the clothier's gain was uncertain, especially given the 'boom and bust' nature of the European cloth trade in the sixteenth century, subject as it was to the vagaries of war and changes in currencies. If trade with the continent was disrupted, clothiers or merchants might need to hold back their cloth until the economy improved. Although clothiers were sometimes criticised for exploiting their workers by paying them insufficient wages, their businesses involved a high level of financial risk and the ability to lay out money for supplies and wages for a considerable period before gaining payment.[54]

Hadleigh's successful clothiers commonly wanted to buy land and turn themselves and their sons into gentlemen. Their ability to do so was enhanced by the cash or credit available to them during the first decade after the dissolution of the monasteries and the subsequent sale of land by the crown. The estates they acquired generally lay in Suffolk but not in Hadleigh itself. Thus, three members of the Clerke family made substantial purchases in the mid 1540s: John bought the reversion of the lordship of Layham for £255 in 1544, and his son Walter Clerke and grandson Stephen acquired the reversion of the manor of Kettlebaston for £620.[55] The impact of these purchases upon their local status is seen in the terms used to describe them. John Clerke, although he was the third wealthiest person in Hadleigh in 1524, assessed at £100 in goods, always called himself

---

52. It was said in the early seventeenth century that the 84 lbs of wool needed to produce a finished broadcloth, requiring the labour of 14 people, would give employment to 40 to 50 people when used for stuffs and stockings, and the wages the latter received were higher (George Unwin, *Studies in economic history: the collected papers of George Unwin*, ed. R.H. Tawney (1927; London, 1958), p. 292).

53. See Chapter 4, 'Training and discipline in the workhouse', below.

54. See Chapter 6, 'The ongoing influence of Christian social teachings', below for Thomas Carew's 'Caveat'.

55. *L&P*, vol. xix, pt. 1, p. 627 and vol. xx, pt. 2, p. 543. A reversion was a purchase that would take effect when the current lease expired. For Walter as an opponent of Rowland Taylor, see Chapter 6, 'The impact of Rowland Taylor and opposition to him, 1544–54', below.

a clothmaker or clothier.[56] Walter was termed a clothmaker through the 1540s but a gentleman by the early 1550s. Stephen died young, but his cousin Edward was termed an esquire from the later 1550s onwards. The (ex-) clothier families continued to buy smaller pieces of land later in the century, in some cases from each other.[57] Whereas only 8 or 9 gentlemen appear in the records each decade between 1520 and 1549, the number of gentlemen, esquires or knights rose to 14 or 15 during the 1550s and 1560s and had reached 28 by the 1580s. The transformation of clothiers into members of the upper ranks had an impact upon Hadleigh's social and political life.[58]

We can observe this process in more detail through the experiences of Hadleigh's wealthiest family, the Forths (sometimes spelled Foorthe or Forde). Robert was an extremely wealthy cloth merchant during the first three decades of the sixteenth century, assessed at £267 in goods in 1524 – the largest amount of anyone in Hadleigh.[59] Although he was already termed a gentleman, his son Robert, assessed at £30 in goods and hence in the top 10 per cent of Hadleigh's tax payers, was still described at that time as a draper or merchant. When Robert the younger died in 1540, now called a gentleman, he held scattered pieces of land, mainly in Essex.[60]

A greater elevation of status occurred in 1544, when William Forth, Robert's son, paid £910 for the buildings and lands of the recently dissolved Butley Priory in east Suffolk, together with a water mill and the rectories and advowsons of two parishes.[61] In the following year he gave the crown £488 for half of the reversion of the manor of Boynton, Suffolk, with the accompanying advowson. By 1547, now termed an esquire, he had moved into the ranks of the Chief Inhabitants of Hadleigh, helping to audit the town accounts.[62] Perhaps owing in part to his support for the reformist cause in religion and his backing of Rowland Taylor, William was appointed a Justice of the Peace for West Suffolk starting in 1550/51, but was dismissed with Mary's accession. At the time of his death in 1559, though he still identified himself as 'of Hadleigh', he had extensive holdings not only in Suffolk but in Essex and London as well, having used his new properties for income as well as prestige.[63]

---

56. *Suffolk in 1524*, p. 153.

57. Clothier Julian Beamonde bought houses from Edward Clerke sometime before writing his will in 1586; Robert Rolfe purchased holdings from William Forth and Edward Clerke before 1588; Thomas Alabaster gained property from Edward Clerke and clothier Thomas Parkins before 1591 (TNA PRO PROB 11/70/1; PROB 11/72/20; PROB 11/80/51; and C 2/Eliz. I/A1/35).

58. See Chapter 6, 'Worry about control and cost, 1576–85', below.

59. *Suffolk in 1524*, p. 153.

60. TNA PRO PROB 11/28.

61. *L&P*, vol. xix, pt. 1, p. 493. An advowson was the right to appoint a clergyman to a particular living. For below, see *ibid.*, vol. xx, pt. 2, p. 119.

62. HadlA 004/A/01, p. 35. For below, see Diarmaid MacCulloch, *Suffolk and the Tudors* (Oxford, 1986), Apps I and III.

63. TNA PRO PROB 11/43. In 1547, he had brought suit against William Reedham for refusing to become the tenant of his manor of Butley (TNA PRO C 1/1177/65). Their agreement, Forth claimed, had been that Reedham would lease the manor, feeding and tending the cattle and at least 500 sheep, but he had not taken over the tenancy. Forth was probably raising animals as meat, for which there would have been high demand in Ipswich and the smaller east Suffolk towns, and perhaps for their hides and wool.

All of William's four sons were under age at their father's death, so for the next 15 years no Forth was active in town or county affairs. But, starting in 1575, William's third son, another William and an esquire, played an important role in Hadleigh's political and charitable life.[64] He also sat as a JP for Suffolk from 1589 until his death in 1599 and was the only justice from the western part of the county to attend sessions in the north-east as well as in Bury. His younger brother Israel, gent., to whom he bequeathed the house in which Israel then lived plus a 'beer house', began to audit town accounts in 1596.[65]

A young cousin of Hadleigh's Forth family, who lived in nearby Layham, fared less well. Richard Forth, gent., a younger son of the second Robert Forth of Hadleigh, died in 1558, leaving his own son Robert, then aged less than 21 years, to the supervision of his mother, Elizabeth.[66] Robert wanted a more lively existence than simply being a country gentleman, as we learn from a suit heard by Chancery sometime in the 1560s or 1570s. Initiated by Thomas Swyneborne, a draper of Hadleigh, the dispute concerned the George Inn and other properties in and around the town.[67] Swyneborne alleged that Forth had granted a 20-year lease of the inn and land to him but was now trying to get out of their contract on the grounds that he had not been of full age when he signed it. Swyneborne said he had already bought a horse for Robert, paid a 40s debt to Edward Clerke on his behalf, delivered timber from some woodlands to him and given him other items and cash amounting to £25. In his response, Robert said that Swyneborne had taken advantage of him, 'being a poor infant of the age of 19 years or thereabout' and ignorant of the world.

Swyneborne replied with righteous indignation that Robert had told him that his mother 'was over hard and straight unto him and would not give him or suffer him to have any thing whereby he might maintain his living according to the degree and estate of a gentleman'. Robert therefore decided to go to London but needed money in order to live there 'without fear and danger of arrest' by his creditors. Because Robert was a gentleman and from a good family, Swynborne gave him clothing, a felt hat, some trade goods and cash. But, once in the capital, Robert began 'to accompany himself with light, unthrifty, and ill disposed persons and being so accompanied and matched he hath with dicing and carding and other riotous, lascivious manner and behaviour consumed, spent, and cast away the said sums of money and wares'. Now, hoping to raise funds that would allow him to 'depart out of this realm into the parts beyond the seas', thereby escaping his creditors, Robert was trying to revoke his previous leases and grant them out to other people. We do not know the outcome of the suit, but Robert does not appear in later records.

---

64. HadlA 004/A/01, p. 107 (2) ff. He was accused of 'unconscionable practises' in 1589 concerning his efforts to avoid repaying a debt of £130 owed to John Dey of Southwold, including collusion and deceit (*APC*, vol. xvii, pp. 29–30). For below, see MacCulloch, *Suffolk and the Tudors*, App. I and p. 36.

65. TNA PRO PROB 11/94/73.

66. TNA PRO PROB 11/42A. In 1550 Richard Forth had sold to Hadleigh's Chief Inhabitants Mascalls Farm in Offton, land that was henceforth a major component of the town's endowment for the poor (see Chapter 2, 'An endowment of landed property for the poor', below). I am grateful to Sue Andrews for pointing this out to me (personal communication).

67. TNA PRO C 3/164/76 for the next two paragraphs.

While Hadleigh's wealthiest clothiers were major producers and exporters of cloth, storing finished cloths in their houses or in London, other clothmakers functioned on a much more modest level.[68] Some were just starting in business or were having trouble keeping afloat, while certain people who called themselves clothiers were not actually the organisers and financiers of the entire process. They might, for example, buy yarn and hire just a few weavers, or they could purchase raw cloth and merely finish it. If one examines the levels at which people were assessed for poor rates, 21 clothiers were among the upper groups who had to pay 1d or more per week, but 5 others paid only by the quarter.[69]

Community wealth, occupational distribution and gendered absences

Hadleigh's cloth industry created an atypically large number of wealthy residents, leading to a very high economic valuation for the town as a whole. In the national subsidy of 1524 Hadleigh's total assessed wealth came to just under £2,500.[70] Of that amount, the Forth family owned one-eighth, while the next sixteen families together owned another third. The town's total subsidy payments between 1524 and 1527 placed it twenty-fourth among English provincial towns, tied with Southampton; in Suffolk it was below Ipswich, Bury St Edmunds and Lavenham but above Long Melford and Sudbury.[71]

But cloth manufacture relied upon the labour of many people who gained an unpredictable and generally low income. Among sixteenth-century subsidies that of 1524 was unusual, for its assessments included people who paid on their wages, not just on land or goods. It thereby gives us a picture of the distribution of wealth across a wide range of household heads.[72] At the bottom level were those who paid on wages of less than £2, followed by people assessed for £2 on wages, goods or land. In the listing for Hadleigh, which included rural as well as urban parts of the community, 38 per cent of the payers fell into the bottom category and another 26 per cent into the second. That pattern was close to the distribution found in a study of sixteen country towns, but it contained a much heavier weighting of people in the bottom category

---

68. Among leading clothiers, John Raven bequeathed '20 coarse cloths, of blankets and russets' in his will written in 1552; when Robert Rolfe senior added a codicil to his will in 1552, he said that eight broadcloths currently lying in a house in London should be sold, with the profits going to the poor; in 1556 John Clerke left to his wife and others 25 'plunket' broadcloths, 25 'azure' cloths, 10 plain needle wool cloths and 10 needle cloths woaded and dyed (TNA PRO PROB 11/36, PROB 11/35 and PROB 11/38). Although sixteenth-century local documents nearly always place an 's' at the end of the surname Ravens and sometimes spell it Ravence, the name will be written here as Raven, in conformity with other modern studies. For lesser clothiers, see Pilgrim, 'Cloth industry', pp. 51–3 and 144–9.

69. See Table 2.4 below.

70. *Suffolk in 1524*, pp. 153–7.

71. A&S, *Hadleigh*, p. 12. In the subsidy of 1568, which taxed only more prosperous people, Hadleigh's assessed wealth was third in Suffolk, behind Ipswich and Bury St Edmunds (*Suffolk in 1568*, pp. 107–10).

72. See App. 1.2 for this paragraph.

than was seen in the suburban market town of Romford, Essex, even when Romford's agricultural hinterland is included. A quarter of Hadleigh's payers were in the middling category of £3 to £19, slightly lower than found in the country towns and well below the 41 per cent seen in Romford. Hadleigh also included 12 per cent who were assessed at £20 or more, above the level in both other places. This distribution accords with the presence of many wealthy clothiers and a substantial number of workers dependent upon limited wages.

Although we lack a full listing of the occupations of Hadleigh people, we gain at least occasional snippets of information. Such entries are skewed in favour of wealthier people who were more likely to leave wills and to be identified in other sources by their line of work or a status designation. The problem is compounded by the fact that for most periods we have only those wills proved by the Prerogative Court of Canterbury, used for people with property in several jurisdictions; wills from the lower probate office, for the Deanery of Bocking, survive only from 1545 to 1554. I have assembled all the occupational references encountered in the Hadleigh records, but we must recognise that the numbers are incomplete.

As Appendix 1.3 shows, by far the largest occupational cluster in the town produced or sold cloth.[73] In addition to the many clothiers, drapers, merchants and brokers, and a somewhat smaller number of weavers, we see a range of subsidiary workers, many of them involved in cloth finishing. Canterbury Cathedral Priory already had a water-powered fulling mill in Hadleigh in 1287, and references in wills between 1453 and 1500 document the presence of woad- and dyehouses and fields with 'taynturs' [tenterhooks] in them, together with the skilled craftsmen who utilised them.[74] Between 1540 and the end of the century Hadleigh contained woadsetters, dyers and stainers; fullers and leaseholders of the fulling mill; wringers (presumably of wet cloths); and burlers, curriers and shermen. Other occupations were dependent upon this industry, such as the woodworkers who made looms, the metalworkers who produced combs and shears, and carriers or carters.[75] The second largest occupational/status group, those involved in agriculture, consisted of the gentry, yeomen and husbandmen, followed by people who worked in the food or drink trades or made candles.

The unusual features of Hadleigh's occupational structure are highlighted if we again compare its pattern with suburban Romford and its agricultural hinterland, 1560–1619.[76] In Hadleigh a third of all men of known occupations in the best-documented decades were engaged in some aspect of the manufacture or sale of

---

73. For known occupations by neighbourhood, see notes 23–25 above. Even during the first half of the 1620s 37 per cent of the people who appeared before the magistrates' court in Hadleigh were in the cloth trade, as compared with 14 per cent in agriculture and 11 per cent general labourers (A&S, *Hadleigh*, p. 152).

74. Jones, *Hadleigh*, p. 16, and CCA DCc-ChAnt/H/87/A; TNA PRO PROB 11/4/1/8–9, PROB 11/11/30/240–41, PROB 11/11/34, 275 and PROB 11/12/12/92.

75. In 1637, carriers from Hadleigh commonly arrived in London on Thursdays, spending the night at the George Inn on Lombard Street (John Taylor, *Carriers cosmographie* [London, 1637], fol. B3r). I am grateful to Lyn Boothman for this reference.

76. McIntosh, *A community transformed*, pp. 96–7.

woollen cloth or in making clothing, joined probably by some of the retailers; in Romford, only 5 per cent made or sold cloth. Romford, located on a main road leading into London, had a large concentration (25 per cent) of people who worked in the areas of food, drink and lodging, but Hadleigh had only 9 per cent.[77] Because wealthy clothiers in Hadleigh had commonly bought landed estates for their families in the previous generation, 15 per cent of its residents with known occupations or status designations were gentlemen, esquires or knights; in Romford, only 8 per cent were in those ranks.

A significant feature of the known occupations for Hadleigh is the almost complete absence from our sources of the women who prepared wool and spun it into yarn, work in which they were often joined by children. Men were commonly described by their occupations, but women were not, especially if their activity was part-time and done at home.[78] We know, however, that a great deal of labour was required to produce yarn. One indication of the relative figures comes from Thomas Deloney's novel *Jack of Newbury*, published in 1597 and clearly reflecting contemporary conditions, though nominally set in the reign of Henry VIII. Deloney, an unemployed weaver, offered a detailed account of the manufacturing setup of John Winchcombe, described as a wealthy and generous clothmaker. In one great room Jack had 200 looms, each worked by a male weaver assisted by a boy who sat beside him making quills.[79] To supply those looms with yarn, Jack employed three kinds of people. The first consisted of 150 needy children – the offspring of 'poore silly men' – who sat in an adjacent room sorting or 'picking wooll, the finest from the course to cull'. The children received food and drink plus a penny every day, 'which was to them a wondrous stay'.[80] In the main room 100 women carded wool, while 200 'maidens' (younger women or girls) spun it, singing as they worked. All of Jack's workers were fed while on the job with beef, fish, bread, butter, cheese and ale or beer.

While the numbers of workers presented by Deloney are exceptionally large – and the rewards and good cheer of his employees exceptionally high – the relative proportions of the sexes involved in the preparatory stages may be roughly correct. In Hadleigh each clothier bought the products of multiple male weavers: to avoid exaggeration, let us use a figure of three to five weavers per clothier. Since a minimum of 15 clothiers were at work in each decade during Elizabeth's reign, that should have

---

77. In Warwick, 1571–1602, 20 per cent of men with known occupations made or sold cloth and 13 per cent were victuallers (Beier, 'Social problems').

78. Marjorie Keniston McIntosh, *Working women in English society, 1300–1620* (Cambridge, 2005), esp. pp. 28–37 and 122–3.

79. Thomas Deloney, *The novels of Thomas Deloney*, ed. Merritt E. Lawlis (Bloomington, IN, 1961), pp. 26–7, for this and below. Deloney also described the various cloth finishers employed by Jack (20 people in his fulling mill, 40 men in his dyehouse, 80 rowers who raised the nap on the cloth and 50 shermen who trimmed it to a level surface) and the people he hired to feed all these workers (*ibid.*, pp. 27–8).

80. Thomas Carew of Bildeston, the author of a sermon delivered around 1600, said that children working within their own families, some of whom also carded wool and spun it, earned around a penny per day without food and drink ('A caveat for craftesmen and clothiers' in his *Certaine godly and necessarie sermons* [London, 1603], fol. V1r). See Chapter 6, 'The ongoing influence of Christian social teachings', below.

yielded a total of 45–75 weavers per decade. The occupational summary, however, shows no more than 15, probably because the records are skewed in favour of more prosperous men and because some of the cloths were woven in nearby villages.[81] In giving numbers for the people who produced the yarn needed by those weavers, Deloney shows women and children working full-time within a large clothmaking establishment, whereas in Hadleigh and most other Elizabethan areas those earlier stages would normally have been carried out within the workers' own households and on a part-time basis. Let us therefore double the number of part-time people required to prepare yarn for our 45–75 hypothetical looms. The labour of around 70–110 youngsters would have been needed to pick the wool, while 45–75 women or children carded it and 90–150 spun it. Those numbers are minimal, for among poor people in Norwich in 1570 91 men were described as weavers of various kinds of woollen cloth while 538 women carded or spun, a ratio of 5.9 carders/spinners per weaver.[82]

These highly tentative figures suggest that the labour of around 205–440 women and children would have been necessary to produce yarn for 45–75 weavers in and near Hadleigh.[83] Robert Reyce, a local observer who described Suffolk's woollen cloth production in 1618, commented that clothiers 'sett many poore persons a-worke, which other wise knew nott how to live, especially of the women kind, whereof whole villages and townes, doe live and maintaine themselves by spinning'.[84] But of the people who carried out the preliminary stages in Hadleigh, we know almost nothing. The only mentions of anyone sorting and carding wool come from accounts of the town's workhouse beginning in 1589, where children and young people were set to those tasks. Spinning, too, was taught in the workhouse, but we have only three other references to it, in bequests by clothiers or their widows probably influenced by Rowland Taylor.[85] The additional economic activities of women are entirely hidden from our view, with the exception of women paid by the town to board children or look after sick people. Other women presumably assisted their husbands in the food and drink trades, in running alehouses and inns or in making clothing or light leather items, but of those contributions to the economies of their family and town we remain ignorant.

---

81. See App. 1.3.

82. *The Norwich census of the poor, 1570*, ed. John F. Pound, Norfolk Record Society, vol. 40 (Norwich, 1971), pp. 97 and 99.

83. Robert Reyce calculated in 1618 that a Suffolk clothier who made twenty broadcloths every week employed at least 500 workers in addition to the labour of his own family: sorters, spinners, weavers, woadsetters, dyers, wringers, burlers, shermen and carriers (*Suffolk in the XVIIth century: the breviary of Suffolk*, ed. Francis Hervey [London, 1902], p. 22).

84. *Ibid.* In 1637, John Alabaster of Hadleigh referred in his will to 'my spinning houses' in the village of Baylham and elsewhere, which may have been warehouses where clothiers distributed wool and collected spun yarn; he was thus employing workers in communities 15 miles away from Hadleigh (A&S, *Hadleigh*, p. 148).

85. TNA PRO PROB 11/31 (James Hawle, 1547) and 11/37 (John Raven, 1555), ERO D/ABW 18/67, and see Chapter 6, 'The impact of Rowland Taylor and opposition to him, 1544–54', below.

Religion

Hadleigh's religious life during the Reformation period has interested outside observers since the 1560s. Its leading reformers and their martyrdom under Mary are described with great feeling and powerful woodcuts in John Foxe's enormously influential *Actes and Monuments of ... the Church*, generally known as *The Book of Martyrs*. Beginning with the first edition of his book, published in 1563, Foxe described Hadleigh as a cradle of early Protestantism:

> The towne of Hadley was one of the firste that receyved the woorde of God in al England, at the preachynge of Mayster Thomas Bylney: [and suche gracious successe had it[86]] that a great number of that parishe became excedyng well learned in the holy scriptures, as wel women as men, so that a man myghte have founde amonge them many that had often red the whole Bible thorow, and that could have sayde a great part of S. Paules Epistles by hart, and verye wel and readely have geven a godlye learned sentence in any matter of controversy.[87]

These lay reformers spread the word and put their new beliefs into practice:

> Their children and servauntes were also broughte up, and trayned so diligentlye in the ryghte knowledge of Gods woorde, that the whole towne seemed rather an Universitye of the learned, then a towne of Clothmaking, or labouring people. And that moste is to be commended, they were for the more part faithfull followers of Gods woord in their lyvyng.

The reason for the robust presence of early reformers in Hadleigh lay in the parish's unusual position within the ecclesiastical structure of the country. Rather than being subject to the authority of the bishop of Norwich, as were many parishes in Suffolk and Norfolk, Hadleigh was a 'peculiar', responsible directly to the archbishop of Canterbury. Hadleigh's rectors were appointed by the archbishop and commonly held other church livings and offices as well, including, from 1556 onwards, the (co-) Deanery of Bocking; those who did not live regularly in Hadleigh fulfilled their obligations to the parish by naming curates. Thomas Bilney, one of the first Cambridge reformers, caused a stir in the county in 1527 through his preaching in Hadleigh, and Thomas Rose, another 'evangelical pioneer', made the town his base shortly thereafter.[88] After Thomas Cranmer became archbishop in 1532, he named several charismatic supporters of the new faith as rectors, sheltering them and their curates from the wrath of the conservative bishops of Norwich.[89] In 1534 Cranmer intervened on Rose's behalf after the radical curate had

---

86. Changed in the 1570 and 1583 editions, with slightly different spellings, to: 'by whose industrye the Gospell of Christ had such gracious successe, and took such root there'.

87. John Foxe, *Actes and monuments of matters most special and memorable, happenyng in the church* (London, 1563), p. 1065, for this and the quotation below.

88. MacCulloch, *Thomas Cranmer: a life* (New Haven, CT, 1996), p. 110.

89. Conversely, in 1536 Cranmer ordered Hugh Payne, a vehemently Catholic curate in Hadleigh, to cease preaching (*ibid.*, 143). Payne disregarded that order, and when he preached in 1537 that 'one Paternoster said by a priest's commandment was worth 1,000 said voluntarily' he was reported to Cranmer, questioned by the archbishop and sent by him to Thomas Cromwell for punishment (*L&P*, vol. xii, pt. 1, p. 121).

incited the anger of some of his parishioners by questioning the spiritual merits of charitable bequests.[90] English was said to have been used in 'the masse and consecration of the sacrament of the aultar' in Hadleigh as early as 1538, the same year in which royal injunctions ordered that an English bible be placed in every parish church. After 1538, none of the limited number of surviving wills from Hadleigh contains bequests for intercessory masses or references to purgatory, apart from one possible exception in 1545. People who remained loyal to traditional beliefs or were uncertain apparently resorted to minimal, neutral wordings, as did Margaret Tourner, widow of Roger, who in 1535 said simply that she left her soul 'into the hands of my lord God'.[91] One of Cranmer's protégés was Dr Nicholas Shaxton, temporarily bishop of Sarum (Salisbury) in the later 1530s, who came to Hadleigh in 1540 after resigning his episcopal position and being forbidden to preach; he worked as an unofficial curate in St Mary's church for six years and through his sister's marriage became uncle to Thomas Alabaster, later one of Hadleigh's leading clothiers and staunchest Protestants.

Foxe drew special attention to the preaching, charitable activities and death of Dr Rowland Taylor, Hadleigh's rector from 1544 to 1554 and one of the town's Marian martyrs.[92] Presenting Taylor as a model Christian minister, Foxe noted that when he was appointed to the office, having previously been a member of Cranmer's household, he did not follow the common pattern of leasing out his benefice (especially the income from tithes) to a layperson and appointing 'an ignorant unlearned Priest to serve the cure'. Instead Taylor

> made hys personal abode and dwelling in Hadley among ye people committed to his charge. Where he as a good shepheard, abiding and dwelling among his sheepe, gave himself wholly to the study of holy scriptures, most faythfull endevouring himselfe to fulfill that charge, which the Lord gave unto Peter, saying, *Peter lovest thou me? Feede my Lambes, Feede my sheepe.*

As part of that charge, Taylor preached 'the worde of God, the doctrine of their salvation' to his congregation every Sunday and holy day; his life and conversation were 'an example of unfayned christian life and true holyness'. Under Mary, however, Taylor's

---

90. Rose had reportedly said that 'a man's goods spent for his soul after his death prevaileth him not'. Cranmer wrote to Hadleigh's inhabitants, offering a more innocuous interpretation of Rose's statement: the curate was only referring to people who had made their bequests 'while out of charity and were buried in hell'. Cranmer encouraged the parishioners to 'leave their grudges' and accept Rose favourably (*L&P*, vol. vii, p. 148). For below, see Charles Wriothesley, *A chronicle of England during the reigns of the Tudors*, vol. i, ed. W.D. Hamilton, Camden Society, new series (London, 1875); vol. i, pp. 83 and 85, and *Visitation articles and injunctions of the period of the Reformation*, vol. ii, ed. Walter H. Frere and W.M. Kennedy (London, 1910), vol. ii, pp. 34–43.

91. TNA PRO PROB 11/25 and a similar wording in PROB 11/27 (Thomas Rotheman, 1538). For below, see John Craig, *Reformation, politics and polemics* (Aldershot, 2001), pp. 156–62, and A&S, *Hadleigh*, ch. 2.

92. Foxe, *Actes and monuments*, 1583 (4th edition), pp. 1518–19, for this paragraph. For a fuller discussion of Taylor, his followers and opponents, and their probable impact upon poor relief, see Chapter 6, 'The impact of Rowland Taylor and opposition to him, 1544–54', below.

enemies were able to obtain his arrest by the Privy Council, leading to his execution as a heretic, burned at the stake at Aldham Common on the edge of Hadleigh in 1555. Richard Yeoman, his loyally Protestant former curate, and two lay followers from Hadleigh were likewise taken prisoner; two of them were later martyred, while the other died in prison.

Although most subsequent commentators have given Taylor credit for much of Hadleigh's early support of Protestant ideas, John Craig called that assessment into question.[93] Accepting that Taylor was a powerful preacher, a vigorous controversialist on behalf of the new religion and a man of keen wit, Craig noted that Taylor – like his predecessors – held positions other than the rectorship of Hadleigh. During his many absences, while carrying out the duties of his other offices, preaching or serving on national commissions, he left the parish in the hands of Yeoman and, late in Edward's reign, David Whitehead, a staunch Protestant who was to flee England under Mary.[94] In 1551 Taylor leased out 'the parsonage and rectory of Hadley' to two local men, which to Craig indicates that he was not in regular residence, but may be interpreted differently.[95] He signed only a few wills of his parishioners and seems to have taken no direct part in town government other than its charitable activities, unlike several Elizabethan ministers who followed him.

Nevertheless, Taylor, Yeoman and Whitehead clearly continued the progress of the Reformation in Hadleigh. We gain some evidence from the testaments of faith that opened most wills. The first surviving will for which Taylor served as scribe, written in 1547, contains a moderately reformed religious statement: 'I commend my soul unto Christ Jesus, my maker and redeemer, by whom and by the merits of whose blessed passion is all my whole trust of clean remission and forgiveness of my sins, and my body to be buried in the church yard of Hadley.'[96] The testator – Thomas Brounsmythe, a prosperous woadsetter or dyer – went on to give instructions for a distinctly Protestant burial, proscribing the service associated with prayer for the dead: 'I will that my body shall be brought to my burial in the morning after my decease or shortly after; Item I will there be rung one sole knell with one bell without any dirge to be sung or said.' Strikingly, Brounsmythe requested a sermon:

---

93. Craig, *Reformation*, ch. 6. For discussion of Craig's assessment, see Chapter 6, 'The impact of Rowland Taylor and opposition to him, 1544–54', below. Taylor's most important office in Suffolk, below, was the newly created office of Archdeacon of Bury St Edmunds (MacCulloch, *Thomas Cranmer*, pp. 456–7).

94. In 1552 'Mr Whitehead of Hadley' received Cranmer's highest recommendation for an archbishopric in Ireland, due to his 'good knowledge, special honesty, fervent zeal, and politic wisdom' (Thomas Cranmer, *Miscellaneous writings and letters of Thomas Cranmer*, vol. ii, ed. J.E. Cox, Parker Society [Cambridge, 1846], vol. ii, p. 438). I am grateful to Diarmaid MacCulloch for this reference. Whitehead wrote the will of John Raven in 1552, which left a substantial sum to the poor (TNA PRO PROB 11/36).

95. TNA PRO REQ 2/18/26. Taylor may actually have been trying to shield his possession of the parsonage, which had previously been leased to Nicholas Shaxton, whose properties were seized when he lost religious favour. Taylor's lessees were Steven Gardiner, a cloth maker and office holder in the town, and Thomas Alabaster, who had recently come to Hadleigh with Shaxton, his uncle, and was soon to become a firmly Protestant trustee for many civic and charitable causes (A&S, *Hadleigh*, chs 2 and 6).

96. ERO D/ABW 3/135.

Immediately after my body be buried, I will that a sermon be preached by one whom my executor shall think best or most convenient to the laud and praise of my lord and saviour Jesus Christ and setting forth of his blessed and holy word and to the declaring and testimony of my faith towards the same.

The other will for which Taylor served as a witness, as did Yeoman, was left by merchant John Freeman in 1551.[97] Freeman bequeathed two parcels of land 'commonly called the Maundy Land' to the churchwardens; the income was to support Maundy Thursday rituals if they were still in use or, if not, to provide a sermon to be delivered annually in Hadleigh's church and to assist the poor.

Richard Yeoman apparently favoured a more elaborate wording, as seen in the 1551 will of William Broke, clothier, to which Yeoman served as a witness and probable scribe:

I bequeath my soul to almighty God to have the fruition of his most glorious Godhead by the merits and passion of our only saviour, Jesus Christ, and my body to be buried in the church yard of Hadleigh aforesaid, or else in that church yard in the which parish it shall please almighty God to call me to his mercy.[98]

Yeoman's wording continued to influence wills during Mary's reign, even after the return to Catholicism and his own subsequent departure from the parish. Three wills written in the first few years after Mary's accession include a similar statement, including 'the fruition of his Godhead', but also – probably to avoid trouble from the new religious authorities – a Catholic reference to 'the Blessed Virgin Mary and all the holy company of saints'.[99]

A quantitative analysis of testaments of faith in the surviving sixteenth-century wills is shown in Table 1.1.[100] Whereas all those written during the first third of the century were traditional/Catholic, as early as 1534–47 a quarter were mildly or probably reformist and two-fifths were neutral. Under Edward half of the testaments were strongly or mildly Protestant, with the others neutral or mixed. In Mary's reign only one person wrote a Protestant will, while the majority sheltered under a neutral or mixed statement; interestingly, there were no Catholic ones.

The intensity and hostility that surrounded religious belief in Hadleigh between around 1540 and 1558, including the Marian attacks on Taylor and his followers, decreased thereafter.[101] The first Elizabethan rector, Dr Thomas Spencer, was a committed reformer and an active preacher throughout Suffolk, though he also held the office of archdeacon of Chichester. Spencer participated in Hadleigh's governance, helping to audit the annual accounts between 1563 and 1570, but he

---

97. TNA PRO PROB 11/34.

98. ERO D/ABW 3/201. For other wills that use a similar wording, see TNA PRO PROB 11/31 (Joan Quintyne, 1546) and ERO D/ABW 3/110.

99. ERO D/ABW 8/183, D/ABW 13/38 and TNA PRO PROB 11/38 (John Clerke, 1556).

100. I have used the categories for analysing religious testaments that John Craig and I developed together in the early 1990s and that he employed in his *Reformation, Politics and Polemics*, p. 170. Because I excluded wills from people living outside Hadleigh, in order to assess local sentiments, my total number is slightly lower than his 100.

101. See Ch. 6A and 6E below for the pre-1559 years. For below, see Jones, *Hadleigh*, pp. 46–7.

Table 1.1

Religious testaments, by period, Hadleigh wills, 1500–99.

Periods	Traditional/ Catholic	Neutral/ none/mixed	Mildly/probably reformist	Definitely Protestant	Total
1500–33, Catholic	15 = 100% of period	0	0	0	15 = 16% of all wills
1534–47, early reformed influences in Hadleigh	5 = 38%	5 = 38%	3 = 23%	0	13 = 14%
1547–53, Edward VI	0	11 * = 52%	5 = 24%	5 = 24%	21 = 22%
1553–8, Mary	0	8 *** = 89%	1 = 11%	0	9 = 9%
1558–79, early Elizabethan	0	10 = 43%	6 = 26%	7 = 30%	23 = 24%
1580–99, late Elizabethan	0	4 = 27%	3 = 20%	8 = 53%	15 = 16%
Total	20 = 21% of all wills	38 = 40%	18 = 19%	20 = 21%	96

Notes: This analysis excludes wills written by people who held land in Hadleigh or left bequests there but did not actually live in the community or hold local office. The number of wills is therefore slightly smaller than that given by Craig (*Reformation*, p. 170). The dates refer to when the will was written, not when it was proved.

* Each asterisk designates a mixed testament of faith, containing both traditional and Protestant elements.

does not appear to have caused religious discord within the community. He was followed in 1571 by Dr John Still, who remained as Hadleigh's rector until 1592, when he was named bishop of Bath and Wells.[102] A pragmatic man who held many other church offices, including the mastership of St John's and Trinity Colleges in Cambridge, Still acted as a moderate in religious terms, though his own personal beliefs are unclear. Showing no eagerness to stir up controversy, he became heavily involved in Hadleigh's civic life. Around 1574 he married Anne Alabaster, daughter of Thomas, then one of the town's leading clothiers, and most of their eight children were baptised in Hadleigh. Still audited town accounts for the next sixteen years and joined the efforts of some of the Chief Inhabitants during the later 1570s and 1580s to impose greater control and order.[103]

Elizabethan wills reflect generically Protestant beliefs but provide relatively little evidence of active pressure for further reform along Calvinist or puritan lines.[104] During the first 20 years of Elizabeth's reign, although no Hadleigh wills contained Catholic testaments, 43 per cent were neutral and 26 per cent mildly Protestant. John Water, who died in 1564, was the only person to leave money for sermons, one to be preached at his burial, the other at a later time.[105] Between 1580 and 1599 27 per cent of the wills were still neutral, with 20 per cent mildly Protestant and 53 per cent definitely so. Thomas Alabaster the elder, who wrote his will in 1591, was atypical in his detailed (and trinitarian) religious testament:

> I do commend my soul into the hands of almighty God, the father, the son, and the holy ghost, in whose name I was baptised and through whose free mercy and grace by the death and passion of my lord and saviour Jesus Christ I only hope to obtain remission of all my sins and undoubtedly believe to be saved. And as touching my body I will that it be decently committed to the earth, there to rest until the Last Judgement day, at which time I certainly believe that it shall rise again in the same form and substance and be joined again with my soul and live together eternally with my saviour Jesus Christ in joy and glory.[106]

Alabaster began the more practical side of his will: 'Now concerning the disposing of that portion of lands and goods which it hath pleased almighty God to make me a steward of here in this world, … '. Based on the wills and other evidence, John Craig suggested that the tumult of the Marian period 'pushed Hadleigh into a state of quiescence. Like a child once burned and twice shy, religiously, Elizabethan Hadleigh

---

102. A&S, *Hadleigh*, ch. 12.
103. See Chapter 6, 'Worry about control and cost, 1576–85', below.
104. See Table 1.1.
105. TNA PRO PROB 11/47.
106. TNA PRO PROB 11/80/51. Alabaster had recently purchased land in Hadleigh from Stephen Upcher of Dedham, Essex, one of the signatories of the puritan orders issued in Dedham in 1585/6. The only other distinctive testament was left by clothier Julian Beamonde in 1586: 'I commend my soul into the hands of almighty God, my maker and redeemer, hoping to be saved by his grace through the merits of Jesus Christ, my Lord God and only saviour, and my body to the earth whence I was taken out, in hope of the glorious appearing and coming of our saviour Jesus Christ to judge both the quick and the dead' (TNA PRO PROB 11/70/1, and see Chapter 6, 'The ongoing influence of Christian social teachings', below).

seemed in a state of arrested development.'[107] As will be discussed below, that assessment is exaggerated.

Although bequests to the church ceased temporarily at the Reformation, in the late 1570s they begin to appear again, though now only for physical repairs to St Mary's. John Turner, a clothier who died in 1577, left 20s that may have been applied to the work done the following year, for which a special church rate was levied.[108] Additional repairs were done in 1585, including mending the steeple, bells and glass windows, and in 1589, on both of which occasions rates were imposed. Thomas Alabaster left £5 towards the reparations of the church in 1591, but the money was delivered to the churchwardens only in 1599, when it was used for lead, nails and work done on the south and west sides of 'the cradle of the steeple'.[109]

Town government

During the Elizabethan period Hadleigh's form of government was unusual though not unique, in that the men who ran the town had no formal legal authority to do so. The town was not yet an incorporated borough, so it could not appoint civic officers, but neither did it function through the parish or the Chief Pledges within a View of Frankpledge, like some other communities.[110] The 20–25 men who styled themselves the Chief Inhabitants – who might be joined by the rector if he was in town – were an extra-legal group. Although there is no indication of when and how they selected new men to join their company, their authority within the town appears to have been unquestioned. Their high socio-economic positions and their obvious willingness to spend considerable time and effort on behalf of the town may have persuaded their neighbours that they were working for the good of the whole and should be accepted as having *de facto* legitimacy.

The body of Chief Inhabitants appears to have grown out of three previous groups, which in practice probably had heavily overlapping memberships: the 'most honest persons' of Hadleigh, whom Rector and Archdeacon William Pykenham had named in 1497 as the present and future feoffees of the land that supported the almshouses he established; the feoffees who held the market property; and the men who headed Hadleigh's pre-Reformation religious' guilds or fraternities. The successors to Pykenham's initial feoffees and those who handled the market properties were accustomed to serving as trustees, managing land and running a charitable or civic activity; the guild heads, some of whom were feoffees as well, had likewise been

---

107. Craig, *Reformation*, p. 174. For below, see Chapter 6, 'The ongoing influence of Christian social teachings', below.

108. TNA PRO PROB 11/59/36 and HadlA 004/A/01, pp. 125 and 129. For below, see HadlA 004/A/01, pp. 169 and 201.

109. TNA PRO PROB 11/80/51 and HadlA 004/A/01, pp. 226 and 267.

110. See Chapter 6, 'Civic identity, civic competition', below, and, e.g., McIntosh, *A Community Transformed*, ch. 5. The only hint of an alternative source of authority within Hadleigh was when the Chief Inhabitants who signed an order in 1577 called themselves 'the headboroughs and inhabitants' of the town (HadlA 004/A/01, p. 122, and Chapter 6, 'Worry about control and cost, 1576–85', below).

organising activities on behalf of larger groups within the community.[111] In Hadleigh we know the names of only six guild heads, from 1542–5 (two esquires, two gentlemen and two clothiers), but all of them audited town accounts, the criterion I have used to identify Chief Inhabitants.

During the rest of the sixteenth century the Chief Inhabitants held great power within the town. They handled the properties held in trust to support the market and charitable activities, supervised the operation of the market, maintained order within the town, repaired local bridges and some roads and administered the town's system of poor relief.[112] They also selected the working officials: two market bailiffs and two churchwardens (who served for staggered two-year terms), and a chief collector and two subcollectors for the poor (all of whom had one-year terms).[113] It is a reflection of the integration of civic and religious authority within Hadleigh that churchwardens and poor relief officers were appointed by the Chief Inhabitants, for they were supposed to be chosen by the parish except in incorporated boroughs. Some of the working officers were themselves Chief Inhabitants, while others were well-regarded men of slightly lower status. Special orders in Hadleigh's town book were signed by those Chief Inhabitants present at the time. At the end of each year the Chief Inhabitants audited the accounts at a formal reckoning and signed new leases, followed by a bang-up dinner for themselves, the officers and the tenants of larger town properties.

The Chief Inhabitants and officers came from the upper ranks of the community. Of the 35 men known to have held those positions between 1537 and 1553, 81 per cent were from wealthy clothier families or were gentlemen, esquires or knights.[114] By the period 1576–85 73 per cent came from those backgrounds, joined now by a somewhat larger fraction of men in other crafts or trades. The market bailiffs and chief collectors were generally clothiers or other successful businessmen; the churchwardens were of slightly lower rank; and the subcollectors for the poor, who interacted on a regular basis with needy people, were commonly crafts- or tradesmen. Of 19 Chief Inhabitants between 1537 and 1553, just under half – all men of gentry or other high local status – accepted no functional working offices in the town. (Sir) Henry Doyle (or Doyly) signed first among the auditors of accounts in 1535 and continued to do so until his death in 1564; although he later became a Justice of the Peace for West Suffolk, he never held a working office in the town.[115] The ten Chief Inhabitants who did serve as officers in the earlier period, in nearly all cases for only a single term, were joined by sixteen other men who were not Chief Inhabitants. By 1576–92 only a third

---

111.   In some towns, the heads of guilds became the *de facto* governors of the community after the Reformation (e.g., Bury St Edmunds, Stratford upon Avon, and Louth, Lincs.) For below, see HadlA 026/C/06–08 and 026/D/04–05.

112.   A&S, *Hadleigh*, ch. 5. For maintenance of order, see Chapter 6, 'Worry about control and cost, 1576–85', below; for poor relief officials, see Chapter 2, 'The forms of aid, in-kind distributions and services', below.

113.   A working office carried actual responsibilities throughout the year, whereas auditing the accounts and electing new officers normally occurred only once annually.

114.   See Table 6.1 below.

115.   A&S, *Hadleigh*, term him the 'chairman' of the Chief Inhabitants (p. 60), but he is not given that title in the records.

of the 26 Chief Inhabitants accepted a working office, while 28 other officers generally served as churchwardens or subcollectors for the poor.

Although Hadleigh did not obtain a royal charter that incorporated the town as a legal entity until 1618, it had previously received two economically important charters. One, as we have seen, confirmed the town's right to hold a market and fair. The other renewed a privilege enjoyed by Hadleigh's carriers: a long-standing exemption from paying tolls on goods that they took into London for sale or export. Since the eleventh century all vassals and tenants of land belonging to the archbishop of Canterbury had been free from those tolls, and in 1414/15 four Hadleigh carriers appeared and were authorised before the Lord Mayor's court.[116] The exemption was confirmed by Edward VI and Elizabeth, and local carriers were approved in London in 1548 and 1567.[117] Early in Elizabeth's reign Hadleigh's Chief Inhabitants began issuing their own certificates to local people.

Three notations in the town book between 1580 and 1590 refer to delivery of a charter into the hands of leading residents for safe keeping.[118] The first and third references speak of 'the charter for the town' or 'the town charter' – probably the earlier market charter – while the second confirmed the exemption from tolls. In 1571, however, the market bailiffs paid £4 to John Smyth 'for that he have laid out about the charter', and in 1586 or 1587 a memorandum notes that William Forth, gent., held £10 due to the town, 'part of that money which was gathered for the charter'.[119] Those statements have been taken as indications that Hadleigh was already trying to obtain a charter of incorporation, which is possible. But it is equally likely that during this period the Chief Inhabitants were only trying to secure a renewal of their market charter or their exemption from London tolls: there is no other evidence that they found formal borough status necessary for themselves or the town.

Hadleigh was nominally subject to the authority of the Justices of the Peace for West Suffolk, appointments that during the central years of the century were at least partially dependent upon one's religious position. Between 1536/7 and 1561 the town had an important resident JP, Sir Henry Doyle. Although himself a Catholic, Doyle was able to accommodate himself to diverse official religions.[120] He was joined on the late Henrician bench by Thomas Tilney, an associate of the conservative duke of Norfolk, who was removed when Edward VI came to the throne. As we have seen, Protestant William Forth was named as a JP under Edward but removed under Mary; he was replaced by Walter and Edward Clerke, strong supporters of the old faith.[121] Between

---

116. HadlA 001/C/03 and SRO-BSE TEM 129/132, temporary deposit, March, 1956, item 11, an inspeximus by the Lord Mayor of London, 1625, granting inhabitants of Hadleigh freedom from London tolls, citing earlier documents.

117. HadlA 001/C/01–03. For below, see A&S, *Hadleigh*, p. 66.

118. HadlA 004/A/01, pp. 136, 193 and 205.

119. *Ibid.*, pp. 91 and 178. For below, see, e.g., A&S, *Hadleigh*, p. 240.

120. MacCulloch, *Suffolk and the Tudors*, esp. pp. 93 and 167, and A&S, *Hadleigh*, p. 290. Doyle was also sheriff of Norfolk and Suffolk in the mid 1550s; in a year of dearth during Mary's reign he promoted Hadleigh's market at the expense of neighbouring Bildeston. For the rest of this paragraph, see MacCulloch, *Suffolk and the Tudors*, pp. 166–7, 232–3, 416 and App. I.

121. For the Clerkes, see Chapter 6, 'The impact of Rowland Taylor and opposition to him, 1544–54', below.

1561 and the late 1580s Hadleigh had no representation among the JPs, but William Forth the younger was named in 1589, Edward Doyle in 1591 and Robert Rolfe (from a clothier family who had become gentlemen and then esquires) in 1599. Perhaps owing to Forth's appointment, the Justices had dinner with local gentlemen at Hadleigh's Angel Inn in 1589.[122] It was within this small geographic area, with its complex demographic, economic, religious and political patterns, that the town's system of poor relief was to develop and function.

---

122.   HadlA 021/B/09.

Chapter 2

Hadleigh's system of assistance

Before we turn to the people who received assistance in Hadleigh, to be considered in the next three chapters, it will be helpful to know how the system of relief functioned. This chapter first describes the officers responsible for administering assistance, together with their duties and the kinds of decisions they had to make. We look then at the types of aid offered, especially in-kind distributions and provision of services. A final section shows how this expensive array of aid was financed.

Officers and decision-making

From the mid 1560s onwards three unpaid officers were chosen each year by the Chief Inhabitants to administer the system of relief. These men had primary responsibility for maintaining the properties that provided income for the poor, collecting rents, bequests and rates, and distributing assistance to needy people. The chief collector paid for repair of buildings, ditches, woodlands, the almshouses and, after 1589, the workhouse; he gathered rents from the properties held as a charitable trust by the Chief Inhabitants, delivering out-rents to the manorial lords from whom the lands were held; and he transferred the bulk of his income to lesser officers for distribution.[1] If the market bailiffs had excess funds they commonly gave them to the chief collector, as did the churchwardens on occasion. In 1570 Thomas Alabaster, as chief collector, itemised the income he had received from other officers plus rents from thirteen separate units of land and houses located in Hadleigh and five other communities, together coming to nearly £106. Chief collectors were also responsible for seeing that gifts and bequests to the town for the use of the poor were actually delivered, and they commonly worked to find homes for orphans and to set up positions as servants or apprentices for other children. Some collectors played a more direct role in helping needy people, giving supplemental payments to certain individuals or having clothes made for them.

Although those were serious responsibilities, most of the work of running the system of relief on a daily basis was assigned to two subcollectors for the poor.[2] They were given several difficult and potentially unpopular assignments. Probably with the advice or at least the approval of the chief collector, they had to assess Hadleigh's more prosperous household heads for poor rates and to collect the sums due each week or quarter. It was also their job to give out assistance, which meant knowing which poor individuals or families needed help: how much, of what kind and for how long. They had to ensure that help was going to needy and deserving people but was

---

1. A&S, *Hadleigh*, pp. 118–22, for this paragraph.
2. *Ibid.*, pp. 122–5.

not overly generous and did not continue when it was no longer essential. Although the choice of people to be given places in an almshouse was nominally assigned to the Chief Inhabitants as feoffees of the property that supported those institutions, poor relief officers were probably involved in that selection process too.

The poor relief offices began evolving in the 1550s. Between the mid 1530s and at least 1549 the churchwardens had received, spent and accounted for the rental income from the land that supported Pykenham's almshouses. By 1559, however, after the creation of the town's new charitable endowment, Robert Rolfe was appointed as 'receiver of all the lands to the use of the poor folks', and three years later the office was described as 'collector for the poor inhabitants'.[3] The 'head', 'high' or 'chief collector' accounted for income in 1566; in 1569 he was described as 'chief collector for the provision of the poor'. The office of subcollector was meanwhile developing beneath that position. In 1557 the churchwardens delivered the balance in their hands after submitting their account to two named 'collectors', and from 1564 onwards these officers were always described as subcollectors.[4] At the end of their annual term, the chief collector and subcollectors were required to submit detailed accounts of all expenses, down to the last penny, at the annual reckoning or audit held by the Chief Inhabitants.

In total, 74 men are known to have held the poor relief offices between 1557 and 1600. Of these, 15 served as chief collector only, 43 as subcollector only and 16 held both offices, in all but one case starting as a subcollector and some years later moving to the higher office. Perhaps because these positions were so demanding of time and commitment but received no salary, most men served for only a single year. Of the 31 chief collectors, 7 held office for two non-consecutive years and 1 for three. William Gale was in a class by himself, named to this position in 1570–72, 1575–6, 1579–81 and 1585–6.[5] Most of the 59 subcollectors likewise held office for just one year, though 6 men were appointed twice and 3 men served three times.

The chief collectors were generally of higher status and probably older than their assistants. Of 31 men who held this office, two-thirds were already Chief Inhabitants at the time (as measured by their inclusion among the group of men who audited the annual accounts) and another fifth became so later; only 5 of the 31 never became Chief Inhabitants. Many held the position of churchwarden or market bailiff in other years. Of the 29 chief collectors whose occupations or levels of wealth are known, 6 were termed gentlemen (though 4 of them were clothiers or headed families that had previously been clothiers), 13 were currently clothiers and 3 were drapers, haberdashers or yeomen. The remaining 7 were among the upper half of the Hadleigh

---

3. HadlA 004/A/01, pp. 50 and 62. For below, see *ibid.*, pp. 69–70; *ibid.*, p. 80.

4. *Ibid.*, pp. 48 and 65. According to a statute of 1552, modified slightly in 1563, every parish or incorporated urban community was to appoint two Collectors for the Poor responsible for gathering money from more prosperous members of the community and distributing it to the needy: 5 & 6 Edward VI, c. 2, and 5 Elizabeth, c. 3 (*SR*, vol. iv, pp. 131–2 and 411–14).

5. Gale also audited accounts as a Chief Inhabitant from 1572 to 1603, was market bailiff in 1575–6 and 1587–8, was named to keep order in his neighbourhood in 1580 and 1586 and to oversee bridge repair in 1587, distributed charitable goods in 1592, and was an overseer of the workhouse in 1596.

people assessed for the national subsidy of 1568, indicating that they were some of the town's wealthier people.[6]

The subcollectors came from respectable but less elevated families, presumably because the position involved more burdensome duties as well as intimate contact with needy people and the reality of poverty. Fewer than a third of the 59 ever became Chief Inhabitants, and 44 per cent held no other town offices, though 34 per cent went from being a subcollector to a higher office later. The occupations of those who held this position but were not chosen subsequently as chief collectors were more modest. Four men were described later in their lives as clothiers, but they were just beginning their careers at this time. The remainder included two tanners, a miller, a smith, a fishmonger, a yeoman and someone who rented a market stall from the town. Six other men rated for the subsidy of 1568 covered a wider economic range.[7]

The willingness of Hadleigh's leaders to accept the heavy burden of administering the town's elaborate system of poor relief deserves our respect. They may have gained status from their peers for agreeing to accept these offices, but they received no direct financial reward and had to take time away from their own occupations to carry out their duties. Although the chief collector perhaps had some opportunities for patronage (such as suggesting who should receive leases of property or a place in an almshouse), he was obliged to account for and justify his actions to the other Chief Inhabitants at the end of the year. The subcollectors may have been under pressure to offer preferential treatment to their friends, relatives and certain powerful men in the community; when they demanded that fellow townspeople pay their rates they faced considerable potential resentment. Thomas Carew, the minister of the neighbouring village of Bildeston, wrote in 1603: 'Some townesmen doe not rate themselves and their neighbours conscionably and proportionably, as they may provide for the poore, but as they may satisfie their owne humors.'[8] One can imagine that certain poor people may have objected to the amount of assistance they were given and pestered the officers for more. Unlike the situation in seventeenth-century England, however, when some poor people felt entitled to relief and submitted written complaints if they did not receive it, there is no indication that needy people in Elizabethan Hadleigh protested formally.[9]

These officers apparently had considerable freedom to exercise their own judgement in distributing benefits to the needy. We have no verbal descriptions of how they selected recipients and decided how much they should receive, but certain features seem clear. The subcollectors must have been in regular personal contact with the town's poor families. The types of assistance awarded and the variable amounts and frequency indicate that officials were responding to immediate and

---

6. Three were assessed on lands or goods worth £8 (in the upper 87th–91st percentile of the 92 people rated in the town), two on goods worth £6 (the 76th–85th percentile), and two on goods worth £5 (the 54th–75th percentile): *Suffolk in 1568*, pp. 107–10.

7. One was assessed at £6 in goods (in the upper 76th–85th percentile), three at £5 in goods (54th–75th percentile), and two on £3 in goods (21st–48th percentile): *ibid.*

8. Thomas Carew, 'The reward of godlinesse', in his *Certaine godly and necesssarie sermons* (London, 1603), fol. N6r.

9. Steve Hindle, *On the parish? The micro-politics of poor relief in rural England, c. 1550–1750* (Oxford, 2004), pp. 398–428.

changing needs of individuals and households. Even among those people who received regular weekly payments, the size of the stipend sometimes altered over the course of a year. This level of specificity indicates that the subcollectors did not merely sit in the Guildhall making up an annual list of people to be helped. Instead, they must have been going into people's homes, seeing how they actually lived and what their true needs were and then delivering an appropriate payment. The occasional assistance given by the chief collector and even the market bailiffs suggests that they, too, were aware of the specific situation of some people and their families.

The criteria used by poor relief officials in selecting the particular people and households to be assisted from among the larger body of need can only be inferred. Because the chief collector and subcollectors were chosen for single-year terms and most did not serve in the same position again, any tendency to favour certain people on purely personal grounds may have been lessened. Some kind of requirement concerning length of residence in Hadleigh was apparently imposed, as reflected in the efforts of the Chief Inhabitants after 1575 to prohibit poor people from settling in the town who might subsequently qualify for relief.[10] Although we do not know how long a newcomer needed to live in the town to qualify for relief, three years was commonly the standard elsewhere during the Elizabethan period and may have been used here as well. An especially interesting issue is whether the town was prepared to help working men and women who were at least temporarily out of employment or who could not find enough employment to sustain their families. Given the 'boom and bust' cyles of woollen cloth manufacture and export, there must have been times when some of the women in Hadleigh who prepared yarn and some of the male craftsmen who used it to weave or finish cloth had little if any work. Such people probably account for most of the 62 women and 80 men aged 20–49 years who received help between 1579 and 1596 (24 per cent).[11]

The question of religious or behavioural requirements is also unanswered in the records. An occasional private bequest specified that help was to be handed out after church services, implicitly restricting recipients to attenders. Thomas Alabaster said in his 1591 will that 2s was to be distributed every Sunday 'amongst twelve honest, aged, impotent poor men and women of the said town immediately after evening prayer within the south chapel of the church of Hadley aforesaid, two pence to every one of them, exhorting them to be thankful unto God for the same'.[12] But no evidence suggests that the town itself imposed similar requirements, and some of the families that received public aid do not appear likely to have been regular church goers. Poor relief officials may have been reluctant to support adults who would spend their assistance on drink or gambling, but under some circumstances they were willing to help illegitimate children or the mother or grandparent with whom they were living.[13] Young people who misbehaved seriously were candidates for the workhouse, not for

---

10. See Chapters 4, 'Granted to a different family or expelled from Hadleigh', and 6, 'Worry about control and cost', 1576–85, below. For below, see McIntosh, *Poor relief in England*, e.g., pp. 168, 246 and 250.

11. See Chapter 6, 'Relations between clothiers and workers', below. For 50 years as the cutoff between younger and older adults, see Chapter 3, note 4, below.

12. TNA PRO PROB 11/80/51.

13. See Chapter 4, 'Aid while living at home', below.

normal relief. The almshouse residents were all older people and poor, but their social situations covered a considerable range. While widow Ann Bartholomew, who entered an almshouse in the early 1590s, was clearly hard working and respectable, old Father Gedge, who occupied one of the houses from before 1579 until his death in 1584, was the senior member of an extended and apparently dysfunctional family with nine members on relief over three generations.[14]

The need for assistance in Hadleigh may have been influenced not only by the specific situation of particular individuals and households but also by some wider economic, seasonal and demographic factors. Although we do not have information about prices, wages and piece-rates for Hadleigh specifically, we know about patterns for the country as a whole. During the period of Rowland Taylor's rectorship, the price of grain, needed for the bread that formed the basis of the diet of the poor, began to rise sharply.[15] By the 1590s, grain cost 4.3 times more than in the later 1530s. The depth of need among people working for wages or paid by the piece was surely intensified by a decline in the purchasing power of their income. Because wage rates were rising far more slowly than prices, the purchasing power of wages in the 1550s was only 75 per cent of its value in the 1530s for both agricultural labourers and building craftsmen; it had dropped to 61–69 per cent by the 1590s.[16] Little correlation is visible, however, between food prices and the amount of poor relief distributed annually in Hadleigh.[17] Seasonality, likewise, appears to have had scant impact. Although one might have expected that demand would be greatest in the winter, when the cost of wood for cooking and perhaps heating was high and when certain foodstuffs were more expensive, that does not seem to have been the case. The town's willingness to provide a decent burial for the destitute poor may, however, have been affected to some extent by the total level of mortality in the town and the presence of epidemics.

The forms of aid, in-kind distributions and services

Some of the total volume of aid for needy people in Hadleigh must have been given informally and privately. Poor people themselves presumably helped their relatives, friends and neighbours: by taking in poor children; by tending the sick, injured and elderly; and by giving or loaning small amounts of food, cash or personal goods. Such assistance would often have been delivered by women, in their roles as providers of food, clothing and care. Some economically comfortable families offered aid to poor neighbours, friends and servants, as well as to less prosperous kinsfolk.[18] While informal help is rarely visible in the records, we must recognise that the aid documented in written sources constitutes an unknown fraction of all relief.

---

14. For these people, see Chapter 5, 'Help for old people', Chapter 4, 'Granted to a different family or expelled from Hadleigh', and App. 5.1 below.

15. In 1544–5, average grain prices were 1.7 times their level in 1536–9; between 1549 and 1554 they averaged 2.3 times higher. See Joan Thirsk (ed.), *Chapters from the agrarian history of England and Wales, 1500–1750*, vol. i, Economic change: prices, wages, profits and rents 1500–1750, ed. Peter J. Bowden (Cambridge, 1990), pp. 150–51, for this and below.

16. *Ibid.*, 167. See also Chapter 6, 'The ongoing influence of Christian social teachings', below.

17. See App. 2.1 for fuller discussion of this issue and the ones below.

18. See, e.g., Chapter 5, 'Care for people who were ill or disabled', below, for people with disabilities.

The assistance provided by the town assumed multiple and sometimes overlapping forms. Most aid was awarded in three ways: regular weekly cash payments; occasional grants of money, household goods, clothing or services; and boarding with another local family. Six years with full or nearly full accounts provide a quantitative overview of these kinds of help, together with the number of people who received them annually and the cost of that aid (Table 2.1). Between 91 and 149 people were helped annually in those years, some in multiple ways. As individuals they received an average of 16s 2d per year, or 3.7d per week, but if we calculate the amount provided to households, some of which contained more than one recipient, the average rises to 19s 10d annually or 4.6d per week. Ongoing cash assistance (defined here as ten or more payments within a calendar year) was given to between 34 and 67 people living in their own homes or one of the almshouses. Their allocations, which averaged 27s 8d annually, or 7.2d per week, consumed 80 per cent of the average total of £90 14s 2d that Hadleigh spent on poor relief each year. Occasional help went to between 52 and 125 recipients with a much lower annual average of 3s 2d; those costs formed 13 per cent of all expenses for relief. Only 3 to 15 people were boarded annually, but because the cost per person was high, averaging 16s 11d, such expenses consumed 7 per cent of the total outlay. In addition, children and teens were eligible for other kinds of help, and some of the elderly received free housing in an almshouse.[19]

Reserving cash assistance for discussion in Chapter 3, we may look here at aid that was given though in-kind items or provision of services. The town itself or private charities that asked the Chief Inhabitants to distribute their benefactions sometimes gave wood for cooking and possibly for heating.[20] Fuel went to almshouse residents (in accordance with their founders' instructions), to the workhouse starting in 1589 and to some individual poor people. In 1551 John Freeman, a merchant, bequeathed a grove at Hadleigh Heath to supply firewood for the poor.[21] Preparation and distribution of the fuel was initially assigned to the churchwardens but later was usually a duty of the chief collector or market bailiffs. A collector in 1566 spent 40s for '40 loads of wood carrying which is his covenant to carry yearly to the poor'.[22]

Help might take the form of cloth or clothing. Several testators left lengths of canvas (made of hemp) or woollen cloth (including broad 'blanket' and narrower 'twill') to the poor. The surviving accounts show that a total of 1,063 ells of canvas were distributed, each piece averaging 67 inches in length, plus 504 yards of woollen cloth averaging 52 inches in length. These fabrics had not been made up into clothing before distribution to the poor: payments for sewing clothes are described as such. While some of the cloth may have been used by recipients for apparel, much of it was probably intended as bedding. Poor relief officers also paid for making clothing and shoes, especially for children and teens going out into service or apprenticeships and

---

19. See Chapter 4, 'Assistance when entering service or apprenticeship'; 'Training and discipline in the workhouse'; 'Granted to a different family or expelled from Hadleigh'; and Chapter 5, 'Help for old people', below.

20. See App. 2.2 for this paragraph and the next.

21. TNA PRO PROB 11/34.

22. HadlA 004/A/01, p. 73.

Table 2.1

Types of assistance given in six years with full or nearly full accounts.

Year	No. of people who received assistance with a money value	Regular weekly payments #				Occasional assistance (goods, money, or services) #		Boarding care #		Aver. total amt received annually per person (in s)	Aver. total amt received annually per household (in s)
		No. of people who received payments	Aver. no. of payments per year	Aver. amt of weekly payments (in pence)	Aver. amt received annually per person (in s)	No. of people who received payments	Aver. amt received annually per person	No. of people who were boarded	Aver. amt paid annually per person (in s)		
[1579]	91	44	42	7.9	27.7	52	7.3	5	31.6	19.3	22.5
1582	149	34	49	7.8	32.1	125	2.7	15	14.3	11.0	14.9
[1585]	93	55	44	8.0	29.2	60	1.6	3	0.9	18.4	22.2
[1590]	101	51	51	6.5	27.7	81	3.2	4	12.0	17.0	20.2
1591	122	59	48	6.4	25.3	73	1.9	8	24.3	15.0	18.5
1594	111	67	44	6.6	24.1	65	2.5	4	18.3	16.7	20.3
Average	111	52	46	7.2	27.7	76	3.2	7	16.9	16.2	19.8
Average annual expended for individuals		£72 16s. = 80%				£12 3s. 2d. = 13%		£5 15s = 7%			

Notes: Full records survive for the three years that are not bracketed; for those in brackets we have only three of the four types of accounts. For the records that survive by year, see App. Intro.2.

Regular payments are defined as paid in 10 or more weeks per year. Regular and occasional payments were made to people living in their own homes or in the almshouses, while boarding was done in other people's homes. The three types of relief shown here were not mutually exclusive: many people received occasional assistance in addition to regular weekly payments or boarding, but few received both regular payments and boarding in a single year.

for certain old people. They provided 95 pairs of shoes, 54 coats, 38 waistcoats and petticoats, 19 pairs of hoses or stockings and 38 smocks and shirts, as well as 20 other kinds of clothing and 59 payments for unspecified items.

Food was almost never provided for the poor either by the town's officers or through private charity. Under normal circumstances, the town preferred to provide money, allowing recipients to employ it as they wished. This pattern contrasts with parishes elsewhere that provided bread to the poor, at least on special holidays or at burials, and with the efforts of some cities during periods of high food prices to import grain for bread and sell it to the poor at a subsidised cost.[23] The only entries for food in Hadleigh's regular accounts come from 1591, when the subcollectors brought together some poor people suffering from illness and hired a woman to look after them, in what may have been some kind of quarantine arrangement.[24] The food purchased for that group and for the young inmates of the workhouse starting in 1589 were atypical: no provisions were purchased for people living in their own homes. Likewise, no perpetual charity established in the sixteenth century gave out food to the poor, and the only temporary bequest seems to have reflected the desire of the donor for humble gratitude more than concern for the hunger of the poor.[25]

Other people received services at the town's expense. Some were cared for in their own homes when they were ill, recovering from giving birth or injured, assisted usually by local people but occasionally by trained surgeons.[26] Practical help was provided too, such as sewing or washing. Poor relief officers were willing to pay for a winding sheet or the burial of extremely poor people.[27] Such payments, which were made for 153 individuals during the years under study, imply either that the deceased person was so destitute that his or her personal possessions were insufficient to cover the cost of a burial, or that poor relief officials were unwilling to burden impoverished relatives with the expense. In 1591 the Chief Inhabitants formalised an arrangement with John Hills, the sexton of Hadleigh's church, that in return for an annual payment of 40s in money plus four loads of wood, he would not only ring the bell for services but also make 'the graves for such persons as shall be buried at the charges of the town and to such as the town shall find sheets for their burial'.[28] At the same time, Dr

---

23. McIntosh, *Poor relief in England*, pp. 241–4 and 31.

24. See Chapter 5, 'Care for people who were ill or disabled', below. For below, see also Chapter 5, 'Help for old people'.

25. See Chapter 6, 'The impact of Rowland Taylor and opposition to him, 1544–54', below. The first and only 'bread dole' was created by a bequest in 1614 (A&S, *Hadleigh*, p. 99).

26. See Chapter 5, 'Care for people who were ill or disabled', below. For below, see App. 2.2.

27. In most cases a person received one or the other, but eight people were given both a sheet and a burial. The town assumed responsibility even when the deceased were not known local people. In 1592 the chief collector reported that he had spent 12d 'for carrying of poor women to church that died at Mr Forthe's' (HadlA 021/C/07). See also Chapter 3, 'Individual recipients of assistance'; 'Recipient households and family relationships', below.

28. HadlA 004/A/01, p. 218, for this and below. The customary charges for a burial, including the ringing of bells, were listed in 1617: the sexton, parish clerk, parson and 'town' all received payments, coming in total to 11s 6d for the normal burial of a 'covered' body in the churchyard. Burial inside the church cost an additional 6s 8d (*ibid.*, p. 396).

John Still, rector of the church, offered to abstain from collecting the fees normally owed to him 'for such persons as shall be buried in manner aforesaid, either for burial or ringing'. (One notes that it was the Chief Inhabitants who signed these agreements, acting on behalf of the town, not the churchwardens, who in most parishes negotiated with the sexton and oversaw burials.)

Poor relief officials sometimes paid another local family to take in adults or children for anything from a few months to a few years, providing them with food, shelter and care. Across the full span between 1579 and 1596, 17 adults and 35 children lived at some point with another household at the town's expense. Recipients of boarding will be examined below, but it is interesting to consider also the people who cared for someone in their own home.[29] Of those 44 people, just over half were given relief themselves: town officials probably saw this as a desirable way to assist two needy people at once. Half of the recipients of relief who were paid for boarding others were men, but we may assume that their wives provided most of the care. Three-quarters of the recipient women who took in boarders and just over half of the men were aged 50 years or more and may have welcomed a way to earn some extra money within the confines of their own homes. The older women were especially likely to take in children, and they engaged in boarding for unusually long periods of time (four of them boarded for four to six years); they received on average £2 6s 9d for such work across the full span. Nearly all of the 20 people who did not receive relief accepted children, including very young ones. Poor relief officials may have sought out households that included a woman already nursing a baby of her own who could feed an orphan or abandoned infant as well. The non-recipient households headed by men received an exceptionally large total amount for boarding, an average of just under £3.

In addition to direct poor relief, Hadleigh opened public employment to the needy. The main job was looking after their peers. In addition to boarding, seven recipients provided services such as sewing or washing. Payment for their work provided a helpful addition to other forms of public assistance and income earned elsewhere. Another group of recipients supplemented their resources by performing manual labour, usually odd jobs, for the town. In this latter kind of hiring, however, there is no indication that the poor received preference.

Financing poor relief

Paying for Hadleigh's ambitious system of aid was expensive. In most years between the mid 1530s and 1549 the churchwardens received and spent £7–10 in income from the landed endowment of Pykenham's almshouses; in 1559 a collector accounted for £9 6s 7d for the almshouses.[30] From 1563 onwards, however, the (chief) collector was responsible for maintenance and collection of rents of all charitable properties administered by the Chief Inhabitants. The £73 11s 7d for which he accounted in that year derived from the older Pykenham endowment, the land purchased in 1550 from

---

29. See Chapter 3, 'Individual recipients of assistance', for adults who were boarded and Chapter 4, 'Short-term boarding in another household', for children.

30. See App. Intro.1 for the rest of this paragraph and the next; for the almshouses, see Chapter 5, 'Help for old people', below.

sale of church and guild property and the new purchases from the Ravens' bequests. That income rose gradually to £162 11s by 1603, thanks to additional gifts and bequests and increasing rents. Although a number of nominally independent charities were endowed during the second half of the sixteenth century, the line between private and public assistance in Hadleigh – as in many settings – was blurred: most of the privately created forms of aid were administered by the Chief Inhabitants or some subset of them, forming an adjunct to the kinds of help that fell fully within the town's purview.[31] Further, the feoffees who administered Hadleigh's charities were commonly replaced by 'their heirs', which in the sixteenth century was taken literally to mean their sons, rather than their successors in office. Direct personal inheritance of office reinforced the oligarchic nature of Hadleigh's mechanisms for managing property for the poor.

Income from land and bequests was supplemented by the poor rates, obligatory local taxes assessed by the subcollectors for the poor on 18–25 per cent of the more prosperous household heads in the town. In most years between 1566 and 1594 rates brought in £16–25. The total amount given to poor people and the almshouses during the 1580s and early 1590s ranged in most years between £80 and £103. After the workhouse was fully operational its expenses raised the total cost of poor relief to £119–136, with the exceptionally high payment of £154 in 1596.[32] We may consider each of the three main sources of income in turn: rents from landed property, other gifts and bequests, and the poor rates.

An endowment of landed property for the poor

The beginning of Hadleigh's endowment for charitable purposes came through William Pykenham's gift of lands to support his almshouses in 1497.[33] Although he left that property to a body of private feoffees, the Chief Inhabitants had become its *de facto* trustees by 1563. A second component of the town's endowment was created in 1550, when the town's leaders bought additional land with the proceeds from the sale of the goods of the parish church and local guilds. Divestment of Hadleigh's religious possessions had begun in the later 1530s but accelerated during the first three years of Edward VI's reign, probably influenced by Rowland Taylor's teachings about charity to the poor and fears that the crown might confiscate the lands and goods of parishes and guilds, as it had of the monasteries.

Hadleigh's parish of St Mary's was quick to read the writing on the wall, shedding its property, both real estate and goods, prior to royal appropriation. Between 1537 and 1542 the churchwardens sold to John Swynborne 'certain houses', described later as two buildings on Churchgate Street formerly called 'the church houses'.[34]

31. McIntosh, *Poor relief in England*, pp. 13 and 268.
32. The average total of £90 14s 2d laid out annually in the six years of good records amounted to 7.3d per capita within the full estimated population. That level of assistance was much higher than the average of 3.1d in the five comparable small towns (McIntosh, 'Poor relief in Elizabethan communities').
33. See Chapter 5, 'Help for old people', below.
34. HadlA 004/A/01, pp. 23, 25 and 29. For below, see *ibid.*, pp. 33 and 37.

Although that prescient sale of property precluded its seizure by the crown, the parish's annual income in the mid 1540s was only £5 or £6. Strikingly, when St Mary's decided to part with its movable goods in September 1547 it was the Chief Inhabitants – not the churchwardens – who handled the transactions and utilised the proceeds 'for the better maintenance and provision of our poor people'.[35] The church plate, which weighed about 48 pounds, was sold for nearly £183, while the copes, other vestments and cloths brought in £70. That income, too, went into the town's fund to buy land that would henceforth support the poor.

In similar fashion, Hadleigh's five religious guilds or fraternities transferred into the town's hands their goods and apparently the money owed to them from outstanding loans. At least one of the guilds held real estate (a tenement with two shops, yards and gardens bequeathed in 1469), and each guild had had a 'stock' of money, animals or land that in 1524 had ranged in value from £6 8s 6d to £12.[36] The guilds' movable goods – religious objects, plate, equipment for cooking and eating and some decorative cloths – were conveyed to the town before the Parliamentary act of late 1547 that terminated the fraternities and authorised the crown to seize their possessions. The guild goods were then sold together with the church plate by the Chief Inhabitants, who referred to them as now belonging to the town.[37] They brought in £271. Moreover, it was later reported that, sometime before 1550, Hadleigh's guilds had loaned out money in small batches, a total of 99 'obligations' which when repaid – presumably with interest – would yield £242 7s 8d.[38] These loans seem to have been distinct from the sale of goods, in which case they were probably the proceeds from sale of items in the guilds' stocks. Although the people who took out these loans had to supply sureties (other people who would guarantee repayment of the money), the Chief Inhabitants were still trying to collect what was due in 1556. Though the Guildhall itself was temporarily lost to the crown, the guilds thus managed to avoid other confiscations through collusion with the town. The combined income from the possessions of the church and guilds came to £524, and if the guild loans were additional the total would have been nearly £767.

It is difficult to describe precisely how the money gained by the town from these sales and repayments was utilised, for we have two separate but not entirely congruent accounts. Certainly, however, the great majority of the income was devoted to the poor, some in immediate payments but most through the purchase of land that would henceforth produce a regular income for their support. The first account entered into the town book is undated but describes five sets of payments, most of which were made no later than 1550 but in one case extended to 1554.[39] Of the total of £518 15s 1½d listed in that reckoning, 92 per cent went to the poor. Dr Taylor gave

---

35. *Ibid.*, p. 408. For below, see *ibid.*, pp. 394, 402–3 and 408–10. Most of the textiles were sold to two Dutchmen in London, but the linen was given to the poor (*ibid.*, p. 411). The items sold and their values were listed in 1556.

36. TNA PRO PROB 11/5/216–17, and *Suffolk in 1524*, pp. 154–5.

37. HadlA 004/A/01, pp. 404 and 412. For below, see *ibid.*, pp. 404 and 412–15.

38. *Ibid.*, pp. 416–25.

39. *Ibid.*, p. 406.

£28 7s 10½d to needy people during Edward's reign, while £449 was laid out to purchase land in nearby Offton. We know from other records that Mascalls Farm, situated on the western boundary of Offton, consisted of 200 acres of arable and pasture plus 20 acres of woodland.[40] Bought by Hadleigh's Chief Inhabitants in 1550, it was subsequently held by them to the use of the poor. The only expressly religious expenditures took place in 1554, during Mary's reign, when £38 1s 7d was delivered to the churchwardens for repairs of the church and to buy 'ornaments' for it, presumably an effort to return the building to a condition more suitable for Catholic worship. The sexton received 5s, and £3 8d was 'lost by the fall of the money', the Edwardian debasement of the currency.

It is not clear how that account relates to a more detailed one compiled on 15 April 1566.[41] The latter notes that on or by 2 November 1549 a total of £348 16s 8d in cash had been granted out to 53 people, many in units of £5–10 each, but with some smaller units and a few of £15–20 each. The people who had received the money included many of Hadleigh's leading townsmen, so these grants, disguised as loans, were probably an attempt to keep some of the income from sale of church and guild goods secure – and safely out of sight of the crown – until it could be spent on the purchase of land. The earlier account had noted that £43 13s 7d was 'left in the chest' in 1549. That money was spent entirely on the poor, in that year and the next. Although the right side of some of the entries cannot be read, legible amounts include £34 6s 8d for purchase and transport of herrings, cheese, malt and barley for the poor. Other sums were delivered to Dr Taylor or 'Sir Richard' (probably Richard Yeoman, Taylor's curate) 'for the poor folks'. If the cash temporarily in the hands of the 53 people was indeed used to pay for land, that amount plus expenses for the poor from the chest would have constituted the full sum laid out in 1549–50.

The 1566 account records also a variety of other expenditures that had been made at unspecified times since 1549–50, coming to a total of about £206. Of these payments, which were probably supported by gradual repayment of the guild loans, at least £53 7s 6d (26 per cent) went to needy people: £24 'paid to Mr. Doctor [presumably Taylor] for the poor', £8 16s 4d handed to individual Chief Inhabitants to be used for the poor, £4 7s 10d given to needy people directly and £16 3s 4d towards the purchase in 1560 of land called Spencers, which later provided wood that was given to the poor. However, with Taylor's arrest shortly after Mary's accession in 1553, followed by the departure of Yeomans and David Whitehead from Hadleigh and the appointment of a Catholic rector, pressure from the pulpit for charitable contributions may have diminished.[42] Some of the later entries are damaged, but a large chunk of money (£43 14s 4d plus some illegible amounts) was delivered to named churchwardens 'for provision of the service and for the church'. All of those wardens held office during Mary's reign, suggesting that the payments were a somewhat expanded version of the ones for ornaments mentioned in the first account. Other

---

40. A&S, *Hadleigh*, p. 111.

41. HadlA 004/A/01, pp. 428–9, for this and the next paragraph.

42. For Taylor's history, see Chapter 6, 'The impact of Rowland Taylor and opposition to him, 1544–54', below.

sums were devoted to work on Hadleigh's market (£11 9s 7d), were lost by 'the fall of money' (£3 8s) or were delivered to named people without explanation. Of the full amount of £598 9s 9½d recorded in the 1566 account, a minimum of £445 17s 9d (75 per cent) went for the poor.

The purchase of Mascalls Farm and Spencers brought in substantial new rental income and fuel for the poor, resources that – unlike Pykenham's foundation – were not restricted to almshouse residents. The provision of alms places expanded in the mid 1550s, when two John Ravens, a father and son, left the cash and then the land that henceforth supported their almshouses for eight people on Benton Street.[43] During the second half of the sixteenth century three additional tenements in the town were given or bequeathed to the Chief Inhabitants, their income to be used for the poor. Hadleigh's endowment, held by the Chief Inhabitants as *de facto* charitable trustees, provided the lion's share of the resources that assisted needy people during the rest of the sixteenth century.

Gifts and bequests

Additional assistance came through gifts and bequests. Some money and goods were distributed to the poor immediately after the donation was received, while others were spread out over a period of years or set up in perpetuity. In her detailed analysis of Hadleigh's charitable benefactions and the administration of private charity, Sue Andrews divided the various contributions into several categories: money given out at burials; other distributions made on single occasions; donations to the alms-box in the church; doles distributed over a period of years; and perpetual charities.[44] Of the 14 perpetual charities created between 1485 and the end of the sixteenth century, 4 were for almshousing and 7 furnished cash, fuel or cloth for needy people or were to be used for the poor in unspecified ways; 1 provided money to help place orphans into a new home, 1 was for education and 1 gave loans to young clothiers.

These legacies were to be distributed in various ways. Some testators instructed their executors or heirs to handle their bequests, especially if the money or goods were to be given out immediately. In 1551 clothier Henry Blosse left £6 13s 4d 'to the poor folk in Hadley', to be paid by his executors; sherman John Posford bequeathed 13s 4d in 1571 to his executors 'to be given to the poor of Hadleigh'.[45] Robert Rolfe, a wealthy clothier, asked his own executors to distribute two white broadcloths and 40 ells of canvas to the poor people of Hadleigh at Christmas for five years, even though he was himself a Chief Inhabitant who had held virtually every local office by the time of his death in 1588.

In other cases, the churchwardens and/or clergymen were asked to carry out charitable bequests. Thomas Orson, a baker who wrote his will early in 1570, said that after the death of his wife Alice a tenement should be given to the parson and churchwardens of the parish church, under condition that they 'yearly distribute and give the profits coming of the said tenement to the poor people of the said town where

---

43. See Chapter 5, 'Help for old people', below. For below, see A&S, *Hadleigh*, p. 99.

44. A&S, *Hadleigh*, chs 7 and 8, esp. pp. 94–8. For below, see *ibid.*, pp. 99–105.

45. TNA PRO PROB 11/35; PROB 11/57/56. For below, see TNA PRO PROB 11/72/20.

most need shall be at their discretion for evermore'.[46] In 1576 Dr John Still, Hadleigh's rector, reported that he had received 40s as a legacy from Widow Raynam, of which he had delivered 29s to Thomas Alabaster, one of the Chief Inhabitants, 'to employ upon the poor children'.[47] In 1591 Alabaster himself bequeathed an annuity of just over £5 in perpetuity, to be distributed by the churchwardens – with the consent of the parson – as grants of 2d each week to twelve poor recipients.

Other gifts and bequests came through the church in different ways. Some were given to the 'alms box' or 'God's chest' in the church, commonly termed the 'poor men's box' as of Edward's reign.[48] During the 1570s the churchwardens delivered money on occasion from that box to poor relief officers for distribution, using the remainder for the church's own needs; by the 1580s, half of the amount in the box each year was handed over to the town to join other income for the poor.[49] 'General alms' donated at communions were assigned to the poor beginning in 1590. Further, at least by the 1570s, 'the Receivers of Canterbury' gave money for the use of Hadleigh's poor and on several occasions clergymen turned over sums collected as penance for wrongdoing.[50]

Increasingly, however, executors assigned responsibility for handling charitable bequests to the town, to be administered as part of its broader system of relief. In 1587, for example, clothier Julian Beamonde left £10 'to be paid into the hands of the collectors', which they were to use in buying wood during the summer when it was inexpensive so that it might be sold to the poor at the same price during the winter.[51] Use of the Chief Inhabitants was especially common for larger gifts, ones that had to be distributed over a period of years, and projects that had already been initiated during the donor's lifetime.[52] Asking town officers to handle the awards was sensible, for by the Elizabethan

---

46. TNA PRO PROB 11/53/22. The bequest of Edward Clerke of Layham in 1583 towards maintaining a schoolmaster was likewise given to the churchwardens (TNA PRO PROB 11/75/37).

47. HadlA 004/A/01, p. 109. For below, see TNA PRO 80/51.

48. See, e.g., the will of Thomas Fulsnape, clothmaker, 1490 (12d every Sunday for 10 years to the alms box of the church, to be dealt among the poor parishioners there, TNA PRO PROB 11/11/30/ 240–41); will of John Bramston, mercer, 1546 (6s 8d to God's chest 'toward the maintenance of the poor people', ERO D/ABW 3/110); and will of Edmund Freeman, yeoman, 1552 (6s 8d to the poor men's chest, D/ABW 14/67). For 50s 'received of the chest' by the churchwardens in 1562, see HadlA 004/A/01, p. 58. For poor boxes, see McIntosh, *Poor relief in England*, pp. 128–30.

49. See, e.g., HadlA 004/A/01, pp. 92, 95, and 124; *ibid.*, pp. 143, 167 and 182. For below, see *ibid.*, pp. 201 and 204.

50. *Ibid.*, pp. 89, 131 and 166; *ibid.*, pp. 86 (20s from Michael Hall as part of his penance for 'his shameful adultery', 1570), and 109 (sums of 5s to 20s from four men for unspecified penances, 1576). Archbishop Whitgift ended the commutation of penance to money fines in 1583 (McIntosh, *Poor relief in England*, p. 239).

51. TNA PRO PROB 11/70/1.

52. Yet the 1583 will of Alice Parkins, widow of Thomas, a clothier who had been very active in Town government, makes no mention of the two tenements she had bought three years before and conveyed to the Chief Inhabitants, with the income to be used for cloth for the poor in perpetuity: TNA PRO PROB 11/66/192 and see HadlA 021/B/07 and Anon., 'Women of Hadleigh V: Alice Parkins', *The Hadleigh Historian*, 5 (2011), pp. 12–14. Her daughter married the son of the younger John Raven who set up the Benton Street almshouses.

period they were recognised by local people as experienced at administering charitable donations. Specialised officials who dealt regularly with the poor and knew their needs would be involved in the decisions and, as a self-perpetuating body, the Chief Inhabitants were able to keep track of bequests that had to be paid over multiple years.[53] The town book includes a memorandum from the end of 1581 that 'John Dyster of London, gent., hath by his last will and testament given to the town of Hadley to the poor there £3 6s 8d to be distributed by the churchwardens and collector every Good Friday'. Payments had begun on 18 May 1577 and were to continue for 40 years, the income coming from Dyster's manor of West Barford.

When bequests were assigned to the Chief Pledges, they worked assiduously to collect the sums granted and use them wisely. They kept careful notes of bequests that had been delivered in full, those that had been paid only in part, and ones not rendered at all.[54] In some years they listed all legacies received over the past 12 months, including bequests in wills that have not survived. They took bonds of people who held money temporarily, until it could be spent as specified by the testator, and made note of bequests to be paid over several years.[55] They paid for searches for wills of which they did not have a copy, sent out agents to extract the full sum due from executors and recorded bequests used to purchase additional land.

We gain a more quantitative picture of the role of charitable bequests in helping the poor through the 96 extant wills written by people living in Hadleigh between 1500 and 1599. As we have seen, not all of the legacies helped to finance the town's own system of relief, but they contributed to the net resources available to help the community's needy people. The evidence is far from robust: the number of wills is small, and we do not know what fraction of all wills these survivors constitute. Further, bequests to be given to the poor only at the testator's burial or obit need to be distinguished from assistance given outright. Because it was thought that God was particularly receptive to prayers by the poor for the soul of the deceased or their prayers of thanksgiving for charity received, conservative testators commonly left a penny or a loaf of bread to every needy person who attended their burial, thus benefiting themselves spiritually as well as the recipients materially. Catholic testators were less likely than those with neutral or mildly/probably reformist religious testaments to leave outright bequests to the poor; wills with definitely Protestant testaments of faith were yet more charitable.[56]

But we do not see mounting bequests to the poor over time. As Table 2.2 shows, between 1534 and 1547, the period of early reformed influence in Hadleigh, the fraction of wills leaving bequests to the poor jumped from 27 per cent to 54 per cent.[57]

---

53. A&S, *Hadleigh*, pp. 111–18. For below, see HadlA 004/A/01, p. 390.

54. See, e.g., HadlA 004/A/01, pp. 68, 77–8, 183 and 220. For below, see *ibid.*, pp. 179 and 226.

55. See, e.g., for this and below, *ibid.*, pp. 189 and 210, HadlA 021/B/09 and 021/C/09 (looking for a will written about 16 years previously).

56. See App. 2.3.

57. For the religious categories used, see Chapter 1, note 100, above. Bequests for Catholic religious purposes (masses, priests, the high altar, lights in churches or guilds) and other charitable causes (repair of roads/bridges, Hadleigh's parish church, education and trade loans) were excluded from this analysis.

Table 2.2

Bequests to the poor, by period, Hadleigh wills, 1500–99.

Periods	Wills with bequests to the poor				Wills with no bequests to the poor	Total
	Only at burial/obit #	Outright only	Burial and outright	Total		
1500–33, Catholic	0	3 = 20% of period	1 = 7%	4 = 27%	11 = 73%	15 = 16% of all wills
1534–47, early reformed influences in Hadleigh	2 = 15%	5 = 38%	0	7 = 54%	6 = 46%	13 = 14%
1547–53, Edward VI	2 = 10%	10 = 48%	3 = 14%	15 = 71%	6 = 29%	21 = 22%
1553–8, Mary	0	4 = 44%	0	4 = 44%	5 = 56%	9 = 9%
1558–79, early Elizabethan	3 = 13%	13 = 57%	2 = 9%	18 = 78%	5 = 22%	23 = 24%
1580–99, late Elizabethan	0	8 = 53%	0	8 = 53%	7 = 47%	15 = 16%
Total	7 = 7% of all wills	43 = 45%	6 = 6%	56 = 58%	40 = 42%	96

Notes:

This table excludes charitable bequests of other kinds, such as for maintenance of the church, roads or bridges and for education.

Bequests leaving food or money to the poor who attended one's burial or commemorative service were of benefit to the testator, for they ensured more prayers on his/her behalf, as well as giving some small aid to needy people. Outright bequests were more directly focused on the wellbeing of the poor themselves.

During Edward's reign, when the impact of Rowland Taylor and his curates was greatest, the fraction rose to 71 per cent. After a considerable decline under Mary, the fraction reached its peak of 78 per cent during the first 20 years of Elizabeth's reign (which rather surprisingly included two bequests only at burial) but then dropped back to just 53 per cent from 1580 to the end of the century.

We can also consider the total amount bequeathed to Hadleigh's poor in the surviving wills, using those same chronological periods.[58] This assessment includes bequests by outsiders, but it is limited because some bequests left food, goods or land for which no cash value was provided. Even so, the analysis reveals a small increase in the cash value of bequests starting in 1534 and a very large jump during Edward's reign in both the total amount and the average amount left per year. Though few wills under Mary left anything to the poor, substantial bequests by the two John Ravens raised the total and annual average further. During Elizabeth's first 20 years the total climbed to its apex, but the average amount per year dropped markedly. Both figures declined in the closing decades of the century.

One might have expected that men facing death who had young children would be less inclined to leave bequests to the poor, thinking that every penny should remain to their wife and/or executors to help raise their own offspring. Interestingly, however, bequests to the poor were not affected negatively by the number of the testator's children. On the contrary, testators who made no mention of any children – either adult or under age – in their wills had the lowest percentage of legacies to the poor. Testators with one or more adult children and those with one to three children still under age were slightly more generous, while a considerably higher fraction of those with four to eight children under age left something to the poor. The 13 female testators were somewhat less likely to include bequests to the poor than were the 83 men (46 per cent as compared to 60 per cent).

Poor rates and rate payers

The Chief Inhabitants supplemented the income received from the town's charitable property and from voluntary gifts and bequests with money levied from compulsory poor rates. Rates formed part of Hadleigh's system of financing relief from early in Elizabeth's reign. The 'collector for the poor inhabitants' in 1563 accounted for income that had come from town rents and 'other collections of the parishioners', a wording that may refer either to rates or to contributions received at church services.[59] We have definite evidence, however, from the account of the subcollectors for a quarter ending at Michaelmas, 1565, which reported income received 'of the weekmen' and 'of the quartermen'. Those terms designate the wealthiest household heads who had to pay each week and the next rank, who paid only quarterly. The list of people assessed was expanded in 1569, for one of the subcollectors accounted for receipts from 'quartermen new created'.[60]

---

58. See App. 2.4.

59. HadlA 004/A/01, p. 62. For below, see *ibid.*, p. 66.

60. *Ibid.*, p. 82.

The fraction of Hadleigh's household heads who were assessed for poor rates between 1579 and 1594 (18–25 per cent) was a little smaller than the average in other places, but they paid slightly more per capita than their peers elsewhere.[61] As shown in Table 2.3, the majority of the 122–195 people rated in various years had to pay only quarterly, giving between 1d and 12d each time (for a total of 4d to 4s annually); a smaller number of more prosperous people were expected to pay every week, giving between 1d and 6d each time (for a total of 4s 4d to 26s annually). In the mid 1560s rates brought in more than £30 annually, but, owing largely to the failure of some of those assessed to render the sums imposed on them, the yield dropped to around £16–20 until the mid 1580s; during the early 1590s it rose to £23–25.[62] That income constituted 21–28 per cent of the total amount disbursed annually to poor people, the almshouses and the workhouse.

Collecting the rates was a challenge right from the beginning. Some people probably claimed economic problems that prevented them from paying the amount due, and it is possible that the questionable legal standing of Hadleigh's Chief Inhabitants weakened their ability to prosecute defaulters: because poor relief officials were chosen neither by a corporate borough nor by a parish, they were not authorised by the statutes of 1552 and 1563 to take non-payers of poor rates before a bishop or Justice of the Peace.[63] As early as the quarter ending in December 1565 the subcollectors reported that they had collected nearly £5 from previous arrears as well as around £4 from current income; in 1576 outgoing collectors prepared a bill listing sums due to the poor, with some unpaid rates extending back for four years.[64] In 1590 the subcollectors included a separate 'bill of arrearages' at the end of their account: it listed 14 weekly payers (including William Forth, esq., and John Raven, gent.) and 38 quarterly payers who together owed the town £5 6s 7d.

Perhaps in response to that problem, the subcollectors changed their method of assessment. Around 160 people had been required to pay rates in 1579 and 1582, and in 1585 the number rose to 195. But, starting in 1590, the number dropped to no more than 128. That decline came entirely from a reduction in the 'quartermen', not the more substantial people who paid weekly. The subcollectors had evidently decided that trying to collect very small individual sums from nearly 200 people was not worth the resulting yield. It was more effective to demand payments from fewer people but ones more likely to fulfil their obligation. Whereas rate payers had formed 20–22 per

---

61. See Table Intro.1 above. In the five comparative towns, an average of 33 per cent of household heads paid rates, as did 27 per cent in St Mary's parish, Warwick in 1582 (McIntosh, 'Poor relief in Elizabethan communities', and Beier, 'Social problems'); in Exeter, 1564–5, 25 per cent of all households were assessed for poor rates, as were 28 per cent in Norwich, 1578–9 (Slack, *Poverty and policy*, p. 178). Hadleigh's average annual payment of 3.1s was above the 2.6s levied in the five towns but far below the average of 6.3s in four cities (McIntosh, *ibid.*).

62. See App. Intro.1.

63. See the Introduction, above. There is no indication that non-payers were taken before any outside authorities. Because of Hadleigh's status as a peculiar, its bishop would have been the archbishop of Canterbury, hardly a person whom one would trouble with defaulting local payers. Perhaps a county JP resident in the town, also a Chief Inhabitant, delivered unofficial reprimands (see Chapter 1, 'Town government', above).

64. HadlA 004/A/01, pp. 66 and 113. For below, see HadlA 021/C/04.

Table 2.3
Payment of rates for the poor.

Year	No. of payers	Weekly payments		Quarterly payments			Aver. amt assessed per person per year (in s)	Total amount paid per year (in pounds)
		No. of people assessed	Aver. amt paid per week (in pence)	No. of people assessed	Aver. amt paid per quarter (in pence)			
1579	165	36	1.6	129	3.4		2.36	19.43
1582	157	37	1.4	120	3.3		2.27	17.80
1585	195	41	1.6	154	3.7		2.41	23.65
1590	128	47	2.0	81	4.0		3.89	25.32
1591	127	47	1.8	80	3.9		3.96	25.15
1594	122	43	2.0	79	3.8		3.81	23.22

Note: All rate payers were men except for 10 widows and 2 women described as 'mistress', several of whom paid in more than one year. Six women paid in 1579, two in 1582, four in 1585, one in 1590, two in 1591 and four in 1594.

cent of all estimated household heads in 1579 and 1582 and 25 per cent in 1585, the fraction dropped to 18–19 per cent in the 1590s.

We may look more closely at the people assessed for poor rates between 1579 and 1594. A total of 351 men and 12 women (10 widows and 2 described as 'mistress') were listed, with a good deal of continuity between years.[65] Those required to contribute weekly paid an average of 1.4d to 2.0d each time, while the quarterly payers gave an average of 3.3d to 4.0d. Although we lack good occupational data for Hadleigh, we do know the types of work pursued by some of the male rate payers and husbands of widows. By arranging people by the level of rates they owed, we can see what occupations fell into each category. As shown in Table 2.4, the 24 per cent assessed at the bottom level, owing just 4d to 8d per year, included some cloth workers as well as a variety of other occupations. The next level up, the 30 per cent who were to pay 1s to 1s 4d annually, again shows various types of work, including a clothier and a cloth broker, occupations that would normally have been much wealthier. The middle level – the 17 per cent who paid 2s to 4s per year – included carters (sometimes described as common carriers), millers and smiths, as well as diverse others. By the time we reach the upper two ranks (the 17 per cent who paid 4s 4d per year and the 11 per cent who paid 8s 8d to £1 6s), clothiers, mercers and gentlemen/esquires dominate the progressively narrower range of occupations.

A fairly complete gap separated those who paid poor rates from those who received relief. Only eight of the 603 recipients are known to have been assessed for rates, usually at a very low level and long before they began receiving assistance. A comparable division is seen for households. In the three years for which we have complete accounts, 18–20 per cent of all estimated household heads were supposed to pay poor rates, and another 14–15 per cent of households contained at least one person who was given relief.[66] In between lay the 65–68 per cent that neither paid for nor received assistance from the town.

It is sometimes thought that in sixteenth-century England extended families were expected to look after their own needy members, including more distant relatives who did not live with them.[67] In Hadleigh, poor relief officials clearly believed that prosperous residents should contribute to relief for the town's poor as a whole, but they were not required to support relatives outside their own immediate families. Thirty-five per cent of the recipients of poor relief had apparent kin (people with the same surname who did not live in the same household) who paid poor rates during the 18 years under study; for 17 per cent of the recipients, two or more probable relatives paid rates. While some of the rate-paying households may not in fact have been relatives (e.g., the multiple families named Smith), in the majority of cases the head of

---

65. The figure of 2 per cent of Hadleigh's payers each year who were women was lower than the average of nearly 6 per cent seen in five other small towns, presumably because so few women owned property or operated workshops here (McIntosh, 'Poor relief in Elizabethan communities').

66. See Table Intro.1. For below, cf. St Mary's, Warwick, where 44 per cent of families in 1582 were able to maintain themselves but were not assessed for rates; another 18 per cent were said to be on the brink of poverty but did not pay rates or get help (Beier, 'Social Problems').

67. But for the contrary, see McIntosh, *Poor relief in England*, e.g., pp. 236, 263–4 and 269.

Table 2.4
Rate payers: amount assessed and known occupations, 1579–94.

Amount and frequency of the rate to be paid	Number of assessments at this level	Known occupations of these men or the husbands of widows
1–2d per quarter (4–8d per year)	219 = 24%	4 weavers, 4 shermen, 2 cobblers/ shoemakers, 2 butchers, 2 coopers, 1 failing clothier, 1 wringer, 1 woadsetter, 1 cardmaker, 1 tailor, 1 tallowchandler, 1 miller, 1 gelder, 1 woodworker, 1 clerk
3–4d per quarter (1s–1s 4d per year)	267 = 30%	3 carters/carriers, 3 millers, 2 shermen, 2 glovers, 2 cobblers/ shoemakers, 1 clothier, 1 cloth broker, 1 weaver, 1 woadsetter, 1 fuller, 1 smith, 1 wheelwright, 1 woodworker
6–12d per quarter (2–4s per year)	156 = 17%	3 clothiers, 2 millers, 2 smiths, 1 cloth broker, 1 sherman, 1 hatter, 1 cobbler, 1 wheelwright, 1 woodworker, 1 fishmonger, 1 merchant, 1 parish clerk
1d per week (4s 4d per year)	153 = 17%	8 clothiers, 3 gentlemen, 2 tanners, 1 cloth broker, 1 mercer, 1 fuller, 1 yeoman, 1 haberdasher, 1 smith, 1 wheelwright
2–6d per week (8s 8d–£1 6s per year)	99 = 11%	13 clothiers, 5 gentlemen, 2 esquires, 2 mercers, 1 yeoman, 1 haberdasher, 1 smith
Total	894	

Note: This analysis pertains to the six surviving listings of rates, from 1579, 1582, 1585, 1590, 1591 and 1594. The number of assessments at each level includes all entries in those listings. People rated at different amounts in various years appear under each category of payment with their occupation at that time.

the household receiving assistance was almost certainly the sibling or cousin of one of the people considered wealthy enough by local standards to be assessed for poor rates. Some recipients probably had additional rate-paying relatives through maternal lines, which are harder to trace.

A sample set of annual accounts

Each of Hadleigh's officers had to submit a formal written account at the end of each year of service to the body of Chief Inhabitants who appointed him.[68] As an example of how the various officers reported their activities on behalf of the poor, we may

---

68. In the mid 1560s the subcollectors generally accounted twice or even four times each year, but later audits were annual.

look at the little packet of accounts for 1582, audited and approved on 2 January 1583.[69] As was true in most years, each officer's account was submitted separately, in various handwritings and on paper of different sizes which were then stitched together. Robert Andrew and Nicholas Strutt, 'under Collectors', prepared the first account, which begins with 'The names of those that are sessed to the poor to pay by the week'. The 39 names that follow were supposed to pay between 1d and 4d every week, but the subcollectors noted that some in fact paid less than the full amount and two 'paid nothing this year'. The weekly payers yielded a total of £11 9s 8d. The next pages list 'Those that pay by the quarter'. The 120 people entered here were meant to pay between 1d and 8d each quarter but, again, some had rendered less. That total came to £6 12s 2d. Andrew and Strutt also reported that they had been given £52 by the chief collector. At the end of the account they entered 17s received from John Marchant and 17s from John Cowper, both for undescribed reasons, and 14s 6d 'out of the chest'. The latter referred to donations to the poor men's box in the church. The grand total of all receipts for the poor for the year was 3 score £12 10s 4d, or £72 10s 4d.

The subcollectors then turned to expenses. The first heading says 'Paid to the poor as followeth weekly'. In that category they listed 38 people, noting how much they received per week, over how many weeks, and what the total amount was. Most of the recipients (29) were paid over the full span of 52 weeks, with the remainder helped for between 24 and 47 weeks. The amount they received each week varied considerably. Eighteen of the recipients were given 6d or 8d, which was probably considered the standard rate at the time for a poor individual or small household, assuming that its members were able to bring in a little income through their own labour. Larger amounts, however, of 10d or 12d weekly, went to four women aged 50 years or more, five old men, and four people who were boarding children. These sums presumably provided full relief for people who were unable to earn money and in some cases needed care as well. The remaining seven people were paid 2d to 4d per week in what must have been seen as supplemental income. The sum of the weekly payments was £58 7s 6d.

The next heading, 'Given in benevolences', is followed by a series of small awards to named people at times of special need. Some of the recipients were already receiving regular payments, but many appear only on this list. 'Benevolences' came to a total of £9 14s 10d for the year. At the end of that section comes a series of miscellaneous entries for such items as burying poor people, making shoes or clothing for the poor, and a new bell rope (presumably for the chapel at Pykenham's almshouses), plus a few payments to people with no cause given. These additional items totalled £3 4s 2d. The total expended by the subcollectors for the year was £72 10s 4d.

The account of the chief collector, Edward Gale, includes further payments for needy people. He reported a total income of £103 8s 4d and total expenses of £106 10d.[70] His reckoning lists rental income from the town's charitable properties and the out-rents due from that land; he reported costs for repairs to buildings, wages, sending people to other places on official business, and food and other expenses for 'the reckoning day'. But Gale also recorded some expenditures for the poor: giving out

---

69. HadlA 021/A/03. The folios are not numbered, and the chief collector's account is divided between two non-adjacent quires.

70. See the last folio in the booklet of accounts and HadlA 004/A/01, p. 148.

cash (usually occasionally but in a few cases over multiple weeks), making and distributing clothing or shoes and preparing and delivering loads of wood. He paid some people for boarding children and gave 'Little the weaver' a total of 20s 'to discharge the town of the dumb boy'.[71] Gale laid out further sums for carrying an unwanted child and an adult man out of Hadleigh and for fetching another man home.

Several other accounts in the booklet for 1582 include entries for needy people. The churchwardens, John Becon and Henry Tottye, recorded no direct expenses for the poor but mentioned the money given to the subcollectors from the poor men's chest. Market bailiffs Thomas Facon and Oliver Chepe listed income from tenements, shops, stalls and standings in the market, together with the out-rents paid. Although they did not describe any direct help to the poor, they delivered their excess profits to the chief collector, some of which were probably used for his charitable expenses. Another sheet records the distribution of 60 ells of canvas purchased from the rental income of the two tenements given to the Chief Inhabitants by Alice Parkins, widow.[72] The canvas was handed out in units of 1½ ells each by the chief collector, the churchwardens, the subcollectors and 'others of the town' to 40 people, most of whom did not receive other forms of relief that year. The total outlay by all officials for the 149 poor helped by the town in 1582 was £83 16s. With this overview of Hadleigh's network of care as a foundation, we turn to the recipients of assistance.

---

71. For the latter, see Chapter 4, 'Granted to a different family or expelled from Hadleigh', below.
72. The account in the 1582 records was duplicated in a separate set of accounts that recorded the distributions of her canvas over the next 20 years (HadlA 011/N/01).

Chapter 3

Recipients of relief and their households

Having seen how Hadleigh's system of poor relief operated from the perspective of those who administered and paid for it, we now shift our focus to those who received relief. This chapter first examines recipients as individuals and then looks at assistance as it functioned for households. The analyses presented here derive from all surviving poor relief accounts and other ancillary sources.[1]

Individual recipients of assistance

The accounts between 1579 and 1596 name 603 people as having been assisted by poor relief officers and through the distribution of privately bequeathed goods as recorded in the town book. (Because the accounts are incomplete for some years, that figure is an absolute minimum. It also excludes children and young people sent temporarily to the workhouse for training and/or punishment from 1589 onwards unless they received direct help as well.[2]) As seen in Part A of Table 3.1, recipients of relief were evenly divided between females and males, though more boys were helped than girls and more adult women than adult men. Hadleigh's summary distribution – 31.7 per cent adult men, 35.5 per cent women and 32.7 per cent children – included fewer women and more children than the average in five other small towns and five cities.[3] In classifying adults by age, 50 years was used as the cutoff between younger and older people.[4] A striking feature of Hadleigh's recipients is that 24 per cent were aged 20 to 49, with more men than women, rather than displaying a heavy weighting of older people. Part B of Table 3.1 shows that, unlike the high concentration of widows among

---

1. See References for a listing of the accounts.

2. The workhouse housed up to 30 children and young people under 24 years at a time (see Chapter 4, 'Training and discipline in the workhouse', below). Of 70 named inmates, 1591–5, 20 had received poor relief previously and are included in the 603. Thirty-nine others were from Hadleigh but had not themselves been assisted before; 11 evidently came from outside of the town. If one regards the institution as providing useful occupational training for the poor, the 39 local youngsters could be added to the total number of people helped.

3. McIntosh, 'Poor relief in Elizabethan communities', and see Apps 3.2 and 3.3 below. The fraction of women among Hadleigh's recipients was, however, rising, from 42 per cent in 1579 to 57 per cent in 1594.

4. Although literary conventions in this period followed the classical pattern of defining old age as starting at age 60, it appears that most poor people in Hadleigh were perceived as 'old' at a younger chronological age, owing presumably to the hardships of their lives. If one examines the ages of those people described as 'Old' someone (e.g., Old Warwicke), all were over 50; nine-tenths of those termed 'Mother' or 'Father' (e.g., Mother Aylocke) were 50 or more when they were first given that designation. For 37 such people of known or probable ages:

Table 3.1
Recipients of relief, by age, sex and marital status.

Part A. Recipients by age and sex

	Females	Males	Sex unknown	Total
Children/teens				
0–4 years	18 = 3%	15 = 2%	0	33 = 5%
5–9 years	24 = 4%	39 = 6%	0	63 = 10%
Child, age unknown	24 = 4%	33 = 5%	12 = 2%	69 = 11%
10–19 years	16 = 3%	16 = 3%	0	32 = 5%
Total	82 = 14%	103 = 17%	12 = 2%	197 = 33%
Adults				
20–49 years	62 = 10%	80 = 13%	0	142 = 24%
50 years or more	105 = 17%	67 = 11%	0	172 = 29%
Adult, age unknown	47 = 8%	44 = 7%	1	92 = 15%
Total	214 = 35%	191 = 32%	1	406 = 67%
Total	296 = 49%	294 = 49%	13 = 2%	603

Part B. Adult recipients of known age and sex by marital status

	Females	Males	Total
Aged 20–49 years			
Single	6 = 10% of sex and age	2 = 3% of sex and age	8 = 6% of age
Married	38 = 61%	57 = 71%	95 = 67%
Widow/widower	12 = 19%	3 = 4%	15 = 11%
Marit. status unknown	6 = 10%	18 = 22%	24 = 17%
Total	62	80	142
Aged 50 years or more			
Single	2 = 2%	0	2 = 1%
Married	29 = 28%	35 = 52%	64 = 37%
Widow/widower	46 = 44%	8 = 12%	54 = 31%
Marit. status unknown	28 = 27%	24 = 36%	52 = 30%
Total	105	67	172

Note: Age and marital status refer to the majority of years in which a person received relief.

recipients in some other communities during the first half of the seventeenth century, only 19 per cent of Hadleigh's younger women were widows, as were 44 per cent of older ones.[5] Two-thirds of the younger recipients and 37 per cent of those aged 50 years or more were married at the time, with higher levels for men than women. Only ten people had apparently never married, but others may be hidden within the category of 'marital status unknown'.

We do not have a census of all poor people in Hadleigh during these years, but we may set these figures for recipients of relief against information about the full complement of the poor in two other urban settings: St Mary's parish in Warwick in 1587 and the city of Norwich in 1570 (Table 3.2).[6] These comparisons show considerable similarities between the communities, suggesting that the poor people assisted in Hadleigh may have reflected fairly accurately the nature of urban poverty. One sees a somewhat smaller fraction of recipient children in Hadleigh, presumably because they were gaining assistance through their parents or grandparents. Among adults, whereas the distribution between women and men was even in Hadleigh, the full population of the poor in Warwick and Norwich had a higher fraction of women. Hadleigh's recipients also included a higher percentage of elderly men and women, unlike the weighting of young and middle-aged adults in the other two places.

An unusual feature of the Hadleigh records is that we can trace the span of years over which people received help, as displayed in Table 3.3.[7] Forty-three per cent of the full group were assisted in just a single year; for children and teens, this figure was

Age	'Mothers'	'Fathers'
45–49 yrs	3 with ages definitely known (1 married to an older man)	1 with age definitely known (married to an older woman)
50–59 yrs	4 definite, 3 probable ages	3 definite
60–69 yrs	6 definite, 5 probable ages	1 definite, 1 probable
70–79 yrs	4 definite, 1 probable ages	3 definite, 1 probable
80 89 yrs	0	1 definite

I have therefore placed all adults termed Old, Mother or Father in the category of 50 years or more unless other information indicated they were younger. (For the marital status of Mothers and Fathers, see App. Intro.3, note 4.) Men and women known to be grandparents also went into the 50+ grouping, while parents of recently born children were placed in the 20–49 category in the absence of contradictory evidence.

5. See, e.g., Tim Wales, 'Poverty, poor relief and the life cycle', in Smith (ed.), *Land, kinship and life-cycle* (Cambridge, 1984), pp. 351–404, W. Newman Brown, 'The receipt of poor relief and family situation', in Smith (ed.), *Land, kinship and life-cycle*, pp. 405–22, and Lynn A. Botelho, *Old age and the English poor law, 1500–1700* (Woodbridge, 2004), p. 116. In the five comparable small towns, 53 per cent of the annual entries for adult female recipients were described as widows or 'mothers' (McIntosh, 'Poor relief in Elizabethan communities').

6. In Warwick, 38 per cent of the poor were aged 0–15 years, 23 per cent were adult men (17 per cent aged 16–60 and 6 per cent aged 61+), and 39 per cent were adult women (27 per cent aged 16–60 and 12 per cent aged 61+): Beier, 'Poverty and progress', p. 215.

7. This analysis measures the span between the first and last year of documented relief, counting each of the terminal years, since the annual accounts are not entirely complete. Thus, help received between 1581 and 1586 was entered as a span of six years even though the accounts for 1584 are largely missing.

Table 3.2

Comparison of Hadleigh's recipients, 1579–96, with all Norwich poor people, 1570.

	Hadleigh recipients (N = 603)				All Norwich poor (N = 2,359)			
	Females	Males	Sex unknown	Total	Females	Males	Sex unspecified	Total
Children/teens								
0–4 yrs (H); 1–5 yrs (N)	3%	2%	0	5%	1%	2%	11%	13%
5–9 yrs (H); 6–10 yrs (N)	4%	6%	0	10%	2%	2%	10%	14%
Child, age unknown/unspecified	4%	5%	2%	11%	1%	0	6%	7%
10–19 yrs (H); 11–20 yrs (N)	3%	3%	0	5%	2%	1%	5%	9%
Total	14%	17%	2%	33%	5%	5%	33%	42%
Adults								
20–49 yrs (H); 21–50 yrs (N)	10%	13%	0	24%	22%	15%	0	37%
50+ yrs (H); 51+ yrs (N)	17%	11%	0	29%	11%	6%	0	18%
Adult, age unknown (H); unspecified (N)	8%	7%	0	15%	2%	1%	0	3%
Total	35%	32%	0	67%	36%	22%	1%	58%
Total	49%	49%	2%		40%	27%	33%	

Note: Source for Norwich information: *Norwich census of the poor*, Apps. I and II.

Table 3.3
Span of years over which individuals received assistance of any type within the eighteen years.

Span of years*	Children and teens	Adult women	Adult men	Total
1 year only	114 = 58%	62 = 29%	80 = 42%	257 = 43% #
2–4 years	39 = 20%	57 = 27%	38 = 20%	134 = 22%
5–9 years	29 = 15%	48 = 22%	40 = 21%	117 = 19%
10–14 years	15 = 8%	31 = 14%	27 = 14%	73 = 12%
15–18 years	0	16 = 7%	6 = 3%	22 = 4%
Total	197 = 33%	214 = 35%	191 = 32%	603 #
	of full group	of full group	of full group	
Average span	3.0 years	5.7 years	4.6 years	4.4 years

Notes:
* Counting the number of years from the first through the last year of relief, including both
  terminal years (e.g., 1579–82 = span of 4 years).
Includes 1 adult of unknown sex who received in a single year.

58 per cent.[8] But 41 per cent gained aid in 2 to 9 years, and 16 per cent were helped for between 10 and at least 18 years (the span of the surviving documents). Adult women received relief over an average span of 5.7 years, as compared to 4.6 years for men and 3.0 years for children.[9]

Analysis of the types of relief given across the full span of 18 years (Table 3.4) shows that 63 per cent of all recipients were helped only occasionally. More than a third never received anything other than household goods or clothes, a pattern especially common among children. Another 28 per cent were given more regular and far more valuable help at some point within the span in the form of weekly payments (defined as ten or more within a given year), with or without occasional help but without being boarded. Among this group, adult women predominated. Fewer than a tenth of all recipients were boarded without receiving regular payments, the great majority of them children. Only a handful of people were both boarded and received regular payments at various times. Examination of the sequenced patterns of relief indicates that 62 per cent of all recipients began with household goods or clothes only, with some then moving on to other kinds of assistance. A sixth of the group first received occasional money or services, while an eighth had been given no other help before starting to receive regular weekly payments. Only 4 per cent were boarded as the initial form of help.

In turning to the money value of the assistance received per year we encounter the impact of missing records. The largest expenditure of funds took the form of regular weekly payments, but accounts of those payments survive for only 6 of the 18 years.[10] For most of the other years, the accounts document distribution of goods and the provision of care, joined sometimes by occasional money payments. If one calculates

8. In four other small towns, 39–70 per cent of all recipients were helped in 1 year only, while no more than 6 per cent received in 10 years or more (McIntosh, 'Poor relief in Elizabethan communities').

9. In three of four comparable towns, women likewise received over longer spans than men, with shorter spans for children (*ibid.*).

10. See Table 2.1 above and App. Intro.2.

Table 3.4

Types of assistance received by individuals over the span of eighteen years.

Types of assistance	Children and teens	Adult women	Adult men	Total
A. Occasional relief only				
Household goods or clothes only	99	59	62	220 = 36%
Occas. money (1–9 payments per year) or services only	12	17	16	45 = 7%
Winding sheet or burial only	14	4	10	28 = 5%
Goods plus money and/or services	21	36	29	86 = 14%
Total, occasional relief only	146 = 74%	116 = 54%	117 = 61%	379 = 63%
B. Regular money payments (10+ per year) at some point within the span, with or without occasional relief but no boarding	13 = 7%	88 = 41%	68 = 36%	169 = 28%
C. Boarding at some point within the span, with or without occasional relief but no regular payments	35 = 18%	6 = 3%	5 = 3%	47 = 8%*
D. Regular payments and boarding at some point, with or without occasional relief	3 = 2%	4 = 2%	1 = 1%	8 = 1%
Total, all types of assistance	197 = 33%	214 = 35%	191 = 32%	603*

Note:
* Includes 1 adult of unknown sex.

the average amount received annually for all years, the resulting values are about half the size of the averages for only the six better documented years (Table 3.5). The latter thus provide a more accurate representation of what kinds of people were awarded help and how much they were given. When analysed by sex and age, average annual payments were higher for girls of all ages, for boys aged 5 to 9 and for older adults than for teens and young adults. Payments for adult women were only very slightly larger than for men.[11] Interestingly, women described as widows or 'mothers' received an average of 1.7d per week, less than the amount given to other women (2.4d), nearly all of whom were married at the time. The pattern found in some seventeenth- and eighteenth-century communities in which elderly widows consumed much of the total expense for relief was not present in Elizabethan Hadleigh.[12] The average annual total for all adults, 14s 11d, would have provided full assistance (at 6d to 7d per week) for half the year or smaller payments for a longer period.

The monetary value of the various types of help awarded may be explored by sex and age (Table 3.6). Among those people who received occasional goods, money or services, boys and male teens were generally given more than girls, and most adult males received more than females. But the low value of such help (no more than 3s 4d annually for the adult categories) suggests that the recipients had additional sources of income, probably through their own labour or that of other household members. We have seen that Hadleigh's weavers required a great deal of yarn, prepared usually within a domestic setting by women and children.[13] Sorting, carding and spinning wool could be done on a full- or part-time basis by people who needed to be at home with young children or were physically unable to undertake more vigorous labour. In Norwich's census of the poor in 1570, 66 per cent of the 514 men aged 21 or more were engaged in some kind of work at the time; the rest said they had an occupation but were not currently employed.[14] Among the 838 adult women, 87 per cent were working, most apparently at home, with by far the largest group (55 per cent) spinning. The annual amounts received by Hadleigh people who were given regular weekly payments were quite similar for adult women and men; elderly people of both sexes, however, received half again as much as younger adults. Among children, girls aged under 5 years were given more in regular payments than boys of that age, whereas boys aged 5 to 9 were given more than girls. Relatively few people

---

11. Hadleigh's averages of 3.4d per week for men, 4.1d for women, and 3d for children, with a combined average of 3.6d, were much larger for adults than in the five comparative small towns (1.8d for men and 1.7d for women) but slightly less for children (3.4d), resulting in a combined average in the other places of 2.2d. In seven cities, however, the combined average was 4.6d (McIntosh, 'Poor relief in Elizabethan communities').

12. See, e.g., Wales, 'Poverty, poor relief', Brown, 'Receipt of poor relief' and Susannah R. Ottaway, *The decline of life: old age in eighteenth-century England* (Cambridge, 2004), pp. 237–45. In the comparative Elizabethan towns, widows and 'mothers' received somewhat more than other women (1.8d per week instead of 1.5d), though in five rural communities the average amount given to both groups of women (1.1d) was the same (McIntosh, *ibid.*)

13. See Chapter 1, 'Cloth manufacturing and clothiers', and 'Community wealth, occupational distribution, and gendered absences', above.

14. *Norwich census of the poor*, Apps III and IV as compared with figures from App. I.

Table 3.5

Average amount received per year and over the full span, by sex and age.

	Females			Males			All recipients		
	Aver. amt received per year for 6 yrs with best records (in s)	Aver. amt received per year, all surviving records (in s)	Aver. total amt received over full span, all records (in s)	Aver. amt received per year for 6 yrs with best records (in s)	Aver. amt received per year, all surviving records (in s)	Aver. total amt received over full span, all records (in s)	Aver. amt received per year for 6 yrs with best records (in s)	Aver. amt received per year, all surviving records (in s)	Aver. total amt received over full span, all records (in s)
Children/teenagers									
0–4 years	17.5	11.9	17.6	5.0	4.8	15.9	11.3	8.0	16.8
5–9 years	21.9	9.9	19.4	14.2	9.4	15.5	17.2	9.6	17.0
Child, age unknown	23.3	12.0	21.0	7.0	7.9	16.8	10.7	9.3	17.5
10–19 years	14.6	7.3	15.2	7.8	5.2	7.2	11.4	6.2	11.2
Adults									
20–49 years	11.5	6.7	18.4	10.8	6.7	18.9	11.1	6.7	18.7
50 years plus	21.0	10.1	47.1	20.0	9.9	39.9	20.5	10.0	44.3
Adult, age unknown	11.5	5.6	15.7	9.1	5.1	8.6	10.5	5.4	12.4
No information about age	n/a	2.4	2.4	3.6	3.5	3.5	3.0	3.0	2.9
Total	17.8	8.9	28.1	13.6	7.8	20.5	15.7	8.4	24.1

Note: Age refers to the person's age during the majority of years in which assistance was received. 'Mother', 'Father', or 'old' plus a surname (e.g., Mother Smith) were counted as 50 years or more unless other information indicates they were younger (see App. Intro.3). For the years included in the 6 with best records, see Table Intro.1 and App. Intro.2. For the number of people in each category, see Table 3.1.

Table 3.6

Type and average amount of assistance received by individuals per year, by sex and age.

| | Average amount received annually, in shillings | | | | | |
| | Females | | | Males | | |
	Occasional goods, money and/or services	Regular weekly payments #	Boarding	Occasional goods, money and/or services	Regular weekly payments #	Boarding
Children/teenagers						
0–4 years	2.8	20.7	38.1	3.2	15.0	15.9
5–9 years	2.8	28.6	24.2	3.6	45.5	19.3
Child, age unknown	4.6	0.9	36.2	3.5	0	16.5
10–19 years	3.3	31.3	1.1	4.0	21.7	0
Adults						
20–49 years	2.7	19.8	12.3	3.3	20.5	5.3
50 years plus	2.8	30.3	0.8	2.9	30.2	3.1
Adult, age unknown	2.9	22.8	0	2.4	17.8	22.8
No information about age	2.4	0	0	3.5	0	0
Total	2.9	27.5	24.6	3.2	26.3	16.0
Average no. of recipients per year	44	31	2	38	21	3

Notes: This analysis is based upon those years for which detailed accounts of such aid survive, not all years.
Regular payments are defined as 10 or more within a given year, usually paid each week.

were boarded, but their care was expensive, especially that of children. Many of those who took in girls were paid more than a pound and a half annually.

We may look more closely at the 177 people who received weekly payments at some time within the 18-year span, the great majority of whom (91 per cent) were adults (Table 3.7). Most children who needed regular assistance were presumably helped through the money given to their parents. Children and teens also received for somewhat fewer years than did adults: on average, 5–6 years for youngsters as opposed to 7–8 years for adults. Elderly people, however, received for longer periods than younger adults. Of those adults whose marital status is known, 81 per cent of the men who were given regular weekly payments were married at the time; 41 per cent of the women were married, but 53 per cent were widows.

There was, however, considerable variation between years in the number and type of recipients of weekly payments. As an illustration, we may compare those assisted on a regular basis in 1579 and 1594. In the former year, which had no special problems with food shortage or disease, 44 people received regular payments: 3 children (7 per cent), 27 adult women (61 per cent) and 14 adult men (32 per cent). Of the adults whose ages and marital status are known, only 16 per cent were under the age of 50, with the rest elderly; three-quarters were currently married and the rest were widows or widowers. Women received an average of 8.7d per week and 24.6s over the course of the year, while males received 9.3d weekly and 34.0s in total.

In 1594, by contrast, the poor were suffering from unusually high grain prices, and some families had been disrupted by high mortality in the plague of 1592. The number of people who received weekly payments in 1594 (67) was half again larger than in 1579, and their situation had shifted somewhat. Only one child was assisted, and the proportion of women to men was about the same as in 1579. But the fraction of adults under the age of 50 years had risen slightly for women and grown to more than a third for men. This suggests that the town was supporting more young families, perhaps including some in which the father was out of work. Currently married women now formed only 28 per cent of the total, as compared with 69 per cent in 1579, and the fraction of married men was down to 63 per cent, as compared with 88 per cent before. The heavier concentration of widows and widowers probably reflects losses from the plague. Yet, although more people were being helped in 1594, the size of their weekly payments had declined. The average amount received by women had dropped from 8.4d to 6.2d, while that for men went from 9.3d to 6.3d, with correspondingly large declines in the total amount received during the year. This reduction in assistance apparently resulted from the realisation by poor relief officials that if they continued to distribute aid at the level given in the early months of the year their annual expenses would far exceed their income: hence they reduced the size of all payments in April.

In 1594 the most fully supported of all the poor were those 40 recipients of weekly help who received a total of 23s 6d or more. Of these, 30 lived in the almshouses and are described below.[15] The remainder included one teenaged girl whose widowed mother or grandmother and two younger siblings received other kinds of assistance that year; one married woman with young children and/or stepchildren whose

---

15. See Chapter 5, 'Help for old people', below.

Table 3.7

Individual recipients of regular weekly payments, 1579–96: span of years received, by sex, age and marital status.

	Females		Males		Total #	
	No. of people and % of total	Aver. span of years received	No. of people and % of total	Aver. span of years received	No. of people and % of total	Aver. span of years received
A. Age						
Children/teenagers						
0–4 years	3 = 3% of females	5.0	2 = 3% of males	6.0	5 = 3% of total	5.4
5–9 years	3 = 3%	3.0	3 = 4%	5.3	6 = 3%	4.2
Child, but age unknown	0		1 = 1%	2.0	2 # = 1%	6.5
10–19 years	3 = 3%	9.7	0		3 = 2%	9.7
Total	9 = 9%	5.9	6 = 8%	5.0	16 = 9%	5.9
Adults						
20–49 years	22 = 22% of females	5.9	25 = 33% of males	7.1	47 = 27% of total	6.5
50 years or more	61 = 60%	8.9	38 = 51%	7.4	99 = 56%	8.3
Adult, but age unknown	9 = 9%	3.9	6 = 8%	5.7	15 = 8%	4.6
Total	92 = 91%	7.7	69 = 92%	7.1	161 = 91%	7.4
Total	101 = 57% of full group	7.5	75 = 42% of full group	7.0	177 #	7.3
B. Marital status of adults *when known*						
Never married	5 = 7% of females	5.2	1 = 2% of males	1.0	6 = 5% of total	4.5
Currently married	30 = 41%	7.3	39 = 81%	7.8	69 = 57%	7.8
Widow or widower	39 = 53%	9.0	8 = 17%	8.0	47 = 39%	8.8
Total	74 = 61% of known marital status		48 = 39% of known marital status		122	

Notes: Regular payments are defined as 10 or more within a given year, usually paid each week. Age and marital status refer to the person's situation during the majority of years in which relief was received.
Includes 1 child of unknown sex and age with the unusually long span of 11 years.

husband was evidently unable to provide for them; two married men and three widows, all with young children at home; one elderly widow; and two elderly blind men.

Turning now to adults who were boarded, we find that of the 10 women and 6 men who received such care 5 were probably self-sufficient under normal circumstances: they were the only members of their households to be helped, and they were boarded only temporarily in a single year.[16] Of the 9 women with known ages who were boarded, 6 were 20–49 years and were boarded for an average of six months, and 5 are known to have been ill or to have had a recent and difficult childbirth. Their boarding care cost the town much more than did the 3 older women (an average of 12.3s per year as compared to 0.8s), largely because women over 50 were boarded for much shorter periods. Of 5 men of known age who were boarded, only 1 was under 50 years, and he was boarded for three months, care that cost the town 5.3s. The 4 older men were boarded for shorter periods, at an average cost of just 3.1s. The surprisingly limited use of boarding for elderly adults may well have been related to the availability of almshouse places for vulnerable old people.

Poor relief officials were prepared to provide a decent burial for exceptionally needy people. In 15 years between 1579 and 1596 poor relief officials reported payments for winding sheets and/or burials for 153 individuals. Of that full group, we have information about the sex and age of 99; the remainder were described only as poor people, without individual names.[17] Most of those identified were either children/teenagers (29 per cent) or elderly adults (37 per cent); slightly more adult men than women were buried.

Hadleigh's recipients may be compared with those in East Anglia's leading city of Norwich and in the nearby town of Ipswich. During the Elizabethan years Norwich had a number of residential institutions for the poor (nine medieval hospitals that had survived the dissolution and two or three newer almshouses), but the city also provided assistance to people living in their own homes.[18] Those who were given relief as described in Norwich's census of the poor of 1570 can be set against Hadleigh's recipients in 1579, the first year of full records. In Norwich only 165 of the needy people recorded in the census (7 per cent) received assistance, at an average level of 3.2d per week. Hadleigh had 91 recipients of relief, despite the great difference in size between the two communities, and its adults were given 1.8 times more each week. No children or teens were assisted directly in Norwich, but a slightly larger fraction of the city's recipients were women aged under 50 years. While nearly all of Norwich's men were married – a few of them described as unable to find work – most of the women were widows or had been abandoned by their husbands. Among older people a quarter were disabled or ill, and women were more common than in Hadleigh.

---

16. For boarding of children, see Chapter 4, 'Short-term boarding in another household', below.

17. See App. 3.1, Pt. A. In three years sheets or burials were provided for unnamed poor folk or people: an unspecified number in 1590 (entered as 4 in this analysis, based on the size of the payment); 38 in 1591; and an unspecified number in 1592 (entered as 12 based on the size of the payment).

18. Information from my database of English hospitals and almshouses active 1350–1600 (as described in Online App. 1 to McIntosh, *Poor relief in England*), for Norwich and Ipswich (next paragraph). For below, see App. 3.2.

Ipswich, a substantial trading and manufacturing port with which Hadleigh had close economic contacts, likewise offered multiple forms of relief. Its medieval hospital of St Leonard was still active, and three almshouses were founded between 1515 and 1569, two of which helped people living in their own homes as well. The town began its Register of the Poor in 1569 and was assessing poor rates and making weekly payments by 1574.[19] A detailed listing of recipients and the amount they received in 1597 may be compared with the help provided by Hadleigh in 1594, the latest year of full records. Ipswich had obviously decided to provide larger amounts of assistance to a limited group of needy recipients. It gave relief to only 46 poor people (as compared to 111 in Hadleigh) even though it was a much larger town, but it provided more to them each week: 1.5 times more for female recipients, and 2.5 times more for males. Ipswich assisted no children or teens directly and, although both communities were willing to help younger adults, in Ipswich those aged 20–49 were either men who were unable to work or women. Among older people, Ipswich gave relief primarily to widows and married men, with a much higher concentration of elderly people who were disabled or ill than in Hadleigh.

Recipient households and family relationships

One of the great benefits of the various Hadleigh records is that they enable us to place individual recipients of relief into households. While some of these assignments are probable rather than certain, they give us a broad picture of how needy domestic units were assisted.[20] This is a rare opportunity.

The 603 recipients of relief in Hadleigh between 1579 and 1596 were members of 320 households, with an average of 1.9 assisted people per unit. If we exclude the sixteen unnamed people for whom a specific household cannot be identified, 30 per cent of the recipients were the only person in their household who was helped, but 42 per cent lived in families with two or three recipients and 28 per cent were in families with four to seven recipients. Children and teenagers were members of units with the largest number of people receiving assistance: an average of 3.6. Men and women aged 20–49 averaged 2.8 recipients in their households, while older people had fewer, just 2.0. In addition to other recipients living in the same household with them, two-thirds had a probable relative (someone with the same surname who appears to have been a member of the same extended family) who was helped as a member of a different domestic unit.

As seen in Table 3.8, the family relationships of recipients within their residential households show considerable variety, but most included either a married couple or a parent/grandparent plus child as basic components of the unit. Table 3.9 shows the average amount received per household for the three years with full records, for all years, and across the full span. Using the numbers for fully documented years, the average value of annual assistance rose from 14s 1d for units in which only one person was helped to 24s 9d for units with two recipients and 52s 2d for those with three or

---

19. *Poor relief in Elizabethan Ipswich*, ed. John Webb, Suffolk Records Society, vol. 9 (Ipswich, 1966). For below, see App. 3.3.

20. See App. Intro.3 for how I grouped people into households.

Table 3.8

Recipients of relief as members of household units.

		No. of households
1 recipient per household (N = 177 = 55% of the 320 households)		
Adult woman	Aged 20–49	11
	Aged 50+	47
	Age unknown	24
Adult man	Aged 20–49	19
	Aged 50+	27
	Age unknown	23
Child or teen		20
Age unknown		6
2 recipients per household (N = 80 = 25% of households)		
Married couple	Aged 20–49	12
	Aged 50+	29
	Age unknown	5
Adult woman + 1 child	Aged 20–49	4
	Aged 50+	5
	Age unknown	5
Adult man + 1 child/teen	Aged 20–49	9
	Aged 50+	3
	Age unknown	4
2 children/teens		3
Other	2 women aged 50+	1
3 recipients per household (N = 29 = 9% of households)		
Married couple + 1 child	Aged 20–49	11
	Aged 50+	9
Adult woman + 2 children	Aged 20–49	3
	Aged 50+	3
	Age unknown	1
Adult man + 2 children	Aged 20–49	1
	Aged 50+	1
4 recipients per household (N = 19 = 6% of households)		
Married couple + 2 children	Aged 20–49	8
	Aged 50+	9
Adult woman + 3 children	Aged 50+	1
4 children		1
5–7 recipients per household (N = 15 = 5% of households)		
Couple aged 20–49	plus 3 or 4 children	6
Couple aged 50+	plus 3 children	6
Woman aged 50+	plus 4 children	1
Other	Man plus 2 successive wives plus 3 or 4 children	2

Note: Couples were placed in the 50+ category if either of them was of this age. Children/teens may have been children or grandchildren of the adult(s).

Table 3.9
Average amount received per household, by year and during full span, by number of recipients in the household.

Number of recipients in the household	Numbers per year for 3 yrs with full accounts #		Numbers per year for all years		Numbers for full span	
	No. of annual entries for households	Aver. amt received (s)	No. of annual entries for households	Aver. amt received (s)	No. of households	Aver. amt received (s)
1	234	14.1	1,168	8.5	174	23.7
2	53	24.9	176	15.5	80	54.6
3–4	13	52.2	51	30.1	48	77.5
5–7	0	0	4	35.1	15	144.1
Total	300	17.7	1,399	10.3	317*	45.3

Notes:
* Excludes 3 households that received only cloth or clothing for which no money value was given.
# The years with entirely complete accounts are 1582, 1591 and 1594.

four. Single-recipient households were thus receiving about 3d per week, while those with two people were given about 6d weekly. In both cases, the amount of relief was about half of what was regarded as full support, not surprising since many of those helped were given only occasional assistance and their family may have had other sources of income. Households with more recipients were given 12d per week. Over the full span, for which the numbers are incomplete, the average amount received ranged from £1 3s 8d for one-recipient households to £7 4s 1d for those with five to seven recipients.

Analysis of households permits some observations about marriage patterns among the poor. The marriages of a considerable fraction of men in Hadleigh who received assistance at some time between 1579 and 1596 do not appear in the parish register, although the latter records the baptism of their children. While some of these men probably married simply by the exchange of vows in the presence of witnesses, rather than through a church ceremony, others may have chosen wives from different communities, with the wedding taking place in the woman's home parish.[21] The suggestion of an exogamous marriage pattern is supported by the frequent listing in the parish register of the marriages of the daughters of local poor relief families to men whose names do not appear elsewhere in the records and were apparently outsiders. Exogamous marriages may have been facilitated by regular contact with other woollen cloth-manufacturing communities in the area. When male recipients of relief in Hadleigh did marry local women, however, their brides were often from other families that received assistance. We know the first name and natal family for the wife or mother of 71 recipients. Of those women, 59 per cent were members of families that were given relief; the others came either from economically self-sufficient families in Hadleigh or from other places.

We can examine the impact of marital status on the amount of assistance received and the span of years over which recipients received help, recognising that it is difficult to identify those people who never married (Table 3.10). The few women who had apparently not married were given more help annually than were currently married women or widows, regardless of age, but the span of years over which they were helped was generally shorter. Among people aged 20–49, married women and men received help for slightly longer periods than widows or widowers, with relatively little difference in the amount paid annually. Of people aged 50 or more, currently married women received more than widows but were paid over a shorter span, whereas widowers received more than currently married men and were assisted over a longer period.

Children were direct recipients in more than a third of the households that were assisted. Twenty-one per cent of all households included one or two recipient children, while 14 per cent had anywhere from three to six youngsters who were helped. The average of 2.5 children does not include additional offspring who did not receive relief and any other young relatives or servants who may have been living with that family. The adult recipients who headed these units were evenly divided between men and women, but – a most interesting observation – in nearly half the cases they appear to

---

21. For unrecorded marriages, see Chapter 1, 'The estimated population and demographic information', above.

Table 3.10

The impact of marital status on relief.

	Women			Men		
	Aver. amt received per year, all types of relief	Span of years received	Total amt received, full span	Aver. amt received per year, all types of relief	Span of years received	Total amt received, full span
People aged 20–49 years #						
Never married	10.4	4.2	24.4	1.0	1.0	23.2
Currently married	6.5	4.6	16.1	6.8	5.1	23.0
Widow/widower	6.7	4.2	22.8	6.4	4.0	19.0
Marital status unknown	5.0	5.0	18.4	6.4	4.7	17.2
People aged 50 years or more #						
Never married	15.3	6.0	48.2	n/a		
Currently married	10.1	7.6	44.0	9.3	5.6	39.5
Widow/widower	8.7	8.6	47.8	12.8	7.5	63.4
Marital status unknown	12.6	5.2	48.9	9.7	4.5	32.8

Notes: Excludes adults of unknown sex and/or age. For the number of people in each category, see Table 3.1. All numbers are in shillings.
For annual figures, age is at time of receiving relief; for full span figures, age is during majority of years in which relief was received.

have been grandparents rather than parents of the recipient children.[22] The amount of assistance awarded to adult recipients was affected by the total number of children living in the family, whether or not the latter received relief. If we analyse how much help was awarded to adults over the full span of years in terms of the full number of children or grandchildren under age 13 who lived with them, we find that younger men and women (aged 20–49 years) received much more relief if they had one or two children than if they were childless; for men but not women the amount received rose further if they had three to six children. For recipients aged 50 or more, the number of children made no difference for women, while for men the amount received increased with two or three children but not with additional ones.

If we move to the end of recipients' lives, the known people who were buried at the town's expense were members of 78 different households.[23] In just over three-quarters of cases only a single person was buried. But in another 21 per cent two family members were buried (a husband and wife, a parent and child or pairs of child siblings) and in one household a father and three of his children were buried. We can trace the sequence of poor relief within those 78 households as related to the point at which one or more of their members were buried. The great majority of the town-sponsored burials were given to people living in households that were already receiving relief. For 40 per cent of the units, payment for one or more burials came as part of a longer history of assistance provided both before and after death. In another 45 per cent, the burial terminated relief to that household, usually because the person who had died was its last surviving member. Rather surprisingly, in only five cases (6 per cent) did a burial initiate subsequent relief for surviving members of a household that had previously not been assisted. Seven households (9 per cent) were self-sufficient apart from the burial itself and perhaps a little help shortly before the person's death.

A sample year: individuals and households in 1582

We gain a more detailed picture by looking at recipients and their households in 1582, the first year for which full accounts survive.[24] In total, 149 people were assisted, in addition to the unnamed 'poor people' who were given some clothing and the wood delivered to the almshouses. The recipients included 38 children, 54 adult women, 56 adult men and 1 person of unknown sex and age.[25] Around two-thirds of both male and female recipients were given only occasional assistance; the remainder gained fuller help in the form of regular weekly payments and/or boarding. People aged 50 years or more were especially likely to be given multiple forms of substantial help.

Of the 109 households that received some kind of assistance in 1582, more than two-thirds contained only a single recipient. Thirty-one units had two recipients and four had three people who were helped. Most households (61 per cent) received only

---

22. See Chapter 4, 'Aid while living at home', below.

23. See App. 3.1, Pt. B.

24. For the accounts from 1582, see Chapter 2, 'A sample set of annual accounts', above.

25. See App. 3.4 for this and below.

Table 3.11
Family relationships within multi-recipient households, 1582.

	Number of households	Number of individual recipients
2 recipients per household		
Husband and wife		
Both aged 20–49	3	6
Both aged 50+	6	12
One of each age	3	6
Both of unknown age	1	2
Total	13	26
Father/grandfather + 1 child		
Father aged 20–49	5	10
Father/grandfather aged 50+	2	4
Total	7	14
Mother/grandmother + 1 child/teen		
Mother aged 20–49	3	6
Mother/grandmother aged 50+	3	6
Total	6	12
2 children, siblings	5	10
Total, 2 recipients/household	31	62
3 recipients per household		
Husband, wife, + 1 child		
Both parents aged 20–49	1	3
1 parent of each age	1	3
Total	2	6
Mother/grandmother + 2 children		
Mother aged 20–49	1	3
Mother/grandmother aged 50+	1	3
Total	2	6
Total, 3 recipients/household	4	12
Total	35 = 32% of all households helped that year	74 = 50% of all recipients that year*

Note:
* Percentage excludes from total recipients one boy of unknown name and age who was not assigned to a household. Some of those aged 50 years or more were grandparents, not parents, of the children being helped.

occasional assistance. Twenty-eight per cent received just household goods and fourteen per cent received just occasional money. But in 28 per cent of the households at least one person received regular weekly payments – and generally other aid as well – while 12 per cent included a member who was boarded.

Table 3.11 shows the family relationships of recipients within the 35 households that contained two or three members receiving relief in 1582. In the 31 two-recipient units, the most common pairings consisted of a husband and wife (42 per cent), followed by a man (father or grandfather) plus one child (23 per cent), a woman plus one child or teen (19 per cent), or two child siblings (16 per cent). The four three-recipient households included two married couples with one child each and two women with two children each. The seven adults aged 50 years or more living with children were grandparents.

This discussion has made clear that Hadleigh was assisting a large number of needy individuals and households, providing multiple types of aid suited to their individual situations. The next two chapters consider the special provisions offered to certain sub-groups of recipients: children and teens (Chapter 4) and sick, disabled and old people (Chapter 5).

Chapter 4

The care and training of poor children

Hadleigh was unusual both in the number of poor children and teens assisted by the town and in the special forms of care and training available to them. Although growing concern with needy children, especially orphans, was visible in other Elizabethan English communities, in neither Norwich in 1570 nor Ipswich in 1597 did any children receive direct assistance.[1] In Hadleigh, by contrast, 197 children and teens were helped individually between 1579 and 1596, constituting 33 per cent of the full group of recipients, in addition to whatever aid might have been given to their parents or grandparents.[2] They lived in 116 households, the great majority of which contained two or more people who were being assisted by the town. Although poor relief officers had various methods for helping needy youngsters or providing training that offered the chance for a somewhat better future, financial considerations may in some cases have outweighed concern for the wellbeing of the children.

Hadleigh's officials were able to choose between five strategies for attending to poor children. Many were assisted while living with their own families, receiving money, household goods, clothing or – if seriously ill or injured – medical care. Other children were helped through the aid given to their parents. Most of the 62 female and 80 male recipients between the ages of 20 and 49 had children, and some of the 172 older adults were taking care of their youngest children or grandchildren. In a second type of relief, children might be boarded with another local family. This form of care was used for young orphans, illegitimate children and youngsters from families who had more offspring than they could support or who seemed to be providing inadequate care and supervision for their children.

The remaining approaches were motivated by the combination of a desire to provide support or discipline-cum-training while also holding down the cost of present and future relief. In one arrangement, the town provided an initial set of clothing and shoes for a poor child – usually aged around 7 to 12 – who was about to leave home to become a residential servant in another household.[3] Poor relief officials helped to set up some of those positions, and occasionally they paid for boys to be formally apprenticed. From 1589 onwards another option was to send children and young people to the town's workhouse. During their stay there – usually less than a year – the residents were

---

1. McIntosh, *Poor relief in England*, pp. 245–50, her 'Poor relief in Elizabethan communities', and see Apps 3.2 and 3.3 below.

2. See Table 3.1. For below, see Table 3.8.

3. Brown has suggested that the increase in orphaned children assisted in Aldenham, Herts., in 1651 was related to high mortality during the 1640s ('Receipt of poor relief', pp. 411–12). The only indication of that pattern in Hadleigh may be the unusually large number of teens assisted in 1585–9, who had perhaps lost one or both parents during the morality crisis of 1582–3 and needed help as they entered service.

supposed to acquire not only discipline and good work habits but also basic skills in preparing woollen yarn and knitting stockings; these skills might enable them to bring in some money for their home families or make them more desirable as young servants or adult employees. Finally, some orphaned or illegitimate children were granted into the keeping of an unrelated person until they were old enough to go into service or reached adulthood. The men who took them in, who were not always from Hadleigh, received a money payment in return for caring for the child and ensuring that he or she would not need further poor relief from the town. Occasionally children were sent out of Hadleigh to another family or community that was legally obligated to support them, and town officials tried to ensure that poor children who might later qualify for relief were not allowed to settle in Hadleigh. We will look at each of these five approaches in turn.

Aid while living at home

Of the 197 poor children who received direct assistance while still living with their own families between 1579 and 1596, 42 per cent were girls and 52 per cent boys (additionally there were twelve whose sex was not described). As Table 3.1 shows, 17 per cent of the children were aged no more than 4 years, with slightly more girls than boys in this group. Another 32 per cent were between the ages of 5 and 9, with many more boys than girls. The exact ages of 35 per cent described as children are unknown, while a final 16 per cent were between 10 and 19 years, almost all of them younger than 15. The help given to children and teens living at home must have been intended to supplement their own earnings: even fairly young children were able to sort or card wool, spin yarn or make simple lace.[4]

The households in which these recipients lived were usually headed by immediate relatives, but not necessarily by their parents. We can examine this issue by looking at those children aged under 10 years who lived in a domestic unit in which at least one of the adult heads also received relief. The household heads for 44 per cent of the girls and 62 per cent of the boys had the same surname as the child and were aged under 50 years, which implies that the children were living with one or both parents. But for a surprising 48 per cent of the full group, the head of the unit was aged 50 years or more and hence was probably a grandparent, though possibly a mother who was in her later 40s when the child was born. Girls were especially likely to live with elderly relatives (56 per cent, as opposed to 38 per cent for boys). While the composition of many poor households may indeed have diverged from a nuclear family model, poor relief officials were probably particularly likely to assist those children who lived with elderly relatives, thus addressing several types of need simultaneously.

Hadleigh was at least occasionally prepared to help illegitimate children and the adults looking after them. Six of the 197 child or teen recipients (3 per cent) were described in the parish register as born to unwed mothers ('baseborn' or 'child of the people') or were said to be 'bastards' in the poor relief accounts. They constituted one-sixth of the 38 newborns noted as illegitimate in the parish register between 1570 and

---

4. For children as young as 5 to 7 years engaging in such work, see *Norwich census of the poor*, passim; for Carew's inclusion of children among those whose activity contributed to clothiers' profits, see Chapter 6, 'The ongoing influence of Christian social teachings', below.

1596. One girl was aged 0–4, two boys were aged 5–9, one boy was of unspecified age, and two girls were aged 10–19. Nine adults were the parents or grandparents of illegitimate children living with them at the time they received relief (2 per cent of all adult recipients). Of the seven women, five were mothers who appear to have been heading their own households at the time of assistance, while one was living with her parents and child. Three recipients (two men and one woman) were the grandparents of an illegitimate child, and all of their daughters were living with them.

The types of direct help given to children and teens were not identical to those provided to adults. Nearly three-quarters of the youngsters received only occasional assistance, a higher fraction than for older people.[5] Most were given bedding, clothing or fuel, and the town assisted fourteen others only after their deaths by paying for a winding sheet or burial. Another 7 per cent received regular money payments, in most cases at a higher weekly value than for young adults but slightly less than for old people.[6] The span of years over which children and teens were assisted was shorter than for adults, so the total value of help received across the full span was for most groups of children slightly less than for young adults and much less than for the elderly.

Short-term boarding in another local household

If a child was left as an orphan, abandoned (perhaps due to illegitimacy) or could not be adequately cared for by its parents, poor relief officials were prepared to pay another local family to board him or her for anywhere between a few months and six years. A fifth of the young recipients between 1579 and 1596, nearly all of them aged under 10, were boarded with another family at some point.[7] The families that took in these children were paid a weekly amount, presumably based upon the amount of care required as set against the amount of help the child could offer within the household.

Because boarding of children is normally poorly documented, we may look more closely at the Hadleigh evidence, though the numbers are small. Table 4.1 shows the average number of months for which children were boarded and the average cost per year. The average period of care was in sum slightly longer for girls than boys, and the cost of boarding them was almost twice as much. For girls, those aged 0–4 years were boarded longer and were more expensive than older ones, but for boys the reverse was true. The average annual cost for boarding children was much higher than for adults, for they remained in care for longer periods.[8] Nor was boarding used only during these eighteen years. The account of the market bailiffs for 1571 includes two payments of 20s each for 'keeping' children; boarding was still used for younger children between 1599 and 1618, a period in which Overseers of the Poor were dealing with some aspects of poor relief.[9]

---

5.   See Table 3.4.

6.   See Table 3.6. For below, see Tables 3.3 and 3.5.

7.   See Table 3.4.

8.   See Table 3.6.

9.   HadlA 004/A/01, p. 91; *ibid.*, pp. 261–357, passim. During the latter years, thirteen children aged from 1 to 8 years were boarded by the town. For Overseers, see the end of Chapter 6, below.

Table 4.1
Children who were boarded with another family, 1579–96: duration and cost.

Age of child when boarding started	No. of children	Aver. no. of months boarded	Aver. cost of care per year (s)
Girls			
0–4 years	5 #	18	38.1
5–9 years	4	16	24.2
Girls, age unspecified	4	26	36.2
Total	13	20	32.3
Boys			
0–4 years	2	12	15.9
5–9 years	8	19	19.3
Boys, age unspecified	12	18	16.5
Total	22	18	17.6
Total	35	19	23.0

Notes: The table excludes 3 children of unknown sex.
Includes 2 girls boarded also when aged 5–9 and 1 girl boarded also when aged 5–9 and 10–19.

Although we have little explicit evidence as to why Hadleigh's poor relief officials decided to pay to board children with other families, we can identify some probable factors. As one might expect, about a third of the children had recently lost their mother or both parents; another quarter were sick or disabled or their parents/grandparents were elderly or disabled. But the most common single feature of these children's natal families – especially for boys aged 5–9 – was that they were burdened with many offspring. In those cases, we cannot be sure whether poor relief officials hoped that removing one or more children by boarding them elsewhere would lessen the economic problems of the natal family or whether they thought the children were receiving inadequate attention and discipline at home and would be more closely supervised in a different household. A few of the birth families clearly faced multiple challenges: they contained many members who received poor relief, some of whom were disabled; they had many young children; and/or they were headed by a single adult.

The people who boarded children in return for payment by the town covered a considerable socio-economic range. Taking in a poor youngster provided welcome income for some needy households. Sixteen local recipients of poor relief were paid for boarding a total of 23 children between 1579 and 1596.[10] Whereas younger adults were particularly likely to take in infants who still needed to be breastfed, the majority were aged 50 years or more, and they were much more likely to board more than a single child in a given year. For elderly people, the company of the youngsters – and perhaps the help they could provide – may have been as important as the money received.

More prosperous families probably had different reasons for boarding a needy child. Eighteen people who did not receive relief – 4 women, 11 men and 3 people of

---

10. A few people from other communities were also paid to board: e.g., the 20s given to Hawkins of Kersey in 1594 and 1595 for care of Wortham's boy (HadlA 021/D/03–04).

unspecified sex – were paid by the town for taking poor children into their households. Some may have regarded this simply as a charitable act, while others perhaps valued the labour that could be obtained from a somewhat older child. (By around 5 or 6 years of age youngsters could carry out simple duties within a household or craft operation, acting as an unpaid junior servant; somewhat older ones might be capable of more skilled activities.) We gain some sense of the probable role of children's labour by examining the occupations of the 11 non-recipient men or husbands and whether they paid poor rates (indicating that they were among the upper 18–25 per cent of Hadleigh's household heads in economic level). Four men were in cloth-related occupations, where children's labour might have been employed, but two of them took in a blind girl at various times, and a weaver boarded a girl too young to be useful. John Alabaster, an extremely wealthy clothier and one of Hadleigh's most active Chief Inhabitants, was unlikely to have set to any serious work the young girl whom he took in for part of a year. The four other men with known occupations (brewer, gelder, shoemaker and craftsman/shopkeeper) might possibly have valued the domestic help of their young boarders but would probably not have used them in their own types of specialised work. Eagerness for additional labour thus does not appear to have been a primary factor in the willingness of these men to board children. Nor was extra income evidently important, for 9 of the 11 men paid rates. It therefore seems likely that many of the non-recipient households were willing to board needy children out of some sense of compassion and perhaps a desire to give them at least a brief exposure to proper religion and good discipline.

Boarding poor children formed part of a wider social pattern in early modern England whereby households contained members other than the nuclear family alone. The houses of middling and wealthier people often included relatives, adolescent servants and sometimes apprentices, and children taken in for charitable reasons.[11] Elderly people might make private arrangements to be looked after by another family. We gain indirect glimpses of such people through Hadleigh's provision of goods or services to children or adults said to be living in another household but where poor relief officials did not reimburse the host for boarding them. In this study they have not been included in analyses of the assistance provided by the town, but their presence makes clear that living with another family was a more widespread option than the records of publicly supported boarding indicate.

In total, 25 people are recorded as receiving goods or services from poor relief officials while living in a household that was not paid for keeping them: 7 girls, 9 boys and 3 children of unknown sex, plus 4 adult or elderly women, 1 man and 1 person of unknown sex. Of the 15 families that hosted these people, 5 received direct poor relief themselves and were paid by the town at other times for taking in boarders. The remaining 10 did not get relief and never provided residential care at the town's expense. This latter group included some of Hadleigh's leading citizens: people with large households who probably took in needy children out of charity. Thomas Alabaster, whose household in 1582 contained a child who received a coat from poor relief officials, was one of Hadleigh's leading clothiers. He had already served as market bailiff, constable, subcollector for the poor and chief collector, and was a

---

11. See, e.g., McIntosh, *A community transformed*, pp. 53–65 and 78–81, for this and below.

strong Protestant. A boy who received healing and treatment from a surgeon at the town's expense in 1583 was living with Arthur Vesey, the head of a family of clothiers turned gentlemen. He too had served as subcollector and chief collector and was a committed Protestant, having been a servant of Rowland Taylor's when he was young.[12] Oliver Chepe, whose occupation and religious orientation are unknown, had a boy in his household in 1583 who received a hat. Chepe had recently been market bailiff and subcollector and was to hold higher offices later. The large households of prosperous, civic-minded and charitable men thus provided another kind of informal support for needy youngsters.

Assistance when entering service or apprenticeship

Many young people in Elizabethan England spent a period of five to ten years as live-in servants with another household.[13] Leaving home typically when they were in their early teens, or at a younger age if they were poor, they signed a series of one-year contracts with masters or mistresses that included cash wages as well as board and room. Many continued as servants, though sometimes changing households over time, until they married. When John Freman, a Hadleigh yeoman, died in 1592, he instructed his executor to bring up 'my boy, Robert Whatlocke, in husbandry if he be willing to be an husbandman'; if Robert did not agree, he was to be 'provided of a master to any honest occupation', assisted by a bequest of 40s.[14] Even wealthy people might think that a period as a servant would provide good training for their children following a period of formal schooling. Julian Beamonde, a successful clothier in Hadleigh, said in his 1586 will that the residue of his goods should be used for 'the bringing up of my children in the fear of God and to set them to school to write and read, that they may be the meeter [more ready] to be put to service when they come to age fit for service'.[15] Close personal relationships between masters and their young employees are suggested by bequests in wills, common especially during the period of Rowland Taylor's influence.

Hadleigh's officials helped some poor children to go into service, usually by providing the clothing that new servants were expected to bring with them. Because employers rarely expected a payment for taking a youngster into service we can identify assistance to prospective servants only if their situation is expressly mentioned. In 1588, the chief collector paid 21d for lockram (a kind of linen cloth), buttons and making a doublet (a jacket) for an unnamed boy going into service with a master called Betham, himself a recipient of occasional poor relief at the time; widow Meg Locke received 1¼ yards of

---

12. For Taylor, see Chapter 1, 'Religion', above and Chapter 6, 'The impact of Rowland Taylor and opposition to him, 1544–54', below.

13. Marjorie K. McIntosh, 'Servants and the household unit in an Elizabethan English community', *Journal of Family History*, 9 (1984), pp. 3–23.

14. TNA PRO PROB 11/80/48.

15. TNA PRO PROB 11/70/1. For below, see, e.g., Thomas Cantler, a butcher, 1553 (a house to a former servant, ERO D/ABW 8/179); John Raven, clothier, in 1553 (bequests to three female servants, one male servant and two apprentices, TNA PRO PROB 11/36); and William Forthe, esq., 1554 (various servants and apprentices, PROB 11/43).

cloth in 1596 'for a coat for her girl to go to service'.[16] It is likely that most of the 13 girls and 14 boys in their teens who received clothing and sometimes shoes from poor relief officials were about to become servants or apprentices. In several other East Anglian communities during the Elizabethan period poor children, especially orphans, were sent into service by churchwardens at younger ages, some only 5 to 7 years old.[17] That pattern suggests that some of the 9 girls and 21 boys in the 5–9 age range for whom Hadleigh provided clothes or shoes were likewise taking positions as servants, probably without pay other than their board and room.

Hadleigh gave money to a few masters or mistresses willing to accept poor children in their teens as apprentices. More prosperous families were able to pay the fee demanded for a decade or more of training young people in the skills that would allow them to support themselves as adults. Some Hadleigh parents arranged to have their sons apprenticed to clothworkers in Norwich or London.[18] But we know that in other Elizabethan communities nominal apprentices from poor families were often regarded merely as long-term servants who did not need to be given cash wages. They gained little if any occupational training and were unable to choose a new master each year, as were normal servants. The small size of the payments made by Hadleigh's officials to people who agreed to accept apprentices from needy families and the lack of subsequent supervision by the town over the children's situation suggest that they too may have been valued only for their current labour.

Four apprenticeship contracts survive from Elizabethan Hadleigh. One 'Bill of covenant for service' dated 20 January 1581 was between John Cuffe of Hadleigh, son of Margaret Cuffe who had later married John Randall of Hadleigh, and Nicholas Crowe, a shoemaker of the town.[19] John, then 11 years old, was an illegitimate child; his uncle, aunt and a cousin were all receiving relief at the time. The document records that the Cuffe boy, of his own will 'and with the consent of his friends', had agreed to be a covenant servant with Crowe for one whole year beginning in two weeks and then 'from year to year for 12 years'. (Apprenticeship contracts normally referred to the consent of the youngster's father, not of friends.) Cuffe accepted the usual requirements for a servant or apprentice, binding himself to serve his master well and faithfully, to keep his secrets and willingly and gladly to obey him:

> Taverns nor alehouses, of custom he shall neither haunt or use, except it be about his master's business there to be done. And cards, dice, or any other unlawful games, he shall not play. Fornication within the house of his said master, he shall not commit. Matrimony with any woman within the said term he shall not contract or espouse himself

---

16. HadlA 021/C/02; 021/A/05. Contributions of clothing or shoes by town officials to youngsters aged from 9 to 19 as they went into service continued in the period 1598 through 1618.

17. McIntosh, *Poor relief in England*, pp. 249–50.

18. See, e.g., *An index of indentures of Norwich apprentices enrolled with the Norwich assembly, Henry VII–George II*, eds W.M. Rising and P. Millican, Norfolk Record Society, vol. 29 (Norwich, 1959), pp. 144 and 159, and A&S, *Hadleigh*, p. 159 (for Thomas Alabaster, apprenticed to a skinner of London around 1572). For below, see McIntosh, *Working women*, pp. 135–8, and her *Poor relief in England*, pp. 249–50.

19. SRO-BSE K2/1/2. The back of the document is inscribed, 'Crowes endentor for Cuffes boy his prentties'.

unto. The goods of his said master he shall not waste or spend, nor without his master's consent lend them to any. From the service of his said master neither by night nor by day, he shall absent himself but as a true and faithful servant, as well in word as in deed, shall honestly use and behave himself during all the said term of twelve years.

In return, Crowe undertook to instruct Cuffe in the occupation of shoemaking, to chastise him as needed and to provide him with food, drink and the clothing appropriate for a servant. He contracted to pay Cuffe 6s 6d at the end of his full term, when he would have been 23 years old, and to give him two sets of apparel – one for the holy day, the other for working days – plus 'such working tools as belongeth to a journey man of that occupation'. For taking the boy into his service, 'the township of Hadleigh' paid Crowe 30s.

In a second case we can observe how helping a boy enter an apprenticeship accompanied other kinds of relief. A bill of covenant was signed on 8 February 1595 between Thomas Morris, the son of Thomas Morris, late of Hadleigh, deceased, and Thomas Hargrave of Hadleigh, weaver.[20] With the consent of 'the inhabitants of the town of Hadleigh', young Morris – who was then 14 years old – bound himself a covenant servant, later described as an apprentice, with Hargrave for a term of 10 years. The contract was witnessed by four of the Chief Inhabitants, and Hargrave received 2¾ yards of cloth worth 5s 6d as a reward for accepting Thomas.[21] Widow Morris had been receiving regular weekly payments and household goods since 1590, and Thomas was given a shirt with lining, a hat and shoes, together worth 8s, when he went to Hargrave.

Of the two other contracts, one was between Thomas Wortham, the son of a deceased Hadleigh father, and Edward Lewis of Hadleigh, a cooper, for a term of 13 years beginning early in 1595.[22] Thomas's father Robert had evidently died in late in 1590, just a year after his second marriage. His widow was left with five young step-children ranging in age from 1 to 9 years. The four youngest, including Thomas, received help from the town between 1591 and 1596. Thomas was boarded with the Lambe family for nearly three years, when he was aged 5 to 7, and at the age of 9 he entered his apprenticeship. The youngster in the final arrangement, Nicholas Alcocke, was the son of Nicholas, a Hadleigh sherman, and his wife Margaret. The boy was born in 1585, four months after his parents' marriage. Following the birth of a second boy a few years later his mother began receiving poor relief, including regular weekly payments in 1590 and 1591. In the spring of 1598, when young Nicholas was 12 years old, he contracted to become an apprentice to Robert Lillye, a weaver of Hadleigh, for 12 years.[23] Lillye received 26s 8d from the market bailiff for taking the boy.

Training and discipline in the workhouse

Certainly by 1589 and possibly by 1575 Hadleigh was operating a residential institution for children and young people that taught discipline and some occupational

---

20. SRO-BSE K2/1/4.
21. HadlA 021/D/04.
22. SRO-BSE K2/1/1.
23. SRO-BSE K2/1/3.

skills as well as punishing those who refused to work. In tracing the history of that project, we must be aware of its changing nature and the variety of terms used to describe it. When the institution was first envisioned in the late 1560s and early 1570s its purpose was apparently to house poor people, especially children, for short periods while they learned good work habits and how to prepare the woollen yarn used in weaving.[24] The residential unit that functioned in the Guildhall at least by 1589 fulfilled those functions for some of its inmates, and it was presumably in that sense that its own accounts and those of the chief collectors and subcollectors for the poor sometimes termed it a hospital. But by 1577 the Chief Inhabitants were thinking about a house of correction, into which idlers and vagrants found begging on the streets could be placed if necessary and forced to work.[25] Although the initial attempt at founding such an institution appears to have foundered, by the 1590s the unit in the Guildhall, now commonly called a workhouse, was accepting some older teens and young adults as well as children. Beginning in 1599, that institution was labelled a house of correction in the contract made between the town and its keeper, who was required to take into the house anyone found begging as well as needy children.

Some kind of poor house or Bridewell – distinct from the two sets of almshouses – was evidently under discussion in Hadleigh in the late 1560s. (At that time, 'Bridewell' probably implied an institution that followed the initial purpose of its London model by housing and teaching poor people to work, though the London house was increasingly used to discipline people picked up for misbehaviour.[26]) In her will of 1569 Elizabeth Water, widow of John Water, a husbandman of Hadleigh, left 10s to 'the town towards the building up of one house for the sustentation and helping of the poor and impotent people'.[27] When Robert Becon, a young clothier, wrote his will that same year, he left to the consideration of his brother John Becon of Cambridge the possibility of making a gift to 'the building of a Bridewell in Hadley'. In 1571 the will of Thomas Spencer, rector of Hadleigh, again reflected a charitable conception of the institution. Spencer left 20 marks as a stock to be bestowed initially in wood and grain for the poor and then 'to the maintenance of the hospital, when it shall be erected'.[28]

It is possible that a residential institution that trained children to work began functioning in 1575. On 24 December 1574 the town book notes that four wealthy

---

24. This attempt to teach skills that would enable poor youngsters to find positions as servants or to earn money for themselves was paralleled in other communities in south-east England during the late sixteenth century: e.g., the taskhouse established in the village of Linton, Cambs., and the decision by the collectors of the poor in the rural parish of Eaton Socon, Beds., in 1596 to pay 2d per week to a woman 'that teacheth the poor children to work bone lace' (E.M. Hampson, *The treatment of poverty in Cambridgeshire, 1597–1834* (Cambridge, 1934), p. 10, and BRO P 5/12/1).

25. Norwich had set up a house of correction in the early 1570s and Bury St Edmunds was to do so in 1588 (Slack, *Poverty and policy*, p. 124, and Andy Wood, *The 1549 rebellions and the making of early modern England* [Cambridge, 2007], p. 200).

26. McIntosh, *Poor relief in England*, pp. 126 and 168–9.

27. TNA PRO PROB 11/51/17. For below, see LPL Archbishops' Registers, Parker i, 292.

28. HadlA 004/A/01, p. 388. This bequest was henceforth used to buy wood for the poor, not applied later to the workhouse. For below, see *ibid.*, pp. 104–5 and Chapter 1, 'Hadleigh's physical setting and neighbourhoods', above, for the Guildhall.

clothiers acting on behalf of the community had bought 'the town house otherwise called the gelde hall' from Henry Wentworth.[29] One incentive for acquiring the Guildhall was to use some of its space to establish a workhouse for children. An entry made that same day reads: 'It is agreed by all this assembly that a fit man and his wife shall be chosen which shall have the government of such children as shall be thought good to be appointed to be put to work and that the said party shall have his dwelling in the town house.'[30] But the town book and accounts say nothing more about a workhouse for children during the next fifteen years, and it is unlikely that it went into operation at that time.[31]

A rather different kind of institution – a house of correction – was envisioned in an agreement made on 31 December 1577. Eighteen of the Chief Inhabitants agreed

> that for the restraint of idle and evil disposed persons and rogues in the said town and for the diminishing of the excessive charges of the parishioners aforesaid, they will presently appoint some convenient house and chose some honest man and his wife, who shall have the oversight and governance of all the idle rogues and masterless persons vagrant and begging in the same town, and keep them thoroughly to their work, and in default of their working or for other their disorder duly to correct them, and further they will proceed in other rules and matters necessary hereunto as conveniently they may.[32]

The memorandum goes on to say that the house in which a man called Pease was then living was to serve as the house of correction and that Pease and his wife would be its governors. To supervise the institution, the eighteen signatories appointed four of their own company as overseers. This plan may have been influenced by the passage in the previous year of a Parliamentary statute ordering that a House of Correction be established in every county, to which people arrested as chronic vagrants could be brought and kept; after suitable punishment, inmates were to be set to work on a stock of supplies provided by the house.[33] In 1577 Hadleigh's proposed house of correction, intended for unemployed people and outsiders who were wandering and asking for alms in the town, was evidently seen as distinct from the proposed workhouse for poor local children in the Guildhall. We find no later references to a separate house of correction, which apparently never got off the ground: a simple private house seems an ineffective setting for an institution in which unemployed adults were to be forced to live and work and, in some cases, be punished.

The next information comes from December 1589, when it was agreed at a meeting of the Chief Inhabitants that

> the workhouse and such stipend for the maintenance of those that shall be committed thither shall be taken out of the town stock and that such money as shall be required to

---

29. HadlA 004/A/01, p. 104.

30. *Ibid.*, p. 101.

31. Sue Andrews, however, thinks that the workhouse began to function in 1574 and that it was the same institution mentioned in 1577 (personal communication).

32. HadlA 004/A/01, p. 122, and see Chapter 6, 'Worry about control and cost, 1576–85', below, for the series of negative orders.

33. 18 Elizabeth, c. 3, sec. 5 (*SR*, vol. iv, p. 611).

the said use by six of us shall be speedily paid by the chief collectors … . Work from time to time shall be provided for such poor as shall be committed thither.[34]

This order, which pertained to an institution to be located in the Guildhall, was signed by gentleman and ex-clothier William Forth, rector John Still and six others. The 1589 agreement says that five clothiers – none of whom had signed the memorandum about a house of correction in 1577 – promised 'weekly to provide by conference among themselves work sufficient for the said poor people'. Four of those men indicated their consent with a signature, while the last made his mark. We know that this institution did indeed function. A separate little 'book of accounts for the new erected working house' was included with the other records for 1589, and the unit was frequently mentioned in other accounts over the next decade.[35] In 1592 John Freman bequeathed £5 'to increase the stocks of the workhouse now lately erected for the maintenance of the poor people in Hadleigh', a gift described in the town's account book as 'for the use of the poor of the hospital'.

The house described in 1589 henceforth combined the two functions foreseen in the earlier discussions. It provided temporary care and useful training for just under half of its inmates, those no older than 13 years, as intended by the agreement of 1574. But for inmates aged 15 to 23, whether idle local youth or poor outsiders, the institution combined some measure of education with correction and punishment, as stipulated in 1577. In April 1590, for example, Edward Doyle of Layham, gent., signed a bond for £10 made out to the Chief Inhabitants.[36] The condition of the bond states that

whereas Rose Colbronde was taken vagrant and masterless at Hadleigh and therefore was committed unto the workhouse of the said town, and upon the entreaty of Edward Doyle above was delivered out of the said house, if therefore Rose Colbronde shall not at any time after this date directly or indirectly be chargeable unto the town, either by herself, or by any child to be born of her, that then this present obligation to be void.

Residents of the workhouse were taught how to carry out the early stages in the manufacture of woollen cloth: how to 'pick' raw wool (removing dirt, pulling apart the strands and sorting it by type), card it (in readiness for spinning into yarn for broadcloth), in some periods 'kemb' it (using oil and a stockard frame to prepare the yarn for knitting stockings and other lighter-weight 'stuffs', part of the New Draperies) and spin it, using a spindle or a wheel.[37] In normal circumstances, these jobs were done by adult women and children at home, often on a part-time basis; they were paid by the piece, receiving less than the income gained by male weavers, dyers and other skilled participants in cloth manufacture. When Hadleigh's clothiers decided to provide a physical residence and equipment for youngsters to learn to card and spin wool, they were thus not furnishing training in a skill that would enable the inmates to be entirely self-supporting in the future. The workhouse did, however, provide basic

---

34. HadlA 004/A/01, p. 197.

35. HadlA 021/B/09. For below, see TNA PRO PROB 11/80/48 and HadlA 004/A/01, p. 226.

36. HadlA 026/G/04.

37. See Chapter 1, 'Economic life', above, and Chapter 6, 'The ongoing influence of Christian social teachings', below, for this and below.

Table 4.2
People sent to the workhouse, 1591–5.

	Females	Males	Sex unspecified	Total
A. Number of people named in the records	34 = 47%	36 = 49%	3 = 4%	73
B. Known ages of workhouse inmates				
6–7 years	2	2	0	4
9–13 years	6	9	0	15
Total children	8	11	0	19 = 48%
15–23 years	11^	10	0	21 = 53%
[Elderly sick people in 1592*]	[2]	[1]	[0]	[3]
Total	19 [+ 2]	21 [+ 1]	0	40 [+ 3]
C. Relationship of children/young people sent to the workhouse to recipients of poor relief				
Received relief him/herself	8	12	0	20 = 29%
Did not receive relief, but parents or siblings did	8	5	0	13 = 19%
People with this surname received but relationship unknown	13	12	1	26 = 37%
No one with this surname received, and surname not in parish register = probable outsider	3	6	2	11 = 16%
Total	32	35	3	70

Notes:
^ Unmarried Bridget Thorpe was first sent to the house in 1592 at the age of 23; she was sent again in 1595 at the age of 26.
* In 1592, during an epidemic of what was probably plague, two old women and a man received payments from the workhouse, the first two due to sickness, the last for burial. All three were receiving other kinds of relief, and they were probably housed in a different part of the Guildhall.

food and clothing for its residents, many of whom came from families that had difficulty in supporting them, and it accustomed them to a regular schedule and good work habits (as attested by the presence of a clock with a chiming bell located in the main workroom). This training should have helped them find positions as servants or labourers. In return, their work provided the clothiers with an inexpensive source of yarn they could pass along to the weavers they employed. Only in the mid 1590s do we see a partial shift to a slightly more profitable kind of training for the children: teaching them how to knit woollen stockings. Because we have little information about early local workhouses it is worth looking at who was sent to Hadleigh's institution, how the institution was administered and how it functioned.

The workhouse could take as many as 30 residents at once. Because nearly all remained for less than a year, however, the number who passed through annually was higher, as seen in the 34 pairs of shoes made for the residents in 1592 and the 37 shirts and smocks prepared in 1593.[38] During the course of 1595 at least 37 people lived in the house at some point: 12 were there in the middle of the year, of whom 4 left later and 8 were still there at the end; 25 others entered during the second half of the year, of whom 7 were still there at the end.

We are fortunate that the accounts between 1591 and 1595 give the names of 73 people, almost evenly divided between females and males, who were placed into the workhouse. From other records we can establish the ages of 43 of them. As Table 4.2 shows, virtually all were aged between 6 and 23 years. (The three exceptions were elderly people listed in 1592, the year in which the town experimented with housing some sick poor in one section of the Guildhall.[39]) Four of the normal residents were children aged 6 or 7 years who had recently been orphaned and were presumably sent temporarily to the workhouse to be looked after by the resident matron until longer-term arrangements could be made with a private family to take them.

A larger cluster consisted of somewhat older children, aged 9 to 13 years. This was the stage at which poor children were commonly sent out as domestic servants, so their time in the workhouse was probably intended to teach them how to live under a regular schedule and labour diligently, as well as training them to card and spin wool to enhance their desirability as employees. The institution's accounts sometimes include payments for new clothing or a little cash given to children when they left to go into service and for the cost of writing up their indentures.[40]

The final and largest group consisted of people aged 15 to 23 years who should have been in service or some other kind of employment. These were presumably idle youths picked up off the streets for begging or causing disturbances who were forcibly detained in the workhouse until they showed some willingness and ability to work and live more respectably. The involuntary nature of the institution for young people is supported by the fact that the master of the house laid out money for a lock on the

---

38. HadlA 021/C/07–08. For below, see HadlA 021/A/04.

39. See Chapter 5, 'Care for people who were ill or disabled', below.

40. See, e.g., 8d to Gooden when she went to service, 1592 (HadlA 021/C/07); 1½ yards of cloth for a coat, a pair of hose, a pair of shoes, a smock, a coif, canvas for the coat and making the clothing, which came to 9s 6d, for Wiles' girl when she went to service, 1596 (HadlA 021/A/05); and 8d each for pairs of indentures for Steede's girl and Wiles' girl, 1596 (*ibid.*).

door leading to the room where at least some of the residents slept and in 1595 bought individual locks – or locks and chains – for three of the men and one of the women in this age group.[41] Were the locks attached to their legs?

Five-sixths of the 70 named children and young people sent to the workhouse came from local families, most of whom received poor relief. Twenty youngsters had themselves been assisted before going to the institution, while the parents or siblings of another 13 were relieved. Twenty-six had other apparent relatives (people with the same surname) who were given aid. Only 11 of the 70, all of them in their late teens and early twenties, appear to have been outsiders: no one of their surname appears in the parish register or the records of the poor relief system. Some may have come to Hadleigh looking for employment, while others were probably just passing through the community when they were apprehended for misbehaviour.

The town book and various accounts describe the administration of the workhouse. It had a male head named by the Chief Inhabitants who was officially responsible for the institution. Although the earliest appointments are not mentioned, John Snowden was master from at least 1592 until the middle of 1595. In choosing Snowden, the Chief Inhabitants may have thought that they could achieve multiple ends by naming someone who was himself poor and getting relief from the town. John's first wife had received occasional household goods and money for several years starting in 1587, as did two of their children at ages from 4 to 10 years. John himself was given money in 1590 and again in 1595, probably during the illness that led to his death in July of that year. In 1593 he married the Widow Busker, who was assisted in 1595–6; a child described as 'Snowden's bastard' received cloth and clothing in 1594 and was buried at the town's expense in 1595.

Snowden was not, however, a competent administrator, and he was relieved of his position in the first half of 1595. At his departure, it was found that the equipment for training the youngsters then living in the institution was limited and the household supplies inadequate.[42] There were 13 spinning wheels but no cards for preparing the wool. Bedding consisted of four bedsteads, two flock beds and one straw bed (i.e., cloth bags filled with tufts of wool or straw, placed either on a bedstead or on the floor); three bolsters or pillows, two of them stuffed with flock, the other with straw; and one blanket. No mention was made of supplies for cooking or eating.

The Chief Inhabitants then decided to name a man of somewhat higher economic standing and greater experience. John Allen, a shoemaker, had served as market bailiff in 1591–3 and held that office again in 1595. As bailiff, responsible for collecting the rents and fees due from the market and fair and maintaining market properties, Allen was accustomed to handling money and people. He was probably appointed master of the workhouse immediately upon Snowden's departure, for when the institution's accounts were submitted on 2 January 1596 Allen was one of those who reported, together with three overseers.[43] The audit showed that the town owed Allen £22 2s 9d,

---

41.   HadlA 021/A/04.

42.   HadlA 004/A/01, p. 247.

43.   *Ibid.*, p. 248. In his detailed account, Allen reported a total of £69 2s 9d in expenses, against which he set weekly income described as 'earned' (presumably the income from the markets), which came to £42 (HadlA 021/A/04). He requested and received the remaining £27 from the town.

which Nicholas Strutt, as chief collector, was ordered to pay. At the same session it was agreed between Allen and 'the inhabitants of the town of Hadley' that in return for wages of £20 paid to him by the town over the course of the coming year, Allen would 'keep and maintain with meat, drink, and apparel all such children and other persons whatsoever' that were ordered into the house, up to a total of 30 residents. 'If there wanteth any bedding for that number of 30 persons so sent in by the town for their lodging, the town doth promise to allow him beds for them.' Allen agreed to these terms, setting his hand to the contract, with William Gale and John Alabaster named as overseers. Because Allen was at least initially a more effective master than his predecessor, the Chief Inhabitants continued to reappoint him annually through 1616.[44]

Allen's contracts, which became progressively more specific, indicate that the nature of the workhouse was shifting away from the training of children and teenagers towards a more punitive kind of incarceration. A document dated 31 December 1597 says that he must 'receive all such persons as are sent to the said house from the age of 8 years to 50 and them to keep with meat, drink, and work needful during their abode there'.[45] On 6 January 1599, after Parliament's passage of the Poor Laws of 1598, Allen agreed

> at his own costs and charges to keep and maintain the poor people which now be and hereafter are to be sent unto the house called the House of Correction or workhouse with sufficient and convenient meat, drink, apparel, lodging, and all other utensils according to the orders set down by the Justices of Peace in that case.

The Chief Inhabitants, churchwardens or Overseers for the Poor were henceforth allowed to send to the house 'any person at their pleasure, and to take any out of the said house either to be bound apprentice or put to service according to the statute'. Allen was no longer merely to receive those sent to him by others, however: he was now obligated 'to take and bring into the said house all such persons as he shall find begging within the said town or any other at the appointment of the churchwardens and overseers'. Religious instruction was mandated. 'The one half of the poor in the house shall every Sabbath day both forenoon and afternoon come to church in decent manner to hear divine service.' It must have been thought that having all the residents attend the same service would be too disruptive, and perhaps it was difficult to supervise them adequately when away from the house. Allen also agreed to return to the Chief Inhabitants at the end of his contractual year 'all the bedsteads, beds, bolsters, coverlets, sheets, wheels, and all other implements belonging to the said house, specified in an inventory indented and made betwixt him and the said townsmen'; he was likewise 'to leave all the poor persons which shall be in the said house at the end of the said term well and conveniently apparelled with woollen and linen as shall be thought meet and convenient for them'. In return for those expanded

---

44. See, e.g., HadlA 004/A/01, pp. 268–9, 286, 299, 313 and 344. But Allen too had financial problems, and by 1612 some of his wages were being withheld for failure to pay the rent owed on his house (*ibid.*, pp. 326 and 331). In January 1618 John Sudbury, a sherman, was named 'master and governor of the house of correction' and required to live there in person 'that he may the more carefully provide and see the said poor persons continued in labour' (*ibid.*, p. 352).

45. *Ibid.*, p. 259. For below, see *ibid.*, p. 264.

duties the town appointed him as bailiff of Hadleigh's market for 1599, 'to receive and take to his own use all the rents and profits appertaining to the said market and fair'.[46] By 1600 a second male official, described as the 'beadle to the hospital', was receiving a salary from the town. That title suggests a more explicitly disciplinary role.

While the master of the workhouse was thus officially responsible for the institution, in practice the day-to-day supervision and training of its young residents was assigned to one or more elderly women, some of whom evidently lived in the institution. In 1589 Widow Brigges received weekly wages plus an extra amount depending upon the number of children under her care. Her monthly earnings could amount to as much as 3s 8d.[47] In December of that year the Chief Inhabitants ordered that she was henceforth to receive 4d per day, which amounted to the considerable annual sum of just over £6. In 1591 and 1592, while John Snowden was nominally master of the house, mother Joan Berket (usually termed 'Berket's wife') was in charge of its daily operation.[48] A woman named Sergeant held the position in 1593, and the next year John Snowden's wife submitted four bills to the chief collector and was reimbursed for them. Widow Kedgell received regular wages in 1595, and was assisted by Browne's wife, who looked after the children at least some of the time.[49] By 1598, when knitting hose had been added to the training given to the inmates, three women evidently shared the daily duties: Widow Kedgell, Widow Bowton and 'great Goodin'.

We learn more about how the workhouse actually functioned from the accounts submitted from 1589 onwards. Work was apparently done in a large ground-floor hall in the Guildhall and perhaps an adjacent room, which may have been divided into smaller units; the inmates slept either in the latter or in rooms on the upper floor.[50] Some of the expenses of the house (including food for its young residents) were covered internally and hence were not normally reported in the accounts of town officials, but the (chief) collectors commonly listed certain outlays for the house. In 1589 payments for the workhouse were recorded at the end of the account submitted by John Alabaster, who described himself as 'Collector for the poor for the town of Hadleigh'.[51] In addition to Widow Brigges's wages, he noted sums for equipment: cards and stockard frames, small and regular size spinning wheels, reels on which yarn would be wound and little baskets. Canvas and brown thread were provided for sewing cases for the beds, bolsters, sheets and towels for the residents; one fortunate person – perhaps Widow Brigges herself – slept on a low bedstead, while the other inmates apparently placed their bedding directly on the floor. Canvas was purchased also for smocks for two of the girls, lined with white woollen cloth for warmth. Considerable work was done in that first year on the 'chamber over the kitchen' in the

---

46. *Ibid.,* p. 264. For below, see *ibid.,* p. 273.

47. HadlA 021/B/09. For below, see HadlA 004/A/01, p. 197.

48. HadlA 021/C/06–07. By 1594, she and her much younger husband had entered Pykenham's almshouse. For below, see HadlA 021/C/08 and 021/D/03.

49. HadlA 021/A/04. For below, see HadlA 021/A/06.

50. A&S, *Hadleigh*, p. 69, and the accounts discussed below.

51. HadlA 021/B/09 for the rest of this paragraph. For the New Draperies and stockard frames, below, see Chapter 1,'Economic life', above and A&S, *Hadleigh*, p. 152.

Guildhall, an area clearly intended for sleeping. An external door and new internal partitions were added to the room, with 2s 2d expended upon two locks and two staples plus the labour of setting them in the doors and another shilling for a lock on the door at the top of the stairs. Alabaster's ordinary expenses for the workhouse came to just under £10, plus £1 8s 6d for redeveloping the room over the kitchen.

In 1591 the chief collector included only a few payments for the house in his accounts.[52] To Berket's wife he paid a shilling for each of five children or young people who entered the house that year as well as 2s for unnamed reasons and 6d for cleaning the house, 12d for 'dishelles' and a pail and 7d for I lb of yarn for 'binds' for the spinning wheels. Another 12d went for making two reels, 12d for spindles and whorls, 6d for '2 beds and bottoming' and 6d for four stools and a form (presumably for eating). These payments totalled only 11s 1d.

The fuller account of the chief collector for 1592 provides several kinds of useful information.[53] In addition to revealing the presence in the Guildhall of sick adults during that year of exceptionally high mortality, it gives the names of all those who entered the workhouse, for each of whom the collector paid a shilling. Some inmates received new clothing: 12 shirts and smocks; several coats, petticoats lined with canvas and waistcoats; 12 head coverings, probably caps and scarves; a neckerchief, an apron and a doublet; 34 pairs of shoes; and 18 pairs of woollen hose (those for boys extended up to their waists). The collector paid for the usual array of equipment for carding and spinning yarn and for some bedding, including new straw to fill the beds. Other items include payments for digging the privy, two keys and two staples for locks and the 'reel' of a clock. Master John Snowden and his son received 5s 4d 'for making the bridge', including sawing timber and poles for it. The bridge may have connected the Guildhall and the Market Hall. Expenses for the workhouse came to a total of £19 10s 1d apart from the money laid out for food and drink for the sick people housed there.

In 1593 the chief collector spent £15 1s 1d on normal workhouse expenses.[54] They included the wages of the woman who took care of the house and children, equipment for carding and spinning, bedding and 20d 'for the removing the privy and for making a new one'. New clothing was made for the children: 37 shirts and smocks, 24 caps and head coverings, 13 coats made of woollen cloth and lined with canvas along 'their upper bodies', 10 pairs of shoes and 7 pairs of woollen hose. The 1593 account also records the considerable expense (£3 4s 8d) of rebuilding a wooden fence around the workhouse, which was probably intended to discourage unauthorised attempts to leave the institution. After the old pale had been dismantled and the wood carried to the chapel at Pykenham's almshouses, a sawing pit was dug on site and materials for the new fence delivered to it. Lulpecke sawed 400 feet of board, and Eli Cooke and his helper received 37s 10d for a total of 44½ days of work in putting up the fence. The following year the chief collector's account records a total of £11 13s 5d in workhouse expenses, including payments for cutting and carrying firewood to the house, 11 pairs of hand cards and 2 pairs of stockards, as well as 14d for a winding sheet for Markes' child.[55]

---

52. HadlA 021/C/06.
53. HadlA 021/C/07. For sick people, below, see Chapter 5, 'Help for old people'.
54. HadlA 021/C/08.
55. HadlA 021/D/03.

The only year for which we have a detailed account of expenditures for the 'hospital', including every individual purchase of even small items of food, is 1595.[56] The reckoning was submitted by John Allen, newly appointed as master or governor of the house. Because the equipment, bedding, clothing and food reported in Allen's account have been fully described by Sue Andrews they will not be repeated here, but we may note the reference to four pairs of 'knitting pins', presumably used for making woollen hose. Because Snowden had left the house poorly supplied, Nicholas Strutt, the chief collector, together with John Bretton and Robert Andrew, its two overseers, paid in 1596 for new equipment.[57] Their purchases included two new spinning wheels, the repair of at least three others, six pairs of cards, a stockard frame and five pairs of blade wheels with which to wind yarn after spinning. They also bought a good deal of bedding and household wares for cooking and eating and paid for repair of the bell on the house's clock.

Full workhouse accounts for subsequent years have not survived, but for 1598 we have a summary of the £32 18s 8d laid out by the chief collector.[58] The largest expense was the £20 given to John Allen for his year's wages, with another 40s paid to him for purchase of hand cards, stockards, spindles and whorls. Several spinning wheels were repaired and three more bought, one said expressly to be for a child, another second-hand. The collector accounted for cloth and sewing for sixteen shirts and smocks for the residents, and he reported the making of four new beds, each with a pair of sheets and a bolster. He paid for a winding sheet 'for one dead in the hospital'. The most interesting feature of these accounts is their clear indication that a new kind of activity had emerged within the workhouse: knitting woollen hose. Knitting stockings on needles had started to appear in East Anglia during the 1570s and 1580s, presented from the beginning as a suitable activity for poor women and children.[59] By the early seventeenth century woollen stockings had become a standard item of apparel in England, the manufacture of which employed as many as 100,000 people per year if each worker knitted two pairs of stockings weekly as bye-employment. In 1598 Hadleigh's chief collector delivered a total of 16½ lbs of list yarn (a light worsted yarn commonly used for making hose) to the house's master and a woman who worked there; he then paid 7s 9d for the completed stockings.[60] For the children and young people who moved through the workhouse, learning how to 'kemb' yarn for stockings and the New Draperies and to knit hose offered the chance for somewhat better future earnings than did traditional carding and spinning for broadcloths.

Granted to a different family or expelled from Hadleigh

The remaining strategies for dealing with poor children were heavily influenced by concern over the future costs of poor relief as well as by varying degrees of compassion for their situation. To provide ongoing care within a household unit for

---

56. HadlA 021/A/04. For a full description, see A&S, *Hadleigh*, pp. 69–71.

57. HadlA 021/A/05 and 004/A/01, p. 247.

58. HadlA 021/A/06.

59. McIntosh, *Working women*, pp. 231–2, for this and below.

60. HadlA 021/A/06.

some orphans or illegitimate children Hadleigh's officials paid another family an immediate lump sum to accept a child not just for temporary boarding but until the youngster was old enough to become a paid servant or attained full legal age. In return, the recipient was to furnish adequate care for the child. This approach had the advantage of long-term simplicity: with a single payment, Hadleigh would bear no further responsibility for the child until it was old enough to support itself. Rather troublingly, however, we see no indication that local officials made any subsequent effort to see that the children were well treated. The households that accepted such children had to bear the costs of feeding and clothing them but would be able to utilise their labour as *de facto* servants as they grew older, without paying any wages. While most of these needy youngsters presumably received basic care and had the security of being part of a family unit, some of them probably remained as second-class members of their new households for a decade or more. In a more callous attempt to avoid giving relief later, the town attempted to prevent poor young immigrants from settling in Hadleigh and occasionally paid to have poor children already living in the community expelled.

The town accounts document frequent payments for taking children. In 1580 the chief collector gave 40s to Richard Masselond 'by the appointment of the town for the discharge of a wench', and in 1582 the town paid 20s to a weaver named Little 'to discharge the town of the dumb boy'.[61] Not all of those who accepted poor children lived in Hadleigh itself, making it even less likely that local officials would supervise the quality of care. In 1589 the chief collector gave 30s to Bull of Layham 'to discharge the town of one of Markes children'; an Aldham man received £3 in 1595 'with a child'.[62] This practice continued in later years as well. Between 1598 and 1618 the town paid to have 16 children between the ages of 1 and 8 accepted by other people.[63]

In at least some cases the Chief Inhabitants required that people who took such children post a formal bond that the youngsters would not later become a charge upon Hadleigh's poor relief system. When Nicholas Spincke, a carpenter, received 20s in January 1595 for raising an orphan, he was required to submit a bond for £10 'for the discharge thereof'.[64] The condition of the bond was that

> if Spynke shall exonerate, acquit, discharge, save and keep harmless the inhabitants of Hadleigh of and from all manner of charges and costs for the keeping and bringing up of one John Laye, son of John Laye, late of Hadleigh, until he shall accomplish the age of 21 years, then this obligation is void.

The chief collector's account from 1596 records payments for writing up the bonds to be signed by three people who accepted young children.[65]

Through the experience of five vulnerable children and teens belonging to the extended Gedge family, we can observe how town officials utilised long-term transfer

---

61.   HadlA 021/B/05 and 021/C/07 (bis).

62.   HadlA 021/B/09; 021/D/04.

63.   HadlA 004/A/01, pp. 261–357, passim.

64.   *Ibid.*, p. 238. For below, see HadlA 026/G/05.

65.   HadlA 021/A/05.

to an unrelated family in conjunction with direct assistance at home, boarding and aid to youngsters living in a household that was not paid by the town. What appear to have been three separate households of this dysfunctional family, two of them containing children, received poor relief between 1579 and 1596. One unit consisted of an elderly Widow Gedge, who was given occasional money and household goods between 1579 and 1588, her unmarried daughter Elizabeth and Elizabeth's three illegitimate sons. Two of the boys died soon after birth in 1581 and 1584, but Richard survived to at least the age of 7, when the town paid Ann Bartholomew to board him.

The second Gedge household contained six people assisted by the town.[66] Its male head, who was blind, received aid between 1579 and 1583, his wife Ann was helped between 1585 and 1596 and they had four recipient children, all of whom were removed from their parents' care at some point while growing up. The oldest, Steven, born in 1571, lived with the Carters for three years when in his teens, receiving bedding, cloth, clothing and shoes from poor relief officers. The town paid to have Elizabeth, born in 1573, boarded with Ann Bartholomew for a year when she was 9. Though Ann was not reimbursed thereafter for keeping Elizabeth, the girl remained in her household for eight more years while receiving household goods, clothing and sometimes cash payments. The next child, Mary, was apparently still at home when she began to get regular money payments at age 11, but when she was 14 and 15 she lived first with the Boram family and then with the Brownes, and was given cloth and clothing. The town also paid for cloth, clothing and sewing for the youngest child, Robert, while he was living at home aged 3 and 4, but in late December 1580 Thomas Love, a shoemaker, agreed to take Robert on a long-term basis in return for a payment of 40s from the town; Love gave a bond of £5 that the boy would not become a charge in the future.[67] That contract failed for some reason, and over the following eight years, from the ages of 5 to 13, Robert lived with three different local families while receiving household goods and clothing from the town. We do not know why poor relief officials deemed the home environment of these children undesirable, but it may be significant that none of them was placed into formal service or sent to the workhouse for training. One wonders if they may have been developmentally disabled, rendering them unable to offer the obedience and skills that would have enabled them to earn their own keep.

For orphaned children, a bequest by Edmund Paynter in 1572 offered extra inducement to households willing to take them in. Paynter was the steward of the bishop of Ely and presumably related to the Thomas Paynter, clothier, who held various offices in Hadleigh during the late 1570s. Edmund left £10 to the town as a revolving loan fund, to be granted to a person who accepted an orphan for so long as the child was with him but then given back to the town to be handed over to someone else.[68] We can observe how Paynter's money was used through the Chief Inhabitants' dealings with Michael Welles, a tailor. In December 1586 Welles promised to return at

---

66. The third household consisted of old Father Gedge – not the husband of widow Gedge – who was living in Pykenham's almshouses by 1579 (see App. 5.1). These Gedges later died out or moved away from Hadleigh; another family with the same surname settled in the town in the nineteenth century.

67. HadlA 004/A/01, p. 139.

68. A&S, *Hadleigh*, p. 105 and note 18.

a later date the £10 'which was delivered to me with one orphan'.[69] By December of 1589, however, the child had evidently died, whereupon Welles became responsible for returning the £10. The town decided to accept a cash payment of just £8, requiring Welles to complete his obligation by making clothing for the poor to a value of £2. The chief collector was instructed to take 40s from his own income to bring Paynter's legacy back to its full £10. In the following month the town book includes a note: 'To remember to provide an orphan for the money late in Welles hands'.[70]

As was true in many Elizabethan communities, Hadleigh's leaders were eager to ensure that they would not have to assume responsibility for poor immigrant children. Parishes were legally obliged to support orphaned, illegitimate or abandoned children born within their bounds if their parents could not provide for them, but people of any age who had lived in a given place for at least three years usually qualified for relief.[71] In practice, these policies did not always yield clear answers about financial responsibility, leading to a good deal of negotiation between individuals and communities. In 1569 Hadleigh's chief collector sent a letter to an unknown recipient of high status asking whether the constables had been correct in bringing a child who had been born in Hadleigh back to the town from the village of Buxhall.[72] Buxhall claimed that the 'extraordinary charges' of providing for the child were beyond its ability to pay, but several people in Hadleigh had copies of a letter from Suffolk's Justices of the Peace saying that the charges for a base child were to be met by the town where it was living, not the place where it was born.

The town's leaders kept an eye on the arrival of outside children who might become a burden upon public relief. In some cases they demanded bonds of people who employed poor servants from elsewhere. When Thomas Corbold, a weaver, accepted an orphaned brother and sister from Much Horsley, Essex, as servants in 1588, the Chief Inhabitants were worried that the children 'in time to come may be chargeable to the inhabitants of the said town of Hadleigh by reason of a statute made in the first year of the Queen's Majesty's reign for the relief of impotent, lame, and needy persons'.[73] Corbold and William Turner as his surety were therefore required to post a bond of £10 for each of the youngsters under condition that they would 'exonerate the inhabitants of Hadley from the keeping, finding, or any relief giving' to the children: the boy until he reached 20 years, the girl until she was 16. Even children who moved into the town with their parents might be regarded with suspicion. A bond for £20 was submitted to the Chief Inhabitants in 1588 by George Wylde of Hadleigh, a shoemaker, and William Wylde, a miller.[74] A different George Wylde, his wife Basyll and two of their children, Agnes and Rodee, had recently come from Ipswich 'and do intend to make their dwelling within the said town of Hadleigh'. Because the town feared that some or all of the newcomers might in the future need relief, the condition of the bond was that

69.   HadlA 004/A/01, p. 177. For below, see *ibid.*, p. 195.

70.   *Ibid.*, p. 204.

71.   McIntosh, *Poor relief in England*, pp. 245–50.

72.   HadlA 021/B/01.

73.   HadlA 026/H/05 and 026/E/05.

74.   HadlA 026/G/02.

if the existing residents George and William and their heirs and executors freed Hadleigh from any expense for the immigrant family, the obligation was void.

In the most negative of all responses, Hadleigh was willing to pay to have poor children removed from the town. In 1581 Robert Clefforde and William Wyles of the neighbouring community of Aldham agreed that they would take Alice Webbe, 'a bastard child which was born in Aldham and is now at Geoffery Tawbote his house in Stone Street in Hadley out of the said town by Easter next coming'.[75] Clefforde and Wyles bound themselves to the churchwardens of Hadleigh that the girl 'shall not hereafter be any more chargeable to the said town'. Some children were simply transported elsewhere, one hopes to relatives or communities that did indeed accept them. In 1582 Sandercock received 4d for carrying an unnamed child to nearby Elmsett, and six years later Rayner was given 4s 'for carrying the wench away'.[76] Some of those removed from Hadleigh did not stay away even if they risked being sent to the workhouse. The chief collector paid 4s 8d to Margaret Locke in 1588 'for carrying away the wench thrice', and a bond for £10 signed on 22 January 1590 concerned Dorothy Harvye, daughter of Richard Harvye, a smith of Hadleigh.[77] If Dorothy had left Hadleigh by the following 20 February and did not return again for more than two nights within the next five years, her father and John Holbard, the other signatory to the bond, were excused from their obligation to the Chief Inhabitants. Confirmation of the practice of expelling needy people comes from an entry in the town book in 1601. The market bailiff was instructed to pay Edward Andrewe 'for writing of indentures and passports for poor children and people that were sent away'.[78]

We may end this discussion by looking at how poor relief officials used multiple forms of assistance for the appropriately named Sadde children. Their father William, whose occupation is unknown, probably married initially sometime around 1560 (a daughter Susan lived for only 13 days in 1561), but his wife Elizabeth died in May of 1562. William married once or twice again, and his wife of the time gave birth to at least four children between around 1570 and 1578. Their firstborn son, William, died in April 1572, whereupon they named the boy who was born a month later another William. By the late 1579s the household was already in need, for poor relief officials supplied it with clothing, and in 1580 disaster struck. William the father died in May and his wife at an unknown date that same year. In both cases the town paid for the winding sheets in which they were buried, suggesting deep poverty. The parents left three children behind: William, who had recently turned 8; Alice, aged 6; and Oliver, barely 2 years old. During their parents' illnesses the town had provided blanketing for the two boys as well as having clothes and shoes made for them, but by late 1580 full-time substitute care for all three children was needed.

A new home for the Sadde children was provided by Richard Smyth, a woadsetter (or dyer) of Hadleigh. He had already taken them into his household by the end of 1580, but on 14 January 1581 he signed an unusually formal bond for £6 with the Chief

---

75. HadlA 004/A/01, p. 140.

76. HadlA 021/A/03 and 021/C/02.

77. HadlA 021/C/02 and 026/G/03.

78. HadlA 004/A/01, p. 280.

Inhabitants, prepared by two notaries public.[79] The document explained that Smyth had received £3 from the town on that date. Fully satisfied by that payment, he took 'upon him to educate and to bring up of his own proper costs and charges one Olyver Sadd and one Alys Sadd, the children of one William Sadd, late of Hadleigh, deceased'. He would 'frankly and freely … bring up the said two children, with godly virtuous education and information of the lord especially, as also with sufficient meat, drink, and clothes meet for them, until the said children and either of them do accomplish their several ages of 14 years'. If he fulfilled that obligation and discharged the 'township' of Hadleigh of all costs concerning the children until they were 14, the bond was void. The older boy William was not part of the contract, presumably because he could offer enough help within the household to be regarded as an informal servant. We know, however, that he remained in the Smyth household, for between 1583 and 1589 he received canvas and cloth there. Alice died in 1582, the day before her ninth birthday, but Oliver stayed with the Smyths through the 1580s.

In 1591, when Oliver was 13 years old and William was 19, the town paid to have both boys enter the workhouse. Poor relief officials may have thought that Oliver would profit from some training before going into service, but William was old enough that he should already have taken a position as a paid servant or labourer. We do not know whether he entered the workhouse directly from Smyth's household or was picked up on the streets. Perhaps he had become troublesome to Smyth as he grew older, no longer willing to obey the authority of the man who had sheltered him and his siblings for a decade, or perhaps Smyth had become too old to deal with teenagers, no matter how compliant. But we have no further information, for Oliver and William disappear from our view as they pass through the doors of the workhouse. For the Sadde children, as for so many others, the forms of assistance offered by Hadleigh reflected a flexible mixture of compassion, a desire to give youngsters training that would lead them to become disciplined adults able to earn at least part of their own support, and concern with holding down both present and future costs.

---

79. HadlA 026/E/02. Smyth did not receive poor relief but was not wealthy enough to be assessed for rates.

Chapter 5

Aid to ill, disabled and elderly people

In addition to the provisions for children, Hadleigh's poor relief officials were prepared to give special assistance to several other groups of especially vulnerable people. They paid for help for some who were ill, experimenting with group care and perhaps quarantining, and they gave extra aid to people with a physical disability. The elderly might qualify for a place in one of the town's two sets of almshouses.

Care for people who were ill or disabled

Fifty-five people described as sick or in childbed either received money or goods themselves or were provided with care or healing (where payment was given to those who attended to them).[1] Eight of these recipients were children or teenagers, four girls and four boys. Eight women aged 20–49 were assisted, in some cases while or after giving birth; the thirteen men in that age bracket were generally said to be ill, though some may have been injured. Twelve older women and eight older men were helped, as were six adults of unknown age. Most of the payments during illness were short-term, for a few weeks or occasionally months. Only one girl and one younger man received payments in two consecutive years, though five others were helped in two or three scattered years. Of the 62 payments, 43 took the form of money given to the person who was ill, while two people received wood for fuel or canvas for bedding while ill. Fifteen people were paid for providing healing and three others for boarding sick children.

The people who offered assistance, which extended from simple bedside care to professional treatment, had a wide range of training. Several male and female recipients of poor relief were hired to attend to others, such as William Turner's wife, who received 10s from the collector in 1571 'for looking to Stoken's daughter's leg'.[2] An apothecary named Gage received 4s 11d in 1587 for treating Thomas Morris, and several surgeons were employed over longer periods while receiving much larger payments. James the surgeon was active between 1579 and 1583; surgeon Bretton was hired in 1589–90 to heal people of the French pox (syphilis); and James Legas, apparently the same surgeon described slightly later as Jacob Legar, was employed in most years between 1591 and 1605.[3] Payments were usually made after the work had been completed, but several times in the early seventeenth century town officials contracted with Legar to heal named people and keep them well for the following two years in return for a set amount of money.

---

1. Two other payments were made for caring for or healing unnamed sick and/or poor folk.
2. HadlA 021/B/03, and see 021/C/06 for care given by old King and 021/C/08 by old Mother Thornton. For Gage, below, see 021/B/08.
3. HadlA 021/A/02 and 021/B/07; 021/B/09; 021/C/06, 021/C/08 and 021/D/03. Legas was listed as a foreigner in the subsidy returns of 1568: *Suffolk in 1568*, p. 110. For below, see HadlA 004/A/01, pp. 286 and 299.

Although care was normally provided within private homes, Hadleigh experimented with housing certain sick people in a common location. Such an approach may have started as early as 1586, when the collector paid 3s 4d to Widow Frost 'for keeping of sick folk'.[4] Because previous entries for care had specified the individual names and for how long a period the assistance was given, this may indicate that Widow Frost was being paid to look after multiple people at the same time, and possibly in the same place, though we do not know where.

In 1591 the evidence becomes clear. In his account for that year the chief collector listed some payments to individual people when they were ill, as were found in earlier records, but he also paid 13s 4d to Parmisie 'for the rent of his house when the poor folk were there' and 3s 4d for a load of brush (for fuel) for 'the diseased folk'.[5] He gave a further £4 to James Legas 'for healing the poor folk'. This is the first payment for professional healing that did not list the names of the people being treated, and the amount is very much larger than previous ones. In the only mentions of food for needy adults in all of the Hadleigh accounts, Legas received 5s 10d for 'the diet' of the poor folk, and William Rose was paid the exceptionally large sum of £3 10s 5d 'for bread for the poor folk'.[6] The subcollectors' account for 1591 was likewise atypical. They began by entering the names and amounts received by the people given a weekly stipend and those granted 'benevolences', the standard format.[7] But they went on to record a third list, 'money given to sick folk', with 21 names and a total of £3 in such expenses. These expenses were distinct from the payments made for the workhouse. Collective accounting for sick people continued after their deaths: in 1591 the town paid 31s 4d for 18 winding sheets and 16s for 18 burials of unspecified poor folk, rather than stating for whom they were provided, as in previous years. If Hadleigh had experienced an epidemic in 1591, especially of the plague, one might have regarded this experiment with group housing and care of the sick poor as an early attempt at quarantine. But because the number of deaths was not atypically high in 1591 it may have stemmed only from a desire to make care of the sick more efficient.

As we have seen, the institution described in some local records between 1589 and the late 1590s as a 'hospital', located in one section of the Guildhall, was intended not for sick people but rather for children and young adults sent to the workhouse to learn basic skills in carding and spinning yarn and to acquire better discipline.[8] Indeed, when Sergeant's son became ill in 1589, shortly after entering the institution, the chief collector paid his father 6d for removing the boy from the house.[9] But in 1592, a year that saw a doubling of the average number of deaths, owing almost certainly to bubonic plague, the town apparently used the Guildhall to house contagious people. We find no indication in the poor relief accounts of group housing in an ordinary domestic setting.

---

4.   HadlA 021/D/01.

5.   HadlA 021/C/06.

6.   If a full-sized loaf of bread, the basis of many poor people's diet for one day, cost somewhere around a penny, that sum would have paid for nearly 850 loaves.

7.   HadlA 021/C/05 and see Chapter 2, 'Financing poor relief', above.

8.   See Chapter 4, 'Training and discipline in the workhouse', above.

9.   HadlA 021/B/09. For below, see HadlA 021/C/07, earlier folios.

The collector reported only 7s given to unnamed poor people and 11s spent on the burial of poor folk. But the accounts of the workhouse indicate that sick people other than its usual inmates were now being accommodated and looked after there, one supposes in a different area of the building from where the children and teenagers worked and slept.[10] Berket's wife received a standard 40s for her wages in looking after the house, but she was given additional amounts for caring for sick people. Payments 'for the sick folk' were followed by a long list of special foods for them, some of which went well above the normal diet of the poor.[11] In addition to the institutional staple of oatmeal, we find eggs, butter, cheese, bread and fortifying food such as unspecified meats, a leg and a rack of mutton and four lambs' heads. Extra beverages were supplied as well: ample beer, and raisins, sugar and nutmeg that were probably used to spice hot wine. Purchases of food and drink for sick people totalled £2 11s 7d, constituting about a tenth of all expenses for the workhouse that year. Small sums of money (usually 2–4d at a time) were also given to named adults in the building, 'being sick'. In a sad reminder that such care was not always successful, the chief collector paid 4d 'for mending the palls' at the workhouse.[12] It appears, therefore, that during a period of exceptionally high morbidity the town decided to use some portion of the Guildhall to isolate and care for the sick, among whom must have been poor people whose own families could not provide adequately for them or keep them effectively quarantined.

Over the next few years the town evidently returned to grouping needy people suffering from illness into a single private home. The accounts for the workhouse from 1593, 1594 and 1595 give no indication that it was being used for the sick, apart from an occasional payment for medical care to one of its young inmates.[13] As was true in the past, collectors gave money to some individual people while they were sick and to others for healing them. But in 1594 the collector paid for various repairs on 'the house where the sick folk were kept'.[14] That house was probably the one that the town had been buying from Robert and Alice King since 1591. In 1594 Mother King was paid for giving healing and special residential care, and the chief collector delivered two loads of wood to her; she also received 53s 4d 'for her house this year', an item listed by the Collector under the heading 'the money laid out to the use of the poor'.[15] Additional payments of 53s 4d were made to her in 1595 and 1596, and in the latter year the town paid the out-rent due for her house.

Hadleigh provided extra help for people with physical disabilities. The recipients between 1579 and 1596 included 21 such people (3 per cent of the 603): 5 children

---

10. HadlA 021/C/07, later folios.

11. These entries were specified as 'for them', meaning the sick, whereas the few payments for food for the institution's other residents were described as 'for the house'. For food in hospitals and almshouses more generally, see McIntosh, *Poor relief in England*, pp. 80–81 and 202–3.

12. A pall was the cloth placed over a coffin or body prior to burial.

13. HadlA 021/C/08, 021/D/03 and 021/A/04. The detailed account for 1595 includes two references to 'medson' and a payment to Browne's wife 'for looking to the children's heads', perhaps when they had lice?

14. HadlA 021/D/03. For below, see HadlA 004/A/01, pp. 216–18. The final payment was made in December 1597.

15. HadlA 021/D/03 and 004/A/01, p. 233. For below, see HadlA 021/D/04 and 021/A/05.

under 10 years of age (two of them blind, and one each who was lame, 'dumb' or had a numb hand); 3 men aged 20–49 (one each blind, lame and with a numb limb); 12 men aged 50 years or more or of unknown age (eight blind, three lame and one deaf); and 1 adult woman (blind). While some of the impairments among the older people may have stemmed from age or the nature of their former employment, the disabilities were probably congenital for the children. Calculation of the average span of years over which people received assistance shows that people with a physical disability were helped for longer periods than those of the same age and sex who did not (1.6 times longer), with the exception of younger adult men. A greater difference is seen in the average amount of aid received by the two groups across the full span: disabled people were given 2.6 times more help than those without such problems, again with the exception of younger men.

Hadleigh sometimes made special arrangements for disabled children. In December 1580 Richard Wallis, one of the market bailiffs, was allowed £5 against his account 'for keeping of the blind wench'.[16] A memorandum in the town book records an agreement between Wallis and four of the Chief Inhabitants and rector John Still: in return for the £5 paid to him, Wallis would 'take into his service and custody a blind wench called [blank] Talbot who is now at William Mannyng's the sherman'. Wallis then submitted a bond that he would 'discharge the town of the said blind wench for ever'. As contracted, he looked after Priscilla Talbot for 38 years, throughout his own lifetime, but after his death a different arrangement was set up with his son, another Richard. The younger man obviously did not want to continue sheltering the blind woman directly, but local officials reminded him of his father's agreement to free the town of any expense for her 'for ever'.[17] In December 1618 Wallis agreed that

> in consideration of £5 given to his father from the townsmen for the keeping of Prescilla Tallbott, a blind wench, as appeareth formerly in the book, the said Richard doth now promise to pay weekly unto the overseers of the poor in Hadleighe 6d weekly and every week so long as the said Richard shall live towards the keeping and maintenance of the said Prescilla, the first payment to begin on the 10th of January next.

Mentally and physically disabled people were sometimes cared for by relatives or other individuals who supported them as sheltered servants. In his 1592 will yeoman John Freman instructed his kinsman, William Grimwade of neighbouring Bildeston, to 'either keep or see kept my poor simple servant Maud Rogers for her work during her life, if she will be at his discretion; otherwise he shall give her one bed furnished and 10s every year during her life'.[18] Some kind of disability is suggested by a bequest in 1553 from clothier John Raven of 40s annually 'for the keeping of John Gentill, as long as he lives'; in 1611 the town awarded a 10-year lease to John Heward under the condition 'that he shall have a care to keep his sister to the uttermost he may as usually he hath done'.[19] Sometime in

---

16.   HadA 004/A/01, p. 136. For below, see *ibid.*, p. 139.

17.   *Ibid.*, p. 357.

18.   TNA PRO PROB 11/80/48.

19.   TNA PRO PROB 11/36 and HadlA 004/A/01, p. 325. For below, see TNA PRO REQ 2/291/15. Facon may have been the Chief Inhabitant of that name who held many local offices between 1575 and 1596.

Elizabeth's reign Anne Warde of Lavenham submitted a petition to the Court of Requests alleging mistreatment by her brother-in-law, Thomas Facon (or Faken), a Hadleigh yeoman. She said she had lived with Facon for 15 years, during which he had treated her as a common servant, wasting her youth and strength, and had not given her the payment he had promised. Facon responded that because Anne was lame and diseased she could not get a good place for service. He had therefore taken her in, but he had not given her 'laborious work but used her rather as a sojourner than either child or servant'.

Help for old people

Many elderly people (defined in this study as aged 50 or more) were assisted by Hadleigh's poor relief officials in the same ways as younger adults: through delivery of goods or money while they lived in their own homes, and through temporary care or healing at home or while being boarded with another household.[20] The 105 older women and 67 older men, who together constituted 29 per cent of all recipients between 1579 and 1596, received on average 2.1 to 2.6 times more assistance over that full span than did younger adults aged 20–49.[21] Among the elderly, widows received only slightly more within the 18 years than did currently married women, whereas widowers were given 1.6 times more than currently married men. Elderly women were helped over an average span of 8.9 years, as compared with just 5.9 for younger women; the gap was much smaller for old men. Elderly women and men alike were given 1.5 times more money in the form of regular weekly payments than younger adults of the same sex, though they resembled the latter more closely with respect to the occasional money, goods or services received.[22] Older people were boarded for shorter periods than younger ones – probably because frail elderly people might be admitted to an almshouse rather than being sent to a private family – and the average value of their boarding care was lower.

Alongside these standard kinds of relief lay a particularly desirable possibility: assignment to a place in one of Hadleigh's almshouses. Pykenham's almshouses, founded at the end of the fifteenth century at the far end of Mawdelyn (later George) Street, contained twelve rooms, each shared by two people; the Benton Street almshouses, founded by clothier John Raven in the mid 1550s, had four rooms housing eight people. Those elderly poor fortunate enough to be named to an almsplace received not only free housing but also a weekly cash stipend, firewood and, in some cases, cloth for bedding or clothing.

At least a few almsrooms existed in Hadleigh by the 1430s. In 1438, when a piece of land near the church was conveyed to a group of Hadleigh men who were henceforth to hold it as feoffees (or trustees), it was said to include 'one long house newly constructed next to the cemetery of the church of Hadleigh which is called le markethows, with the chambers existing below the same called Almessehouses'.[23] The last mention of those rooms came in 1469, by which time another form of almshousing

---

20. See Chapter 3, note 4, above, for an explanation of why age 50 was used as the cutoff for the older adult category.
21. See Tables 3.1 and 3.5. For below, see Tables 3.10 and 3.7.
22. See Table 3.6.
23. HadlA 001/B/01, and see Chapter 1, 'Hadleigh's physical setting and neighbourhoods', above.

had been established at the far end of what was then known as Hell Street, later Mawdelyn Street and then George Street. It is possible that when Archdeacon Pykenham began his programme of grand building in the area around the church he moved the almspeople out of the Market House to the more distant set of almshouses.[24]

The latter dwellings appear first in the 1464 will of Matilda Groome, widow of John Groome.[25] She left four marks (£2 13s 4d) to be expended at 6d per week upon 'the poor house [*domus pauperum*] in Hadleigh in the street called Hylstrete'. It appears that Matilda had herself set up these houses, which were 'to remain to the poor in perpetuity, without any gainsaying'. She may have chosen that setting because of its proximity to a medieval wayside chapel on Hell Street dedicated to SS Mary Magdalene and Catherine of Sienna: in addition to the chapel's spiritual benefits, the almspeople would have been well situated to ask for charitable alms from travellers going in or out of the town. In 1465 John Fulsnape instructed his executors to pay 20d each week for 10 years after his death 'to the collector of alms for the sick poor in the almshouse of Hadlcy', a bequesl that probably referred to Groome's foundation.[26] Twenty years later John Brownsmith, sen., left to his son, for life, a meadow in Hell Street called 'Maiden's meadow', from which he was to pay 2d each week to the almshouse; after the younger man's death, the meadow was to be given to the institution.

A more formal set of almshouses was established on a permanent economic base by William Pykenham, rector of Hadleigh from 1469 until his death in 1497 and archdeacon of Suffolk from 1471. Pykenham had apparently decided to create his foundation by 1477, when he began to buy pieces of land in Hadleigh and the nearby communities of Whatfield, Aldham, Naughton, Elmsett and Semer.[27] These properties included a 35-acre farm in Hadleigh, a 139-acre farm in Whatfield and 1 acre of woods in Semer. In 1491 he acquired several tenements in Hell Street containing at least 10 acres, some of which may have been where Groome's houses were located, to be held jointly by himself and 15 other men. In a English charter of 1497, which describes itself as a will but was in fact entirely different from the Latin one that was proved through the church courts, Pykenham left all that property to 24 feoffees for the almshouses, which he described as 'the 12 tenements with appurtenances lately by me the aforesaid William Pykenham of new edified and builded for 12 almshouses'.[28] He

24. A suggestion made by Sue Andrews (personal communication).

25. TNA PRO PROB 11/5/6/45, and see 'Women of Hadleigh VII: Mathilda Groome', *The Hadleigh Historian*, 7 (2011–12), p. 20.

26. TNA PRO PROB 11/5/12. For below, see HadlA 025/A/01, from 1485.

27. A&S, *Hadleigh*, pp. 110–11, and Jones, *Hadleigh*, p. 25.

28. HadlA 025/E/01, which only discusses the foundation of his almshouses and the regulations for them. The English document begins 'This is the last will of me, William Pykenham, Archdeacon of Suffolk' and bears the same date as his Latin will, with the seals of four witnesses. Attached to it is a later conveyance from the reign of Henry VIII of property on Hell Street from the heirs of Pykenham's original feoffees to a group of men recognisable as the Chief Inhabitants. The Latin version of his will, which includes a testament of faith and many other bequests, does not mention the almshouses; it does, however, leave £5 to be distributed by his executors as 12d each to 'needy householders of my parish of Hadleigh', a bequest that would have provided extra money to 100 families (TNA PRO PROB 11/11/9).

ordered that the almshouse feoffees should be perpetuated by new appointments as current members died, with 16 members appointed from among 'the most honest persons for that time dwelling in the town of Hadleigh' and the remainder chosen from the other communities in which the house's lands lay.

In that English 'will' Pykenham laid out detailed regulations for his almshouse and its inhabitants.[29] Residents were to be chosen by the parson, churchwardens and four of 'the most honest and discreet persons of the town of Hadleigh' (i.e., some of the feoffees who held the house's land). The inmates must be local residents 'and there known of good and honest conversation and living and by fortune fall[en] to extreme poverty'. Two men, two women or a married couple were to share each room. The residents were to be given money payments every week after Sunday evening prayer, whatever was left of the income from the landed endowment after necessary charges had been paid. All were to receive the same amount to avoid 'variance and strife' between them. They would hold their place for life, unless evicted after two warnings for bad behaviour or refusal to obey the control of the parson and churchwardens.

In return for these benefits the residents had obligations for prayer that Pykenham expected would consume at least two hours of the day.[30] Late medieval Catholics believed that prayers for the dead would reduce the time the deceased person's soul had to spend in Purgatory, and prayers said by the poor carried particular weight with God. In Pykenham's almshouses the bell on the chapel next to the dwellings, presumably the one dedicated to SS Mary Magdalene and Catherine of Sienna, was to be rung every morning at eight o'clock and every afternoon at four o'clock by the resident of the house living closest to it. All 24 almspeople were then to go to the chapel for an hour of prayer unless prohibited by sickness or weakness. In laying out his specific requirements, Pykenham distinguished between those residents who were literate and those who 'be not lettered', making the interesting assumption that not all of the elderly poor would lack education. Each morning the full group of almspeople was to say '15 Pater Nosters and 15 Aves with the Creed, so that every one of them in one whole year so continuing may worship all the wounds that our Saviour Christ Jesus suffered to the redemption of sinful man'. Those who were illiterate were also to recite Our Lady's Psalter every morning, while those who could read were to offer further prayers: the services of Matins and Primes, the Hours of Our Lady and the Psalm de Profundis. Prayers were to be said for the souls of Pykenham himself ('their founder'), his parents, other named people and all Christians. In the afternoon all the residents were to say five Pater Nosters, five Aves and a Creed, while the literate were also to recite the evensong, Compline of Our Lady and the Psalm de Profundis. Once each week, 'at their best leisure', those who could read were to recite the Seven [Penitential] Psalms, the Litany and the services of Placebo and Dirige. Pykenham thus intended his almshouses to be in effect a lay chantry, ensuring a large number of prayers for his

---

29.   HadlA 025/E/01.

30.   *Ibid.*, and see McIntosh, *Poor relief in England*, pp. 84–6.

31.   Chantries were normally endowed by wealthy testators with a priest who would say masses for the good of the donor's soul, in some cases also assisting in the parish church or teaching children.

soul and those of others in perpetuity.[31] These prayers were presumably abandoned at the Reformation.

Pykenham's foundation seems to have inspired a little burst of interest in the poor. The will of Thomas Bendishe (or Benysh) of Hadleigh, sen., an esquire who died in 1500, indicates that the almspeople sat together in a designated area when they attended the parish church: he asked to be buried in Hadleigh's church 'by Our Lady's chapel towards where the poor men sit'.[32] When William Forth, head of a family of wealthy clothiers, died in 1504, he was eager to ensure the attendance of poor people at his burial and commemorative services, perhaps in part for charitable reasons but also to gain the benefit of their prayers for his soul. The unusually large sum of 40 marks (£26 13s 4d) was to be 'expended on the day of my sepulture, to priests & clerks, poor folks' meat and drink, and in other good deeds'. At the commemorative mass held 30 days after his burial, 40s in alms was to be distributed among '13 poor men and other alms folks of the same town'. For the rest of the year after his death a dirige and mass were to be said every day, with a total of 8 marks (£5 6s 8d) distributed to poor folks of Hadleigh. More closely related to his own occupation was the bequest of John Daniel, sen., a butcher who died in 1507.[33] Daniel left 12d per week for a full year 'to the alms folks at Magdalen chapel or there about ... to be paid every Saturday in flesh, and in Lent, in fish'. Over the following 20 years, however, none of the 11 extant wills mentioned the almshouses or left anything to the poor.

We know, however, that the churchwardens were at work managing Pykenham's institution, as directed in his will. The earliest surviving accounts, from 1535 to 1538, indicate that the wardens received an annual rental income of £7 from its landed endowment.[34] In 1537, when that money was described as 'to the use of the alms people in the almshouse', the wardens paid £3 8s 4d to the almspeople in ready money and laid out £2 8s 10 1/2d for repairs and carrying wood to the houses. If there was a full complement of 24 people in the houses at the time, they would each have received only about two-thirds of a penny per week, forcing them to seek additional funds. Over the next decade the churchwardens' receipts and expenses for the almshouses were £6–7, but in 1547 income jumped to £17 8d, probably owing to initial proceeds from the sale of goods belonging to the church.[35] The more detailed (but partially damaged) churchwardens' account for 1547–9 provides further information. The wardens paid out-rents for some of the almshouse property and gave to the constable the sum due for a national tax. Additional payments went for loads of clay, probably for repairs to the buildings, and for firewood that was cut and carried to the poor folk at Easter, Whitsontide and Michaelmas. The almspeople received cash gifts at each of those times, and the wardens paid for 'a washer for Mother Geyge', presumably in preparation for her burial, and for extra wood for two other elderly women.

Although charitable concern for the poor mounted between 1537 and 1553, as

---

32. TNA PRO PROB 11/12/15. For below, see TNA PRO PROB 11/14/19 and McIntosh, *Poor relief in England*, pp. 15–17.

33. TNA PRO PROB 11/15/29.

34. HadlA 004/A/01, pp. 18, 20–21 and 23, for this and below.

35. *Ibid.*, pp. 33 and 37, and for sale of goods, see Chapter 2, 'An endowment of landed property for the poor'. For below, see HadlA 021/A/01.

seen in bequests in wills, only one testator left anything directly to almshouses.[36] That gift was important, however, for – extending a previous bequest by the donor's father – it created the second set of such dwellings in the town, located at the southern end of Benton Street. Sheltering eight elderly people, these almshouses – like Pykenham's – continued to operate into the early twenty-first century. John Raven, sen., who died in February 1553, was a prosperous clothier who had held many local offices, including being market bailiff in 1535–7, churchwarden in 1539–40 and one of the Chief Inhabitants who audited town accounts starting in 1551. In his will Raven left £100 to the town if 'the honest men of Hadley' within five years after his death proceeded to buy lands and tenements to the use of poor people.[37]

Two years later Raven's adult son, another John, died. (Mortality was very high during the mid 1550s, in Hadleigh as elsewhere.[38]) The younger man, a clothier who had been a churchwarden for the past two years, instructed the executors of his will that the first charge upon his estate should be to see the provisions of his father's will carried out. But the younger Raven also bequeathed to eight of the town's leading men and their heirs and assignees forever 'four messuages or tenements in Benton [Street] in Hadley aforesaid which I have lately builded for alms houses', each with its own small piece of land, as he had laid them out. To his feoffees he granted the property he had purchased in Holton [St Mary] and Raydon, Suffolk, known as Noakes Farm and containing 42 acres, and he ordered his executors to use £100 from his estate within the next three years to buy additional lands and tenements 'toward the keeping of the poor as shall be dwelling in Hadley in the said four houses'. In 1560 the Chief Inhabitants purchased 108 acres of arable and woodland in Polstead for £250, a sum that included the £100 bequeathed by the senior Raven.[39]

By 1558 the endowments for the Pykenham and Benton Street/Raven almshouses had been turned over by the heirs of the original feoffees to the Chief Inhabitants, who acted as charitable trustees. They delegated management of the properties and houses to a (chief) collector appointed by them each year.[40] The collectors' accounts between 1579 and 1594 show them at work: paying the out-rents due from the land; repairing the chapel at Pykenham's almshouses and making a new gate and wall for it; maintaining the dwellings themselves, including purchase of timber, boards and locks for their doors; and giving weekly payments of around 8d to each of the 32 residents of the almshouses.[41] The size of the distributions varied over time, according

---

36. See Chapter 2, 'Gifts and bequests'.

37. TNA PRO PROB 11/36, and see Chapter 2, 'An endowment of landed property for the poor', above, and Chapter 6, 'The impact of Rowland Taylor and opposition to him, 1544–54', below.

38. See Chapter 6, 'The impact of Rowland Taylor and opposition to him, 1544–54', below. For below, see TNA PRO PROB 11/37.

39. A&S, *Hadleigh*, p. 111.

40. *Ibid.*, p. 112. For a detailed calculation of the relationship between the income and the expenses of the almshouses during the 1580s, see *ibid.*, pp. 122–3.

41. HadlA 021/B/07, 021/B/08, 021/C/07, and 021/D/03; 021/C/07, 021/D/03, 004/A/01, 233, and 021/C/03. A concern for privacy and security of possessions was seen in almshouses elsewhere in this period (McIntosh, *Poor relief in England*, pp. 189–90). For below, see *Norwich census of the poor*, for many examples of old people who pursued such work.

to the level of need of individual almspeople and their ability to work for part of their own support, perhaps through carding and spinning yarn. The normal weekly stipend remained at 8d for the rest of the century, though by 1602 seven residents received 10d or 12d for at least part of the year.[42]

Hadleigh's charities were inspected by royal Visitors sometime between May and December of 1594. Fortunately for historians, a contemporary copy of their report survives in the town's archives.[43] The Visitors described the foundation of Pykenham's and Raven's almshouses and concluded that the donors' instructions were being carried out. The parson, churchwardens and other inhabitants of the town appointed residents to places and removed them if necessary, visiting the 'houses and poor people divers and sundry times in the year'. The property that supported the almshouses was in the hands of three named esquires, three gentlemen, five men without status indicators and John Still, now bishop of Bath and Wells. The 11 laymen were all Chief Inhabitants. The records concerning the charitable lands

> are not in the hands and keeping of any private man, but do remain and lie in a chest within the church to which chest are diverse and sundry locks and keys which are in the custody and keeping of each of the churchwardens and other the inhabitants of the said town, so as no one of them come to them without the rest do agree thereunto.

Especially valuable is the listing of the 32 residents in the two almshouses in the Visitors' report from 1594, giving first and last names, marital status and age. That information may be combined with a record of payments made by the collector in 1602 to 37 people who lived in one of the houses for at least part of the year.[44] The latter account provides surname and in some cases first name, marital status and how much each person received for how many weeks. Occasional entries in other accounts give the names of six additional residents in 1582 and two more in 1591.[45] Of the 64 people known from these references, 33 of the women (52 per cent) lived in an alms place without a spouse, presumably sharing a room with another woman; 13 male residents (20 per cent) were similarly there without a spouse. Nine currently married couples (28 per cent) completed the listings.

The ages of the thirty-two residents in 1594 are shown in Table 5.1. Of the sixteen women living in an almshouse without a husband, seven were between 62 and 68, six were between 70 and 74, and three were between 80 and 86. Three of the four men on their own were between 60 and 67; the other was 74. Particularly interesting are the ages of the six married couples. While two couples had similar ages (62 years for the husband

---

42. HadlA 022/A/04.

43. HadlA 037/G/01 for the next two paragraphs. The report is undated, but it refers to a will dated 30 April 1594, and comparison of the almshouse residents it lists with poor relief accounts and the burial register indicates that it was written before the end of that year. We do not know why the inspection was ordered.

44. HadlA 022/A/04. Of those assisted, 27 remained in the house for the full year, while the rest were there for periods of 4 to 49 weeks. The turnover in that year, far greater than in 1594, was presumably due to high mortality due to an epidemic of plague; the alms rooms were filled almost immediately after the death of the current occupant.

45. HadlA 021/A/03 and 021/C/06.

Table 5.1
Ages of almshouse residents, 1594 and 1602.

| | *1594: ages known* | | | | *1602: ages known or estimated* | | |
Age	Women	Men	Total	Age	Women	Men	Total
40s	1	0	1	40s	1	0	1
50s	0	2	2	at least in 50s	2	1	3
60s	10	4	14	at least in 60s	5	3	8
70s	7	3	10	at least in 70s	10	3	13
80s	4	0	4	80s	1	1	2
90s	0	1	1				
Total	22	10	32	Total	19	8	27

and 60 for the wife in one case, 70 and 72 in the other), four show disparities of ten or more years between the partners. The Colbrones, Robert (aged 50) and Margaret (aged 40), were exceptionally young, the only residents aged less than 54 years. We do not know why they were chosen as residents, for there is no indication that either was disabled.[46] John Mychell was aged 74 and his wife Joann was 63, while a much longer gap separated John Cromer, then 90 years, and his wife Katherine, only 63. Joan and Henry Berket provide the most unexpected age contrast, for although they were described as a married couple, she was 83 years but he was just 54.

Of the residents mentioned in 1602, we know the ages of sixteen who were listed in 1594, and we can estimate the ages of eleven others based upon the date of their marriages (see Table 5.1). Only four were under 60 years, and just two are known to have had physical disabilities: blind widow Joan Wolf, who was living in Pykenham's almshouses in 1594 at age 71 and remained there until her death in 1603; and Henry Berket, said to be deaf. Twenty-two of the full list of thirty-seven residents were women living without a spouse, five were men on their own and ten were married couples.

One would like to know more about the backgrounds of these especially favoured elderly people, who must have been selected for admission into the almshouses out of a larger pool of people eager to gain the benefits of residence. While we do not know on what grounds the inmates were chosen, we can trace many of them through the poor relief accounts, the parish register and other town records to produce mini-biographies.[47] A striking feature of these brief life histories is how commonly middle-

---

46. W.A.B. Jones suggested to the author in 1990 that a somewhat younger couple might have been chosen to provide assistance for frail older residents (personal communication). The current feoffees of the almshouses, of which he was one, commonly assigned one of the rooms to a widowed nurse in her 40s or 50s for that reason.

47. See Chapter 2, 'The forms of aid, in-kind distributions and services', for possible criteria and App. 5.1 for some sample narratives. For below, we know or can estimate the age of 18 first and/or later marriages for female almshouse residents and 14 for men. Of the women, 56 per cent of the marriages occurred while they were in their 20s or 30s, most of them probably first marriages, but 22 per cent of the women were in their 40s and 22 per cent in their 60s or 70s. Of the men, 43 per cent of the marriages occurred while in their 20s or 30s, but 29 per cent were in their 40s, 21 per cent in their 50s–70s and 7 per cent in their 90s.

aged and elderly people remarried. Although many English almshouses prohibited the appointment of married couples and certainly did not allow existing residents to wed, Hadleigh seems to have regarded late marriage in a far more favourable light.[48]

Most of the residents had received poor relief prior to entering their alms place. Of 44 whose previous history of assistance can be traced, 4 men and 13 women had themselves been given household goods, occasional money or residential care; 1 woman and 1 man had been assisted in such ways through their spouses. Two of the men and 12 women were already receiving regular weekly payments before they were admitted to the almshouse, while 2 men and 2 women had not received a weekly stipend themselves but their spouses had. Only 3 men and 4 women or their spouses (16 per cent) appear to have gained no assistance from the poor relief system prior to joining the almshouse.

But not all had been poor throughout their lives. A few had been among the upper 18–25 per cent of Hadleigh's household heads during their middle years, as measured by the requirement that they pay rates for the poor. Four of the 22 male residents had paid rates at an earlier stage of their life, as had 2 of the deceased husbands of the 26 widows (13 per cent in sum). Although nearly all had been assessed at very low levels, their presence indicates that almshouse places were assigned not only to the chronically poor and suggests that there was little stigma associated with becoming a resident of one of the houses. But the almspeople were entirely separated from the town's ruling group: none of the men or the husbands of the widows had ever been a Chief Inhabitant or held a public office.

When assigning places in the almshouses poor relief officials may have given priority to those people – or their spouses – who had worked for the town. Of the 22 male residents 3 or 4 had themselves done such work (1 as the sexton of the church, 2 doing odd jobs and an uncertain identification of a bellworker). One of the female residents and a married couple had been employed by the workhouse, and 3 other women were the wives or widows of men who had done odd jobs. Of the 64 residents, 9 and perhaps 10 (14–16 per cent) had thus earned money from the town prior to their entrance into the almshouse.

Ann Bartholomew's life shows how the various components of Hadleigh's network of care for the elderly worked together. Born around 1520, her earlier marital and childbearing history is unknown, but one son died in 1569, and the town paid for the burial of another in 1582, by which point Ann had been widowed. To help support herself while in her 60s and early 70s she boarded poor or orphaned children for the town. Between 1582 and 1594 she took in five children, one of them illegitimate, for periods ranging from three months to several years each. She was also hired to make clothing for people in need, and she received occasional assistance herself in the form of canvas or woollen cloth. Three other children – probably grandchildren whom she was raising – received regular cash payments in 1590 and 1591 and were given clothing or shoes when they went into service. One of them was a girl with a numb hand. In 1590, at the age of 70, Widow Bartholomew began to receive regular weekly payments, and shortly thereafter she moved into Pykenham's almshouses. She was

---

48. McIntosh, *Poor relief in England*, pp. 72 and 194–5, and see, e.g., Ann Berdwell and John Cromer in App. 5.1 below.

still vigorous, however, for in 1592 she received wages for helping with the younger children at the workhouse. By 1594, however, she had apparently become unable to work, for she received the unusually large weekly stipend of 11d. She lived for at least two more years but had died by 1602.

In light of the various forms of relief available to Hadleigh's elderly poor, including the almshouses, it would be interesting to know what fraction of all old people were assisted. We can gain a very rough impression by using the distribution of ages reported in a national study. During the first half of the 1590s people aged 60 years or more constituted 7.41 per cent of the country's estimated population; small towns may well have had a somewhat larger percentage of elderly people.[49] Since Hadleigh contained an estimated 2,778 residents in that quinquennium, a minimum of 206 may have been aged 60 or above, though not all were in economic need. Of the 32 almshouse residents in 1594, 29 were aged at least 60 years. They thus constituted as much as 14 per cent of the town's estimated elderly population. This was an unusually large fraction for the period.[50] Moreover, if we suggest conservatively that 18 of the 24 other old people who received help in 1594 while living on their own were 60 years or more, the full group being assisted may have amounted to as much as 23 per cent of all the elderly.

Through its provisions for children and teens, ill and disabled people and the elderly, Hadleigh supplemented basic assistance with forms of help directed specifically at particularly vulnerable residents. The town's system of relief was thus able to respond to individual needs in a tailored manner, giving extra help to those whom poor relief officers regarded as both needy and deserving.

---

49. E.A. Wrigley *et al.*, *English population history from family reconstitution, 1580–1837* (Cambridge, 1997), App. A9.1; a personal communication from Richard Smith. For below, see App. 1.1.

50. Ian Archer has estimated the number of almshouse places within given communities as compared to their total aged population, 1589–1600, finding that two county towns and one market centre had places for 8–12 per cent, and London had places for 3 per cent ('Hospitals in sixteenth- and seventeenth-century England', in Scheutz *et al.* (eds), *Europaeisches spitalwesen*, pp. 53–74). For below, see App. 3.3.

Chapter 6

Why?

Having seen the complexity and expense of Hadleigh's system of poor relief, one may reasonably ask, 'Why?' Why did this relatively small town feel the need for such an elaborate network of relief? During a period of mounting poverty many of Hadleigh's poor needed assistance and, owing primarily to the wealth of its clothiers, the community had the economic resources with which to provide help, but similar conditions were found in other towns in Elizabethan England that gave far less aid. Why did the Chief Inhabitants of Edward VI's reign decide to invest the proceeds from the sale of church and guild goods in a landed endowment to support the poor, and why did subsequent donors augment those resources? Why were Hadleigh's more prosperous residents willing to be assessed for poor rates (and in most cases to pay those sums), and why were the town's leaders prepared to spend considerable time administering assistance to the needy, time that had to be taken out of their own business activities? Although we rarely have explicit statements describing people's motives for helping the poor, we can identify five main factors that influenced their decisions, addressed in the sections below. Many of these factors were present in certain other Elizabethan communities too, some of which developed their own forms of poor relief. What distinguished Hadleigh was the interaction of these pressures over the course of several generations and the resulting accumulation of assistance, all shaped by the particular characteristics of this town.

The impact of Rowland Taylor and opposition to him, 1544–54

The teachings and example of Hadleigh's early Protestant rectors and curates, especially during the ten-year incumbency of Dr Rowland Taylor (1544–54), almost certainly provided the motive force for the initial establishment of the town's charitable endowment during the reign of Edward VI. Although Taylor was not always present in the community, sometimes attending to his responsibilities in other places, he evidently made a great impact upon the town while there, and he named vigorously reformist curates, Richard Yeoman and David Whitehead.[1] Taylor's and Yeoman's martyrdom under Mary, vividly described by John Foxe, probably served to heighten the respect in which they were held and later remembered.

Taylor believed that an essential component of individual Christianity and of a community's godliness was the charity it offered to those who were in need. As was true for many early English Protestants, he evidently felt that Catholicism not only taught erroneous beliefs but had also failed in the basic responsibility of providing adequately for the poor.[2] Foxe's account stresses Taylor's concern for those in need, including his personal beneficence:

---

1. See Chapter 1, 'Religion', above.
2. McIntosh, *Poor relief in England*, pp. 20–22 and 119–29, passim.

> To the poore that were blinde, lame, sicke, bedred, or that had many children, he was a
> very Father, a carefull patrone, and diligent provider…. He himselfe (beside the continuall
> reliefe that they alwayes found at his house) gave an honest portion yearely, to the
> common almes boxe.[3]

Through his charity to the poor he showed 'hymselfe in all thinges an example to his
flocke, worthy to be folowed: & taught by his deede, what a great treasure almes is to
all such, as cheerfully for Christes sake do it'. When Taylor was last with his son, before
being burned at the stake in 1554, he exhorted the lad: 'Another day when god shall
blesse thee, love & cherish the poore people, & count that thy chiefe riches is to be
rich in almes'.[4] Taylor advocated publicly supported aid as well. Foxe says explicitly
that he 'caused the parishioners to make a generall provision' for the poor, an apparent
reference to his role in the decision made during Edward's reign to use the profits from
the sale of church and guild goods to set up a landed endowment.[5]

Taylor was outspoken in teaching his parishioners the need for true Christian
behaviour. Foxe comments that he was always willing to correct wrongdoing,
regardless of the standing of the miscreant. His demeanor was normally

> humble and meek, … but as occasion, time and place required, he would be stout in
> rebuking the sinfull and evill doers, so that none was so rich but he would tell him playnely
> his fault, with such earnest and grave rebukes as became a good Curate and Pastor.[6]

When he was led on horseback through Hadleigh in 1555 as a prisoner of the sheriff,
on his way to the death awaiting him at Aldham Common, those who lined the roads
called out in his praise that he not only 'so faythfullye hath taught us, so fatherly hath
cared for us' but also 'so godly hath governed us'.

Taylor directed some of his stoutest rebukes at the wealthy, insisting that they
acknowledge the reality of poverty and help those who were suffering. He was
accustomed, says Foxe, to call at least once every two weeks upon 'the rich
Clothmakers' and Sir Henry Doyle, owner of several local manorial estates and
Hadleigh's only resident Justice of the Peace.[7] Taylor then took those men

> to the almes houses, and there to see howe the poore lived: what they lacked in meat,
> drinke, clothing, bedding, or any other necessaries. The like did he also to other poore men
> that had many children, or were sicke. Then would he exhort & comfort them, and where

---

3. Foxe, *Actes and monuments* (1583 edn, but the same wording appear in the earlier two editions),
   p. 1519. All subsequent references are to the 1583 edition unless otherwise noted. For below, see
   ibid., p. 1526.

4. *Ibid.*, p. 1524.

5. *Ibid.*, p. 1519, and see Chapter 2, 'An endowment of landed property for the poor', above.

6. *Ibid.*, p. 1519. For below, see *ibid.*, p. 1526. It may be significant that the memorial brass placed
   in Hadleigh's church some ten years after his death included the observation that he 'kept his
   flock in feare' (Craig, *Reformation*, p. 169).

7. Foxe, *Actes and monuments*, p. 1526, for this and below. Sir Henry Doyle (or Doyly) of Pond Hall,
   Hadleigh sat on the bench from 1536/7 to 1561 and was sheriff in 1555 (MacCulloch, *Suffolk and
   the Tudors*, Apps I and III). He also audited town accounts as a Chief Inhabitant from 1535
   onwards.

he found cause, rebuke the unruely, and what they lacked, that gave he after his power: and what he was not able, he caused the rich and wealthy men to minister unto them.

Taylor's generosity earned him a following among the poor. Foxe reports that as he came across the bridge into Hadleigh on his way to the stake he was greeted by

> a poore man with five small children: who when he saw D. Taylor, he and his children fell down upon theyr knees, and held up their handes, and cryed with a loud voice, and sayd: O deare father, and good shepheard, Doctour Taylor: God helpe & succor thee, as thou hast many a time succoured me, and my poore children. Such witnes had the servant of God of his vertuous & charitable almes geven in his life time. For God would now the poore should testify of his good deeds, to his singuler comfort, to the example of others, and confusion of his persecutors and tyrannous adversaryes. For the Shiriffe and other that lead him to death, were wonderfully astonied at this: and the Shiriffe sore rebuked the poore man for so crying.[8]

When Taylor rode past Pykenham's almshouses, 'which hee well knew', he gave money to each of the residents, who stood in their doorways to see him. 'And comming to the last of the almes houses, and not seing the poore that there dwelt readye in theyr dores, as the other were, he asked: is the blinde man and blinde woman, that dwelt here, alive? It was aunswered yea: they are there within.' Taylor then threw in through their window a glove filled with money that he had prepared in advance.

Taylor's decision to emphasise the moral obligation of Hadleigh's prosperous clothiers and its relatively few gentlemen to help the poor evidently bore fruit. Of 15 wills left by clothiers during the period of Taylor's incumbency and the first decade thereafter, 13 (87 per cent) contained charitable bequests; of 29 wills written during those same years by men in different occupations or women, 18 (62 per cent) left something to the poor.[9] The only references in all of the Hadleigh records to the women who prepared yarn for weaving are three bequests of 4–12d to 'every of my spinners' in the wills of clothiers or their widows probably influenced by Taylor. John Raven senior and junior, successful clothiers, may well have been among those whom Taylor took into the homes of the poor. Such visits presumably contributed to the father's decision in 1553 to leave £100 to the town with which to buy land to assist the needy and the son's decision in 1555 to endow a second set of almshouses.[10]

---

8. Foxe, *Actes and monuments*, p. 1526 for this and below.

9. A&S, *Hadleigh*, p. 97. For below, see James Hawle, 1547 (TNA PRO PROB 11/31); Joan Hall, widow of James, 1547 (ERO D/ABW 18/67); and John Raven [jun.], 1555 (TNA PRO PROB 11/37).

10. See Chapter 5, 'Help for old people', above. In his will, the senior Raven also instructed his executor 'to bestow upon the poor people of Hadley or within 2 miles of Hadley or else other where as great need shall appear at his discretion 20 coarse cloths of blankets and russets' (TNA PRO PROB 11/36). If these were broadcloths, the length of each was probably around seventy to eighty-five feet. The scribe of his will was David Whitehead, Taylor's second curate (see Chapter 1, 'Religion', above). John Raven junior left many additional charitable bequests: £10 to be bestowed among the poor immediately after his death, 10d every Sunday to almspeople of the town for 4 years, a Sunday dinner every week for four poor folk for 1 year, 100 ells of canvas to be made into smocks and shirts for the poor for 5 years, and 20 bushels of wheat to be baked into bread for the poor for 5 years. He ordered that all of his 'tenants and weavers' in Hadleigh should be freed from paying rent for a year and left £40 to assist poor scholars (TNA PRO PROB 11/37).

Table 6.1
Occupations of Chief Inhabitants and officers, 1537–53 and 1576–85,
and proponents of control, 1576–85.

	Chief Inhabitants and officers, 1537–53	All Chief Inhabitants and officers, 1576–85	Issuers of policies about control and cost, 1576–85
Cloth making			
Clothier/clothmaker	17	14	8
Occup. unknown, but father or brother a clothier	3	2	0
Total	20 = 65% of known occups	16 = 53% of known occups	8 = 42% of known occups
Other crafts or trade			
Draper/mercer	0	2	1
Dyer/woadsetter	2	0	0
Cardmaker	1	0	0
Haberdasher	0	1	0
Smith	0	1	0
Rented a market stall or shop	0	2	1
Prob. in some kind of craft or trade	3	2	2
Total	6 = 19% of known occups	8 = 27% of known occups	4 = 21% of known occups
High status or landed occupations			
Gentleman	2	4	4
Esquire/knight	3	0	1
Rector of Hadleigh (Dr of Div.)	0	1	1
Yeoman	0	1	1
Total	5 = 16% of known occups	6 = 20% of known occups	7 = 37% of known occups
Total, known occupation	31 = 89%	30 = 86%	19 = 83%
Occupation unknown	4 = 11%	5 – 14%	4 = 17%
Total	35	35	23

Note: The left column of this table includes churchwardens, bailiffs of the market, and the Chief Inhabitants who audited accounts between 1537 and 1553. The middle column includes churchwardens, market bailiffs, chief and subcollectors for the poor, and the Chief Inhabitants who audited accounts between 1576 and 1585. The right column includes the men who signed orders about idlers, vagrants and poor newcomers in *c*.1576, 1577, 1580, and 1585.

The clothiers and gentlemen were not only Hadleigh's wealthiest residents, they also held local political authority. Between 1537 and 1553, 35 men are known to have been Chief Inhabitants or held the offices of churchwarden or market bailiff; some were also guild heads. As Table 6.1 shows, 20 (65 per cent) were clothiers or the son or brother of a clothier, and five others (16 per cent) were gentlemen or esquires. It is possible, moreover, that heightened concern with the poor was becoming associated in some people's minds with the new reformist theology. Although both Catholicism and Protestantism taught the importance of charity, the religious doctrines preached by Taylor and his curates evidently affected the beliefs of some of those with whom they worked most closely. Analysis of the tiny number of surviving wills of men who held office between 1537 and 1553 shows that four of six churchwardens already espoused Protestant beliefs; most of the market bailiffs and other Chief Inhabitants left neutral or generic testaments of faith (Table 6.2). Taylor was thus thinking strategically when he directed particular attention at men who were in a position to decide how the proceeds from church and guild goods would be used and whose actions might serve as powerful models for others.

But a growing charitable response is seen also among other members of the community, judging by bequests in the full group of early wills, which – though very limited in number – come from a wider segment of Hadleigh's population. Whereas only 27 per cent of the 15 surviving wills from 1500 to 1533 had left anything to the poor, just over half of the 13 wills from 1534 to the end of Henry VIII's reign did so: 38 per cent left outright bequests to needy people, while 15 per cent gave something to those poor who came to their burials (and presumably prayed for their souls).[11] During Edward VI's reign, the total rose to 71 per cent: 62 per cent of 21 testators made direct bequests, with another 2 giving aid at their burials. The fraction then dropped to just 44 per cent during Mary's reign, perhaps reflecting less enthusiastic preaching for charity from the pulpit.

Not surprisingly, Taylor's teaching and actions met with some resistance within Hadleigh. In addition to those who objected on purely theological grounds, he encountered more personal hostility from Walter and John Clerke, staunch Catholics and contentious figures within the community. In 1534 the brothers had denounced and forced the arrest of Thomas Rose, the protégé of Cranmer's who had made Hadleigh the centre of his evangelical preaching. When Dr Nicholas Shaxton, at that time a reformer, resigned his position as bishop of Salisbury in 1539, he moved to Hadleigh.[12] When he was later found guilty of heresy, Walter Clerke, as bailiff and farmer of Canterbury's manor of Hadleigh, seized all the goods Shaxton had in the community, which he was subsequently ordered to restore. At Mary's accession to the throne, when Protestants were removed from the Suffolk bench, Clerke was named as a Justice of the Peace, though his socio-economic position as a clothier would normally have been insufficient for that office.[13] He was probably chosen specifically to be an ally of the crown in the planned removal of Taylor.

---

11. See Table 2.2.

12. A&S, *Hadleigh*, ch. 2, and *L&P*, vol. xxi, pt. 1, pp. 659 and 679.

13. MacCulloch, *Suffolk and the Tudors*, p. 233 and App. I. His cousin Edward Clerke was appointed a JP at the same time.

Table 6.2
Testaments of faith of Chief Inhabitants and officers, 1537–53 and 1576–85,
and proponents of control, 1576–85.

	Churchwardens, 1537–53	Market bailiffs and other Chief Inhabitants, 1537–53	All Chief Inhabitants and officers, 1576–85	Issuers of policies about control and cost, 1576–85
Number of known people who held these offices	16	19	35	23
Religious position in testament of faith in surviving wills				
Traditional/Catholic	0	1	0	0
Neutral/generic	2	5	2	2
Mildly/probably reformist or Protestant	1	1	1	1
Strongly Protestant	3	1	5	4
Total, mildly or strongly Protestant	4 = 67%	2 = 20%	6 = 75%	5 = 71%
Mixed, with both traditional and Protestant elements	0	2	0	0
Number of surviving wills and percentage of all Ch. Inhabts and officeholders	6 = 38%	10 = 53%	8 = 23%	7 = 30%

In 1554 Walter and/or John Clerke set up a religious entrapment.[14] Without Taylor's knowledge, they and an energetic Catholic lawyer from Ipswich arranged for a priest to celebrate the masses of Holy Week in Hadleigh's church using the traditional liturgy. When the church bells rang and Taylor came to investigate, he and his wife Margaret confronted the visiting priest before being forced out of the building by armed men. Foxe illustrates this scene, showing Taylor in a simple black robe speaking out against the priest and a layman who was probably John Clerke. Margaret was on her knees behind him, praying, 'I beseech God the righteous Judge to avenge the Injury that this popish Idolator this day doth to the Blood of Christ'. That episode led to Taylor's arrest by Sir Henry Doyle and another man at the order of the Privy Council and to Taylor's eventual martyrdom.

---

14. A&S, *Hadleigh*, pp. 44–6, for this paragraph, including a reproduction of the Foxe illustration. Walter Clerke died in 1554. Robert Bracher, a priest who had nominally accepted Protestantism under Edward VI but returned to Rome under Mary, came to Hadleigh from London at the time of Walter's funeral, preaching Catholic doctrine. Taylor was in prison, but when his angry supporters told him about Bracher's sermons he sent a long letter to his wife for the townspeople to read, refuting those beliefs (Foxe, *Actes and monuments*, p. 1527).

Walter and John Clerke's conflicts with Taylor formed part of a history of questionable dealings. Sometime around 1530 Walter Clerke had been sued by John Dunton, a clerk, concerning land that had been bequeathed to support repairs to a chapel of Our Lady on Hadleigh's bridge; later that decade a Sudbury grocer claimed that Walter Clerke, clothmaker, who had private knowledge and intended to defraud him, had interrupted a planned sale of land in Hadleigh.[15] Though they were still described as clothiers, Walter and John were buying ex-monastic land heavily during the 1540s and 1550s, in a fashion that led to many lawsuits, and they gained several royal grants of property.[16] Malyn Tylney, widow of Philip, complained to the Lord Chancellor in the mid 1540s that after John Clerke of Hadleigh, clothier, bought the reversion of the manor of Layham from the crown, he refused to acknowledge her ongoing lease of the property. Entering the land, he persuaded its tenants to pay nothing to her. She asked for the Chancellor's assistance, for Clerke was 'rich and very substantial, greatly friended, maintained, and borne by his kindred and alliance dwelling in the county where the lands do lie'. By around 1550 Walter Clerke's conflicts had acquired a religious component, for they now focused upon William Forth, the leading Protestant gentleman in Hadleigh. The resulting 'law suits and secular violence' reached their peak in 1552.[17]

Walter Clerke had problems within his own family too. He was taken to court by the widow of his deceased son during Edward's reign on the grounds that he had failed to perform the conditions of the agreement signed at the time of her marriage.[18] As he approached death, he clearly expected trouble among his relatives. In his will, written in 1553 and proved in 1554, Walter, who now termed himself a gentleman, first offered a conventional Catholic testament of faith. He then revoked all former wills, testaments, legacies and bequests 'to th'intent there shall be no strife' after his death concerning his possessions.[19] He hoped that his brother John, his son Edward and his daughter and her husband, plus all his other kindred, would 'be contented and satisfied with this, my present testament and last will, without any manor of grudge, vexation, or trouble of any of them against other for any of my lands and tenements, goods, chattels, debts, plate, jewels, or ready money'.

Walter's charitable bequests were traditional. He left £20 to be distributed to the poor people of Hadleigh and other communities, but only those who came to his burial, presumably resulting in a large number of prayers for his soul. In a bequest that harkened back to medieval hospitality as offered by lords of manors or monastic houses, Clerke instructed his executors and assignees to distribute 300 loaves of bread worth one penny each at his 'mansion house' in Hadleigh on Christmas Eve for 40 years after his death. Needy people thus had to accept personal charity with suitable

---

15. TNA PRO C 1/626/28; C 1/922/9.

16. See, e.g., TNA PRO C 1/1048/58, C 1/1343/15–17, *L&P*, vol. xix, pt. 1, p. 627, and *ibid.*, vol. xx, pt. 2, p. 543. For below, see TNA PRO C 1/1163/61. The purchaser of a reversion was supposed to wait until existing leases had expired before taking possession of the property.

17. MacCulloch, *Suffolk and the Tudors*, p. 171, citing references from TNA PRO STAC 10 and KB 9. For the Forths, see Chapter 1, 'Cloth manufacturing and clothiers', above.

18. TNA PRO REQ 2/14/82.

19. TNA PRO PROB 11/37.

gratitude and deference.[20] One suspects that some of them may have decided it was not worth coming out on Christmas Eve, walking to Clerke's former residence known as 'The Place', on the east side of the town across from the Green, and standing in line at the gatehouse for the sake of one loaf of bread. Because Clerke was so strongly associated with Catholicism and appears to have been an unpopular figure in Hadleigh, his attacks on Taylor may have served to intensify support for the rector and – in the early years after his death – for the charity he advocated. These conflicts must also have split the Chief Inhabitants: John Clerke had been one of the auditors of town accounts in 1547, as was Walter in 1552, yet other community leaders had accepted Protestantism and worked for the establishment of Hadleigh's charitable endowment.

An image of Catholicism as a persecuting religion was reinforced by several more arrests and martyrdoms of Hadleigh men during Mary's reign. Foxe tells us that John Alcock, a literate young sherman, had attempted to maintain Taylor's teachings after his arrest, reading the service in English.[21] When John Nowell, the newly appointed Marian rector, arrived in the town, he preached a sermon arguing that Taylor's teaching were erroneous and that he had died out of 'stubbornness'. An indignant Alcock failed to remove his hat in the customary sign of respect as the priest moved towards the altar. Nowell was furious and ordered the constable, who was none other than Alcock's employer, clothier Robert Rolfe, to put him in the stocks. Rolfe refused, saying he would vouch for the young man's appearance if charged. But he warned Alcock to be careful, for Nowell would otherwise 'seek his destruction': the new rector was 'malicious, and a bloodsucker, & beareth an old hatred against me, and wil handle you the more cruelly, because of displeasure against me'. Notwithstanding that advice, Alcock, when questioned by Nowell about his religious beliefs, vigorously laid out his critique of Catholic doctrine, ending that 'ye are false idolatrous priests all the sort of you'. The rector, terming him 'a stout heretic', sent him to Newgate Prison in London, where he remained until his death, though continuing to evangelise through letters sent secretly to the people of Hadleigh.

At the time of Taylor's arrest curate Richard Yeoman, who was then 70, fled with his wife.[22] After peddling small wares in Kent – and being arrested as a vagrant – Yeoman returned to Hadleigh, where he was hidden for a year in a room in the Guildhall while his wife smuggled food in to him. (While there he read the Scriptures, prayed and carded wool that his wife spun into thread.) But Nowell learned of Yeoman's presence, broke into the room and ordered that he be placed in the town's cage or lockup. Already in the cage was John Dale, a 46-year-old weaver well read in the bible, who had been there for several days after interrupting Nowell's service with a loud attack upon the 'superstitious religion of Rome'. Sir Henry Doyle, though himself a Catholic, appealed to Nowell to have pity upon Yeoman and Dale, but he refused. 'In a great rage [Nowell] called them pestilent heretikes, vnfitte to lyve in the common wealth of

---

20. Thomas Carew, the minister of neighbouring Bildeston, wrote in 1603 when discussing payment of poor rates that some rich men lacking in godliness 'will not give almes religiously according to the rules of the Scripture, yet for vaineglory, and ostentation they will give to those that come to their doors' ('The reward of godlinesse', fol. N7v).

21. Foxe, *Actes and monuments*, p. 2046, for this paragraph and its quotations unless otherwise noted. For below, see Craig, *Reformation*, p. 173.

22. Foxe, *Actes and monuments*, pp. 2045–6, for this paragraph and its quotations.

Christians.' At his order, the two men were taken to the jail in Bury St Edmunds, where they were 'tied in irons, and for that they continually rebuked Popery, they were throwne into ye lowest dungeon'. Dale died there, but Yeoman lived to be burnt at the stake at Norwich in 1558, shortly before Mary's death.

When Foxe published the first edition of his *Actes and Monuments* in 1563 he included a dismal portrayal of Hadleigh's religious situation under Mary, far removed from his glowing account of the town as an early cradle of Protestantism under Henry VIII and Edward VI:

> Thus see you what lamentable estate the churche of Hadley was in after the death of D. Taylour. Many through weakenes and infirmitie fell to the Poperie: and suche as were more perfect, lyved in great feare and sorowe of hart. Some fled the towne, and wandred from place to place. And some fled beyond the seas, leving all that ever they had to God, and committing them selfes rather to banishment and povertie, then they would against their conscience do any thyng that should displease God, or in any point sound against his holy worde.[23]

His decision to omit that gloomy assessment from later editions of his work probably stemmed from a sense that it undermined his main message, the eventual triumph of Protestantism.

Foxe was certainly right, however, in suggesting that Mary's reign weakened the impact of Hadleigh's intense early Protestant ministers. Nowell's vigorous reprisals against heretics must have dampened the faith of some. At least three families headed by weavers plus a physician and Maud Facon, a single woman, all of them lay people passionately committed to reform, left England entirely; several went to Aarau in Switzerland to join Miles Coverdale.[24] Demographic factors, too, took a toll. Most of Hadleigh's leaders who had been exposed to Taylor's teaching and were involved in the decision to establish a landed endowment for the poor had died by the time Elizabeth came to the throne, owing probably to very high mortality from disease during the 1550s, a pattern found throughout England. Of the 35 Chief Inhabitants or office holders, 1537–53, we know the year of death for 16. Eight had already died by the end of Edward's reign and another five by the end of Mary's. The remaining three died in 1559–61. The burial register for Hadleigh's church begins in only 1559, but none of the other 19 officials is listed as having survived into that period. Only a handful of the town's leaders who had lived through the initial phases of religious reform were thus still alive during the early Elizabethan years.

Relations between clothiers and workers

Hadleigh's economic situation as a clothmaking town created particular need for assistance among some of its residents but also the wealth with which to address

---

23. *Ibid.*, 1563 edition, p. 1663.
24. Craig, *Reformation*, p. 173, and Jones, *Hadleigh*, p. 45. Two of the weavers (William Betts and Richard Cook) may have returned to Hadleigh, listed in the burial register for October 1559, but the others apparently did not; Facon, who went to Geneva, married Thomas Bentham, future bishop of Coventry and Lichfield.

those problems. During the sixteenth century Hadleigh's clothiers, many of whom were heavily involved in town government, were gaining increased control over the people who prepared thread and wove, dyed and fulled the cloth. Whereas the men and women who carried out the various stages of clothmaking had previously been independent workers, receiving supplies from the clothiers and paid by the product, some were now becoming regular employees of the entrepreneurs who organised the process. In both of those positions they had little ability to demand higher pay for their work and were vulnerable to being laid off during periods when cloth exports to the continent fell. The disparity between workers and clothiers increased as the latter continued to prosper. By the time of the tax returns of 1568 Robert Forth of Hadleigh, a clothier who had also purchased monastic lands, was the richest merchant in Suffolk, and the only towns in the county wealthier than Hadleigh were Bury St Edmunds and Ipswich.[25]

Because the clothiers were dependent upon the work of the people who actually carried out the various stages of cloth manufacture, they had a strong economic incentive for helping at least some of their more skilled employees to survive during periods of weak demand for cloth, quite apart from any humanitarian concerns that may have motivated them.[26] If their weavers and cloth finishers received help from the town they would be more likely to remain in Hadleigh, ready to resume work as soon as trade picked up again. The suggestion of economic self-interest on the part of the clothiers is supported by the observation that of the 603 recipients of poor relief between 1579 and 1596, nearly a quarter were adults aged 20 to 49 years: 10 per cent women and 13 per cent men.[27] While a few of those people were physically disabled or had recently lost their spouse, two-thirds had no obvious reasons for relief. Although we have no information about the occupations of women and know relatively little even about men's work, it is striking that two-thirds of the 32 male recipients of relief whose occupation is known were weavers (18) or other cloth workers (3). For clothiers, helping a worker to gain poor relief supported by the town's landed endowment and poor rates would have been far better than paying private wages during periods of unemployment.

---

25. Jones, *Hadleigh*, p. 34.

26. Richard Smith pointed out the structural similarities between Elizabethan Hadleigh in this period and agricultural parishes in south-eastern England in the late eighteenth century (personal communication). In the latter, the primary rate payers (large farmers) were major local employers (of agricultural labourers) and therefore had a vested interest in helping their workers' households to weather periods of un- or underemployment and survive acute need resulting from slumps in trade or poor harvests. Especially in bad years economically, two-parent families headed by men of working age received heightened support, not just the elderly, widows/widowers with children at home, and orphans who were normally given most of the assistance. As in the second half of the sixteenth century, the later eighteenth also experienced rising population and rising food prices, leaving the poor particularly vulnerable. See, e.g., Thomas Sokoll, *Household and family among the poor: the case of two Essex communities in the late eighteenth and early nineteenth centuries* (Bochum, 1993), and Samantha Williams, *Poverty, gender and life-cycle under the English poor law, 1760–1834* (Woodbridge, 2011), esp. Tables 6 and 14.

27. See Table 3.1. If this study had placed people aged 50–59 years into the younger adults category, rather than among the elderly, the fraction of adult recipients of working age would have been even higher.

Concern for the survival of workers during hard times may have been reinforced by residual fear of unrest, or at least worry about a loss of social deference and political obedience if economic need became too great. The gap in wealth between workers and clothiers, found all through the Suffolk clothmaking area, had led to protests and violence on several occasions during the 1520s and 1530s. When Cardinal Wolsey demanded an 'amicable grant' from cloth merchants in 1525, those in Suffolk notified their carders, spinners, weavers, fullers and others that they could no longer provide them with work. 'Then began women to wepe and young folkes to crie, and men that had no woorke began to rage, and assemble theimselfes in compaignies'.[28] Four thousand clothworkers from Hadleigh, Lavenham and Sudbury gathered in Lavenham in a riotous fashion, threatening to kill the Cardinal, the duke of Suffolk and others. When asked later who had organised the protests, their spokesman responded that their captain was 'Povertie, for he and his cosyn Necessitie, hath brought us to this dooyng'. The clothmakers who employed them 'geve us so litle wages for our workmanship, that scarcely we be able to live, and thus in penurie we passe the tyme, we, our wifes and children'. Without any work, 'then must we perishe and dye miserably'.

In the spring of 1528 the duke of Norfolk wrote three times to Wolsey about unrest in Suffolk. A central issue was fear that clothiers would not keep their workers in employment. On 4 March Norfolk reported that he was going to meet with a number of 'the most substantial clothiers of Suffolk', who were upset about a rumour that some English merchants had been detained in Flanders.[29] He commented that he would need to handle them 'with good words, that the cloth-making be not suddenly laid down'. Five days later he told Wolsey that he had now met with 40 of the leading clothiers of the area, one or two from each town, and 'exhorted them to continue their men in work'.[30] Assuring them that the reports from Flanders were false, he finally persuaded them to resume operations and take back the employees they had laid off. Had he not succeeded, he would have had 200 or 300 women coming to him 'to make seute to have the clothiers to set them, their husbandes and chylderne on work as they wer wont to do'. On the clothiers' behalf, Norfolk also asked Wolsey to tell the London merchants not to allow so many cloths to remain in the warehouse unsold. The problems did not go away, however, for on 4 May Norfolk wrote that 'divers substantial clothiers of these parts' had been with him that day, 'complaining that they can have no sale for their cloths at London, and that unless remedy be found, they will be unable to keep their workfolks in work more than a fortnight or three weeks'.[31]

In 1539 the weavers of woollen cloth in Suffolk and Essex, including some from Hadleigh, sent a poignant letter to Thomas Cromwell, then the lord Privy Seal.[32] Their petition bears a striking resemblance to a sermon attacking the immoral gains of

---

28.   Edward Hall, *Hall's chronicle* (London, 1809), pp. 699–700, for this and below.

29.   *L&P*, vol. iv, pt. 2, p. 1781.

30.   TNA PRO SP 1/47, fol. 83r–v, for this and the following sentences (calendared in *L&P*, vol. iv, pt. 2, p. 1796).

31.   *L&P*, vol. iv, pt. 2, p. 1868.

32.   TNA PRO SP 1/151, fols 70–72 (calendared in *L&P*, vol. xiv, pt. 1, p. 408), for this paragraph. For below, see 'The ongoing influence of Christian social teachings', below.

clothiers that was to be delivered in or near Hadleigh some 60 years later. The weavers explained that in accordance with a recent statute, they were obligated to maintain the full quality and size of their cloths. Although that requirement had increased their costs and labour, no allowance had been made for it by their masters, the clothiers. The craft of weaving had therefore become so greatly decayed that 'no man in these parties will put their children to that occupacion, so that w[i]t[h]in few yeres these shires of Suff[olk] & Essex of wyvers [weavers] ys lyke to be frustrate & voyd'. Moreover, because 'the Richmen, the clothiers, have their loomes & weyvers & also their fullers dailie workyng w[i]l[h]in their owne howses', the petitioners, as independent craftsmen, were often left destitute of work, unable to support their wives and children. 'The lenger they lyve, the more they are lyke to growe into extreme pov[er]ty', for the clothiers 'be concluded and aggreed amonge themselves to holde and pay one pryce for weyving' of a cloth. That price is so low that the petitioners 'cannot w[i]t[h] their labour gett wherew[i]t[h] to susteyne & maynteyne theire poore howsholdes although they shold worke incessantly nyght and day, holy day and worke day'. But because they did not want to remain idle the weavers 'are of necessyte compellyd to take their worke at the clothiers owne pryce'. For that reason, many of the petitioners, who previously 'kepte good howsholdes', had now spent all their resources and become other men's servants; more would have to do so too unless some reformation was made. The authors of this letter had previously written and presented a bill to Parliament, 'but as yet have litle comforte theroff'. They therefore asked Cromwell to help further their bill.

More serious were the uprisings of 1549, featuring unrest and sometimes violence in at least 25 counties, including Suffolk. Hadleigh would certainly have been aware of the disruptions, including the camps set up by protesters outside Bury St Edmunds and Ipswich (later moved to Melton).[33] These camps advocated changes in government and settled at least a few legal cases, 'dispensing justice to the people'. Among the communities whose residents joined the camp at Bury was Lavenham, then declining rapidly from its former economic predominance; it had actively resisted the Amicable Grant of 1525 and was to be at the centre of the abortive peasant rising in the summer of 1569. But there is no evidence that anyone from Hadleigh took part in the 1549 protests.[34] The decision of the town's leaders to use church and guild goods to endow a system of poor relief, a process that had begun in 1547, may well have lessened the inclination of local clothworkers to support the rising. During the second half of the sixteenth century active discontent weakened, but memories of earlier conflict may well have lingered in the back of the Chief Inhabitants' minds, promoting attention to the needs of the potentially rebellious poor.

Worry about control and cost, 1576–85

A different set of concerns emerged during the mid Elizabethan period. A series of orders by some of the Chief Inhabitants between 1576 and 1585 demonstrates anxiety

---

33. Diarmaid MacCulloch, 'Kett's rebellion in context', in Slack (ed.), *Rebellion, popular protest and the social order*, pp. 39–62, for this paragraph. The quotation below is from *ibid.*, p. 43.
34. Diarmaid MacCulloch, personal communication. For below, see Chapter 2, 'An endowment of landed property for the poor', above.

about misbehaviour, idleness, the expense of poor relief and the arrival of poor newcomers who might later become a charge upon public assistance. These leaders did not suggest that help for genuinely needy local residents should be curtailed, but they wanted to ensure that people unwilling to work and new immigrants did not take advantage of the town's generosity. The ongoing rise in food prices and decrease in the purchasing power of wages may have intensified their sense that they needed to maintain control over the poor.[35] Similar responses were found elsewhere in the country, but whereas in some settings they were apparently associated with a puritan approach to religion, this does not appear to have been the case in Hadleigh.[36]

The first sign of a new stance came in 'an order and general agreement made by the whole consent of those whose names do follow … for the reformation of certain disorders within our town of Hadley'.[37] Although undated, the document was copied into the town book after entries for 1576 and was probably from the end of that year. The statement, which does not describe the disorders, was signed by 2 men termed 'Mr', 13 other laymen and Dr John Still, the town's moderately Protestant rector; 6 of the signers were chosen to execute the order for the first year. In December 1577 a new agreement was reached by 'the headboroughs and inhabitants' of the town, with 18 signatories, most of them duplicates from the previous order.[38] The memorandum describing this plan said it had been introduced 'for the restraint of idle and evil disposed persons and rogues in the said town and for diminishing the excessive charges of the parishioners aforesaid'. The agreement then ordered the establishment of a workhouse, governed by 'some honest man and his wife, who shall have the oversight and governance of all the idle rogues and masterless persons vagrant and begging in the same town'. That institution was apparently not set up, but a functioning workhouse was in operation from 1589 onwards.[39]

A new approach to disorder on the streets and the arrival of poor newcomers was initiated at the end of 1580. A memorandum in the town book notes that it was agreed by three named Chief Inhabitants, Dr Still and unspecified others that two men dwelling in every area should be chosen 'to foresee that no incomers nor any other abuses' occur in their neighbourhood.[40] As shown on Figure 6.1, the centre part of the town was then divided into five geographical units, based upon streets. The divisions were similar to those used for collection of poor rates, except that the high-activity area adjoining the central public buildings and market was made a separate section, the little streets with poor housing between Angel and George Streets were now specifically included in that section, and Duck or Duke Street leading to Toppesfield Bridge was split off from Benton Street. Two people were assigned to oversee each neighbourhood, most of

---

35. See Chapter 2, 'Officers and decision making', above.

36. Marjorie Keniston McIntosh, *Controlling misbehavior in England, 1370–1600* (Cambridge, 1998), esp. pp. 1–6, 68–96 and 108–24, and Wood, *1549 rebellions*, pp. 199–200.

37. HadlA 004/A/01, p. 114.

38. *Ibid.*, p. 122. The term 'headboroughs' is not found elsewhere in Hadleigh's records, but see 'Civic identity, civic competition', below.

39. See Chapter 4, 'Training and discipline in the workhouse', above.

40. HadlA 004/A/01, p. 138 for this paragraph.

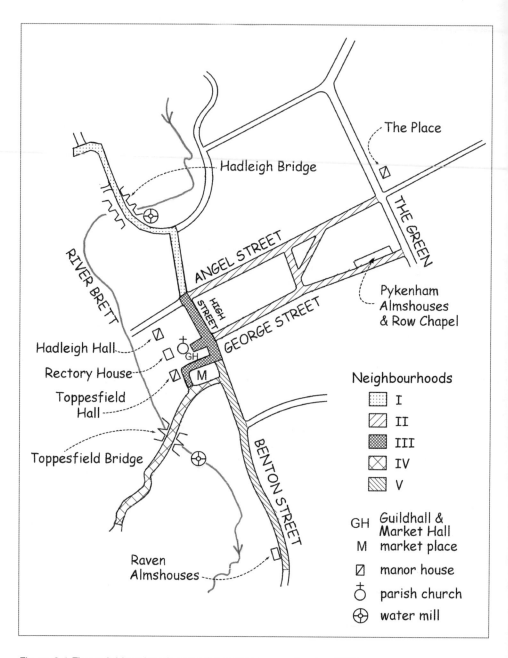

Figure 6.1 Five neighbourhoods used for maintenance of order, 1580.

them Chief Inhabitants. Should any problems occur, the supervisors were 'to signify the same to the rest of the town at the church on Sunday following'. It is not clear whether these leading townsmen – or their servants – actually patrolled their neighbourhoods or were called into action only if trouble was reported to them.

That policy apparently remained in effect, for it was restated and expanded slightly at the end of 1585.[41] The streets were to be viewed by their own prominent residents, looking for 'all new incomers and strangers coming into the town and for all other abuses' and reporting problems at church. Once every six weeks the individual neighbourhood inspectors were to 'join together to visit the whole town and to certify'. Only four geographical units were specified this time, with two to four people named for each. After 1589 much of the concern with public behaviour, idleness and vagrancy in Hadleigh was channelled into the workhouse, whose master was to walk the streets and remove undesirable people into his institution as well as receiving offenders from other officials. We know that for the early 1590s just over half of those put into the workhouse were aged 15 to 23: teens and young adults who should have been working as residential servants or paid labourers and who had probably been picked up as idlers or troublemakers.[42] But town leaders continued to pay attention to the arrival of poor immigrants, including children, and in some cases attempted to expel them or demand bond that they would not require relief in the future; their information may have derived from neighbourhood supervision.

The men who signed one or more of Hadleigh's policies concerning control and cost in 1576–85 formed a sub-set of all Chief Inhabitants and officeholders in that period. The occupations and religious testaments of the 23 signers may be compared with those of the 35 Chief Inhabitants and officeholders in 1537–53 and with the full group of 35 town leaders in 1576–85. This comparison reveals that the group who were pushing for improved regulation after 1576 were quite different from the earlier leaders and not representative of the full company even in their own period (see Table 6.1). Whereas 65 per cent of the earlier figures had been from clothier families and only 16 per cent were gentlemen or esquires, the proponents of order and regulation after 1576 included just 42 per cent clothiers but 37 per cent men of higher or landed status.[43] The full group of Chief Inhabitants and officeholders, 1576–85, lay between these two extremes, with a slightly higher percentage in other crafts or trade. The presence within the control/cost cluster of more people who defined themselves as gentry or better, with fewer clothiers, may be significant: men of higher status lacked the contact with workers and the immediate concern for their wellbeing that probably characterised at least some of the clothiers. In religious terms (see Table 6.2), about three-quarters of both of the later groups were mildly or strongly Protestant based upon the few surviving wills, with the remainder leaving neutral or generic testaments of faith.

---

41. *Ibid.*, p. 170.

42. See Chapter 4, 'Training and discipline in the workhouse', above. For below, see Chapter 4, 'Granted to a different family or expelled from Hadleigh', above.

43. Some of the gentlemen were the sons of clothiers or had themselves previously worked in that occupation.

Other nearby towns and villages were likewise attempting to deal forcibly with disorder and the mobile poor. The small town of Sudbury, lying 10 miles west of Hadleigh, had expelled Nicholas Byron and his wife in 1564 'for their evil conversation and living'; four years later, noting that 'we find much misorder to be in the night used by diverse young men', the town fined Richard Sharpe 'for that he live idly, without a master' and four other men 'for keeping disorder in the night'.[44] In 1572 Sudbury's mayor paid 4d 'for the whipping of rogues', and in the next few years Bess Osborne was whipped three times before the town paid 2s for a horse to carry her out of the town. Sudbury was particularly worried in 1575–6 about residents who were leasing property to poor newcomers, eventually ordering all recent arrivals to leave the town.[45] In 1571 Bury St Edmunds ordered that a search be made once each month within the various wards 'for the resort of vagabonds & new comers'; individuals or families likely to require poor relief were ordered to leave the town unless they could find a citizen willing to post bond that they would not ask for public support.[46]

In Long Melford, a village located immediately north of Sudbury, the constables' accounts from late in Elizabeth's reign document an unusually large number of poor transients but illustrate common practices for dealing with them: whipping rogues, sending some to the county jail in Bury St Edmunds, expelling poor outsiders and escorting undesirable travellers as they passed through the community.[47] (Melford was spread out along an important north–south road that connected Bury and eventually Norwich with Sudbury, Chelmsford and London; another road forked off to Cambridge.) In 1597 Melford's constables spent a total of 37s 7d for 'the conveyance of vagrantes & poore people' through and out of the parish. Some of these travellers carried a licence or passport that permitted travel back to their home communities and authorised local officials to help them along the way, while in other cases the constables probably wanted to ensure that people on the road did not remain in the community. At a standard rate of 2d per person but perhaps including a few for whom a cart and horse might have been required (costing from 4d to 12d), their bill in 1597 must have stemmed from escorting something like 200 people on to the next community. That distressingly large number of poor travellers presumably reflects an increase in the number of needy people on the move owing to the bad harvests and high food prices of the 1590s. In 1602, when Melford's constables noted where the vagrant people they conveyed were going, some of the transients were moving about to seek alms with permission of their local Justices of the Peace or were soldiers or sailors on their way back from a port carrying a licence from their captain, but the majority had evidently been arrested and punished as vagrants or rogues elsewhere

---

44. SRO-BSE EE 501 C141 B/1, fol. 10v; *ibid.*, fols 28v–29r. For below, see *ibid.*, fols 73v–74r, 75r, and 103r. We have no records from the courts in Hadleigh that might have dealt with such issues, but for the borough's Sessions of the Peace, 1619–25, and the Deanery Court during the seventeenth century, see A&S, *Hadleigh*, chs 18 and 14.

45. SRO-BSE EE 501 C141 B/1, fols 112r and 120v.

46. SRO-BSE C2/1, fols 1r, 3r, 4v–8v and 12r.

47. McIntosh, *Poor relief in England*, pp. 141–62, and SRO-BSE FL 509/5/1/63–65. Many other poor people probably passed through Melford, asking for alms, food or lodging, without being picked up by the constables. For below, see SRO-BSE 509/5/1/64.

and were on their way home.[48] Concern on the part of Hadleigh's Chief Inhabitants with maintaining order and keeping poor outsiders from settling in the town was thus part of a wider response to economic and social problems.

Civic identity, civic competition

For Hadleigh's Chief Inhabitants, concern for the poor and operating an efficient system of relief probably served as a unifying element. A powerful lesson of the Edwardian and Marian periods was that religion had become a dangerously divisive force, capable of tearing a community apart. The town's Elizabethan leaders apparently felt that it was wiser to focus on matters about which they could agree: that a well-run community should support those who could not provide for themselves while at the same time maintaining order and holding down costs.[49] These issues may have been especially important for Hadleigh's self-appointed Chief Inhabitants, given the legally precarious nature of their authority. The town's system of poor relief thus reinforced civic identity while granting moral and practical legitimacy to its leaders.

A related consideration may have been a desire to keep up with – and ideally to surpass – other nearby towns and villages as compassionate but careful providers of charity. A cluster of clothmaking communities in south-west Suffolk engaged in a considerable push to assist the poor during the middle and later sixteenth century. While a growing proportion of all English parishes and towns attempted to respond to the needs of the poor during the Elizabethan period, the presence of many impoverished cloth workers and wealthy clothiers in the communities around Hadleigh made such efforts both especially necessary and especially feasible in financial terms.[50] It is likely that Hadleigh's leaders were well aware of how its neighbours were handling provision for the poor and may have taken pride in operating a system that outdid the others. In those places, as in Hadleigh, the need to identify or create a body of men who could collectively hold property on behalf of the community for the use of the poor stimulated the development of quasi-urban institutions.

The kinds of assistance provided in Hadleigh were in use elsewhere, though not in such an organised and comprehensive manner. Two larger centres with which

---

48. SRO-BSE FL 509/5/1/65. Some of the vagrants were sent back to homes close to Melford (in Alpheton, Hartest, Sudbury, Glemsford, Cavendish and Thorpe [Morieux?]), while others were going to Sudbury on their way to destinations in Colchester, London and Kent. A smaller number were headed to places in adjacent counties (Norfolk, Essex and Cambridgeshire), while a few were travelling further (to Warwickshire, London and Yorkshire). A man and his wife passing towards Yarmouth [Suffolk or Norfolk?] had a licence permitting them to request alms along the way, and Melford's constables paid for writing one passport to send a vagrant man to Cambridgeshire and another for a boy who was being removed to Tollesbury, Essex, to join his father. The remainder were soldiers or sailors who were apparently moving with licences towards their homes from the ports at which they had been discharged. Most had come from Ostend [Belgium] and were going to places in Suffolk or Norfolk; two soldiers came from Kent, and a mariner was going from Dunkirk to Lynn.

49. Thornton suggested that in sixteenth-century Clare the necessity of administering urban property for the relief of the poor 'gave a common purpose to the town officials' (*History of Clare*, p. 50). For below, see Introduction and Chapter 1, 'Religion', above.

50. McIntosh, *Poor relief in England*, esp. ch. 8.

Hadleigh had regular economic or administrative contact – Ipswich and Bury St Edmunds – offered multiple but scattered forms of relief, perhaps influenced by Norwich, which from around 1570 provided a model of urban assistance and control of the poor.[51] Closer parallels to Hadleigh's activity come from three small cloth-manufacturing communities lying within about 15 miles to its west: Sudbury, Clare and Long Melford. In these settings we can also observe the diverse institutions used to implement charitable activity. Although in most lesser English communities from 1552 onwards publicly supported poor relief was carried out through the parish, Hadleigh's neighbours utilised other bodies as well: boroughs, a group of feoffees and older leet courts.

Sudbury handled poor relief largely through borough institutions. (The town was formally chartered in 1554 and sent two members to Parliament during the Elizabethan period.) Although Collectors for the Poor – the equivalent of Hadleigh's subcollectors – were normally chosen by and responsible to parishes, Sudbury took advantage of the provision that corporate towns might appoint such officials themselves.[52] In 1572 the mayor paid 2d 'for paper to make books for the collectors'; at a Session of the Peace for the borough held in 1580, two men were chosen as collectors and distributors of the weekly sums given to the poor, while two other men were elected to supervise the poor.[53] The contributions were not voluntary, for several men were fined because they did not pay their 'assessment of ½d weekly to the poor'. During the 1560s and 1570s other town officials – acting like Hadleigh's Chief Inhabitants, chief collectors and market bailiffs – gave occasional sums to individual people, mainly widows, paid a woman for keeping a child and helped several young people when they were apprenticed or sent as servants.[54] Sudbury's tiny medieval hospital of St Leonard, loosely tied to the town, continued to operate after the Reformation, run by private feoffees.

Different ways of providing for the poor are seen in Clare. An old borough and an important cloth-manufacturing centre, with a population of some 600 people around 1600, Clare did not obtain a royal charter of incorporation.[55] Instead it remained a seignorial borough, with burgesses and a court but under the control first of its Clare lords and then, after 1558, of the Duchy of Lancaster. In attending to the needs of the poor its leaders made no use of borough institutions. The first attempt to create a source of income expressly for the poor, managed by feoffees on behalf of the

51. See, for Ipswich, *Poor relief in Elizabethan Ipswich* and App. 3.3 below; for Bury, *Accounts of the feoffees of the town lands of Bury St Edmunds, 1569–1622*, ed. Margaret Statham, Suffolk Records Society, vol. 46 (Woodbridge, 2003), Margaret Statham, *Jankyn Smyth and the Guildhall feoffees*, Guildhall Feoffment Trust (Bury St Edmunds, 1981), and SRO-BSE C2/1, e.g., fols 4v–8v, 39v–40r, 41r, and loose sheet at back, and C2/2. For Norwich, where puritanism was probably a factor, see e.g., Slack, *Poverty and policy*, pp. 149–50, and Wood, *1549 rebellions*, pp. 199–200.

52. McIntosh, *Poor relief in England*, pp. 252–69.

53. SRO-BSE EE 501 C141 B/1, fol. 75r; *ibid.*, fols 173v–174v. These officers were named each subsequent year. For below, see *ibid.*, fol. 182v.

54. SRO-BSE EE 501 C141 B/1, fols 37v, 73v–74r and 136r. For below, see *VCH Suffolk [Victoria county history of Suffolk]*, vol. ii (London, 1907), pp. 140–41 (recte 1372, not 1272).

55. Thornton, *History of Clare*, pp. 27–67 and 121.

inhabitants, came sometime between 1509 and 1534.[56] Four townsmen, two of them successful clothiers, petitioned Queen Katherine, claiming that the town was suffering great hardship because the residents had access to land, fields and pasture only at the will of the men who farmed the manorial demesne. In response, the queen granted a 99-year lease of the demesne lands of Erbury Manor to three townsmen as feoffees at a favourable rent. The condition of the lease was that the common pasture within that holding be used for poor people. When that grant was confirmed in 1554, in return for a payment of 100 marks by three men of Clare on behalf of the community, the main proviso was that those tenants who held less than 15 acres of land were to be allowed to pasture their cows and horses on one part of the common land without charge; the rest of the commons was to be rented out, with the income going to the poor. Town records indicate that the land was used as intended for the rest of the sixteenth century.[57]

A body of headboroughs within the local leet court gradually acquired responsibility for certain other elements of poor relief in Clare. Bequests in 1539 and 1574 left land to 24 inhabitants, acting as feoffees, whose rents would henceforth pay national taxes due from the town or be given to the poor.[58] By the end of the century, and probably well before, that set of feoffees had become identified with the 24 headboroughs of the town, the men who reported offences against the peace and enacted bylaws as Chief Pledges at the court leet.[59] A residual bequest in 1593 said that the land in question should be delivered to the headboroughs as feoffees, with the yearly rent distributed by the ministers and churchwardens to twelve of the poorest households in the town. Most of the headboroughs (like Hadleigh's Chief Inhabitants) were associated with the cloth industry or were gentlemen.

From the mid sixteenth century Clare's parish church was implementing relief through its Collectors for the Poor. (Although there was almost complete overlap in membership between the feoffees of the common pasture, the headboroughs and the vestry that controlled parish affairs, institutionally the groups were distinct.) Obligatory rates may have been imposed by the Collectors as early as 1553 and were certainly in use by 1565.[60] Because we lack regular accounts of the Collectors, we do not know to what extent they were providing weekly payments to some poor people, but we do know that they or the churchwardens distributed occasional gifts and bequests, some made to the poor men's box in the church.[61] As early as 16 December 1552 the parish gave 1d to 6d each to at least 75 poor people: 34 per cent of them were widows, 11

---

56. Clare had evidently had an almshouse in 1462, but there is no mention of it later (*ibid.*, p. 99). For below, see *ibid.*, pp. 49–50 and App. III for the rest of this paragraph.

57. In 1595 a list of people with animals on the common included 110 people described as poor (of whom 24 were women, 18 of them widows), 53 termed 'the better sort' and 38 additional names marked 'purchaser' (SRO-BSE FL 501/11/215).

58. Thornton, *History of Clare*, pp. 50–62, for the rest of this paragraph.

59. For leet courts, see McIntosh, *Controlling misbehavior*, ch. 1.

60. SRO-BSE FL 501/7/36. Parish records include 'damaged and defective' accounts of rates from 1553 and 1562, but they were too fragile to be produced between 1984 and 2007 (FL 501/6/27–28). It is not clear whether these were rates for the church or the poor.

61. Thornton, *History of Clare*, p. 117. For below, see SRO-BSE FL 501/7/34; for later examples, see FL 501/7/21 and FL 501/7/35.

per cent other women and 55 per cent men. In 1589 47 people received aid from Sir Thomas Barniston's gift, which consisted of two bushels of wheat and 19s 2d in money.[62] Six lists of recipients of various bequests between March 1594 and April 1596 show that 116 people were assisted in total: 75 men, 33 women and 8 children. The individual payments were very small, ranging from 1d to 6d, but they added up to as much as 17d per person across those two years.

In the village of Long Melford poor relief was handled at first by feoffees and from the mid sixteenth century onwards by the parish. The subsidy assessments of 1524 and 1568 indicate that Melford had one-half to one-third as many residents as Hadleigh and less total wealth, though its average per capita payments were slightly larger; at the end of the sixteenth century it had around 1,000 inhabitants.[63] Melford was also less strongly Protestant than Hadleigh in the mid and later sixteenth century.[64]

Melford was already providing funds to needy people by around 1500. A large holding called Bower Hall, given by a clothier in 1495, was held by feoffees prior to the Reformation to help pay taxes levied on the community and to the use of the poor; its rental income was augmented by several later charitable bequests.[65] During Edward VI's reign these properties came into the hands of the parish. When the church goods were sold in 1548 the churchwardens resolved that about half of the income should be designated for the poor, and they set up a poor man's box.[66] In the 1550s the wardens reported on income received from rents of parish land and the box and noted how the money had been used.[67] The payments suggest that aid was given out

---

62. SRO-BSE FL 501/11/7. For below, see FL 501/11/12–15. The number of people is not exact, for the streets used in the listings were inconsistent, making it difficult to be sure if some entries were for the same or different people. A list of poor people who were to receive a bequest in 1599 described three of the men as sick and/or having many children, another as very poor, and two women as 'impotent' [unable to provide for themselves] (FL 501/11/19).

63. *Suffolk in 1524*, pp. 29–32 and 153–7, and *Suffolk in 1568*, pp. 13–14 and 107–10. The population estimate is from Lyn Boothman (personal communication).

64. Only 4 per cent of 54 surviving wills from Melford between 1530 and 1553 were even mildly Protestant, as compared to 38 per cent mildly or strongly Protestant in Hadleigh between 1534 and 1553; 44 per cent of 79 Melford wills between 1558 and 1599 were Protestant, as compared to 63 per cent in Hadleigh. Lyn Boothman generously sent me her detailed notes on the 147 surviving Long Melford wills from 1530 to 1599, from the Prerogative Court of Canterbury (TNA PRO PROB 11), the Archdeaconry of Sudbury (at SRO-BSE) and the Norwich Consistory Court (at Norfolk Record Office). She thinks that the continued strength of Catholic beliefs may have been due to its rector, Henry Mallet, appointed by Princess (later Queen) Mary in 1548 and probably the brother of her own chaplain, Francis Mallet (personal communication). For the Hadleigh wills, see Table 1.1 above.

65. SRO-BSE FL 509/1/15, fols 21r, 18r and 24r–v, and further explanation from Lyn Boothman (personal communication).

66. *Ibid.*, fols 27r–v and 41v, and SRO-BSE J545/9/133. The early accounts have been printed in David Dymond and Clive Paine, *The spoil of Melford church: the reformation in a Suffolk parish* (Ipswich, 1992).

67. In 1554, the churchwardens gave 4d to Mother Goodwyne 'in the time of her syckness' and bought 2 hogsheads of beer for the poor; the following year they handed out 23s 4d in cash; in 1556 they bought peas at a cost of 72s that were given to 'the poor folk' during Lent; in 1557 they

whenever it became available, with money, clothing or food awarded to people in particular need.

Relief developed into a more regular system during Elizabeth's reign. By the mid 1560s the parish was appointing Collectors for the Poor to whom much of the charitable income was delivered, an arrangement that continued until the Poor Laws of 1598.[68] Whether the Collectors levied poor rates as well is unknown. As in Hadleigh, the Collectors moved about the community delivering money to the poor in their own homes, rather than having recipients come to them.[69] The amount of relief awarded by Melford's Collectors rose across the later sixteenth century. Between 1575 and 1582 they distributed £2–6 in most years.[70] In 1588/9, a year for which we have a detailed account of payments given each week, the total was £9 4s 8d and by 1595, amidst the stretch of bad harvests and high food prices, the total had risen to £15 16s 3d.

In cases of special need Melford's churchwardens supplemented the assistance provided by Collectors, like the kinds of occasional help given in Hadleigh. In 1586/7, for example, the wardens awarded £1 7s 7d to individual poor people, usually in amounts of 3d to 12d.[71] Some of the entries have notes such as 'geven to mothar hankoke heavenge grate ned', 'geven to greges beynge very seke' or 'to Wyllyam barker at the buryall of his wyeff'. Many of the recipients were described as mother or father, and the wardens paid for the winding sheet and burial of three people, including 'a pore woman that died in a house of mr bokes'. In the next few years the churchwardens paid for such items as buying Kersey cloth and making it into clothing for poor children and healing the head of Spencer's girl; they gave money to mother

---

gave 24s 6d in money to the poor at Whitsontide and the feast of St Peter ad vincula [6–8 June and 1 August] as well as distributing 49s 3d at unspecified other times; in 1558 they handed out 10s 10d 'to the poore folkes in cloth & money' as well as giving cash during the week before Corpus Christi [9 June] and a month after Hallowmas [1 November]: SRO-BSE FL 509/1/15, fols 45r–v and 50r. The 1550s probably saw high morbidity and mortality from disease.

68. *Ibid.*, fols 75v and 119v.

69. The final item on an account dated 12 July 1585 for just over £5 distributed to the poor on a single occasion, probably from a bequest, was a note that Robert Doraunt had been paid 8d 'for walkinge with them [the Collectors], taking ther names, settinge downe the sumes and making this Booke' (SRO-BSE FL 509/5/1/48). A total of 138 named people were given sums ranging from 2d to 18d, with most getting either 6d or 12d. The recipients consisted of 92 women (41 wives, 24 widows, 15 'mothers', and 12 listed in their own names), 44 men (5 'fathers' and 39 in their own names, several of whom were old or bedridden) and 2 children. Money was given also to 'the old maid', two lame maids and three poor women, all unnamed. Father Dorante was the senior resident of Cordell's almshouse, Trinity Hospital.

70. SRO-BSE FL 509/1/15, fol. 108v. For below, see FL 509/5/1/50–51 (and 53–64, passim). In 1588/9, most of the 64 recipients were given 1d to 4d at a time, with only a sixth of them assisted on a fairly regular weekly basis. Women accounted for two-thirds of the total, and two-thirds of them were elderly or widows; a quarter of the men were elderly. The number helped each week varied widely, from only 4–7 in some weeks in June, August and early September to as many as 31–36 during hard weeks in December, February and March. In 1595, many more of the recipients were younger men or married women.

71. SRO-BSE FL 509/5/1/6 for this and the following sentences. Not all needy recipients were identified as such, so my identifications are tentative.

Manhode for her sick daughter, to Fuller 'for the recovery of his sight' and to Wylbe's wife and Garner's wife for 'paynes taking with mother hancok'.[72] The parish also assisted women who were boarding children. High mortality was reflected in payments such as 16d 'for burying of iiij ould folks' in 1593 and winding sheets for six women, two children and one undescribed person in 1596.[73]

During the later Elizabethan years Melford's charitable provisions were augmented by a privately operated almshouse.[74] Sir William Cordell had obtained the manor of Long Melford from Henry VIII after the Dissolution, married a member of the locally important Clopton family, sat in five Parliaments between 1545 and 1571 and served as Solicitor General and Master of the Rolls under Mary. Cordell was already supporting a few poor bedeswomen and bedesmen in Melford by 1565, and he established a hospital (actually an almshouse) there in 1573.[75] His will of 1580 endowed Trinity Hospital with land and named its first trustees; the latter in turn prepared detailed ordinances for the institution, which provided places for 12 respectable poor men from the community.[76] Some cooperation existed between the parish and the almshouse, for when the Collectors bought barley for the village's poor in February and March 1586, 204 bushels transported from Bury St Edmunds were stored temporarily at Trinity Hospital.[77]

We can compare the cash payments given to the poor by Long Melford and Hadleigh for two years in which we have detailed accounts for the Collectors for the Poor and churchwardens for Long Melford (1588/9) and the subcollectors, chief collector and market bailiffs for Hadleigh (1591).[78] That analysis shows that Melford was offering at least occasional help in the form of money to a larger fraction of its population, especially women, than was Hadleigh (6 per cent as compared to 3 per cent). But the average level of payments was very much lower in Melford (an average of 2.9s per person for the year as compared to 17.8s in Hadleigh). Owing to larger awards per person, Hadleigh's total

---

72. SRO-BSE FL 509/5/1/7 (1587); FL 509/5/1/8 (1588). For below, see FL 509/5/1/13, FL 509/5/1/15 and FL 509/5/1/17 (in 1593, 12d to widow Munson for keeping the child that was at Dorantes and 5s 4d for clothing for the child that is at Gellomes; in 1594, monthly sums to Gyllome's wife for keeping Joan Lowes' child and other payments to 'the Acton woman' for keeping a child; in 1596/7, repeated payments to three married women, two widows and one man for keeping children).

73. SRO-BSE FL 509/5/1/13 and FL 509/5/1/17.

74. Elizabeth Wigmore, *Holy Trinity hospital, Long Melford: a 16th-century almshouse* (Long Melford, 1995), pp. 5–25.

75. Lyn Boothman, personal communication.

76. SRO-BSE FL 509/11/10 and OC 88.

77. SRO-BSE FL 509/5/1/49.

78. SRO-BSE FL 509/5/1/8 and FL 509/5/1/50; HadlA 021/C/05–06. Melford had 64 recipients out of an estimated population of around 1,000 in 1600; 67 per cent of those assisted were female and 33 per cent male. In Hadleigh, 85 people were helped out of 2,778 estimated inhabitants in the early 1590s; they included 55 per cent females and 45 per cent males. Melford's female recipients were given an average of 3.4s during the year and its male recipients 1.8s; Hadleigh's female recipients received 18.6s and its males 16.8s. Owing to higher individual awards, Hadleigh spent £75 14s on money payments but Melford only £9 4s.

expenditure for cash-based relief was 8.2 times greater than Melford's for a population that was 2.8 times bigger. Both Melford and Hadleigh offered almsplaces to just over 1 per cent of their residents, but Hadleigh provided extensive assistance through in-kind distributions, boarding and other services, bringing the total of those helped to 5 per cent. Hadleigh's Chief Inhabitants and poor relief officers may well have felt that what gave their town its distinctive identity – and what validated their own positions in the absence of formal borough authority – was the complex network of care they managed efficiently for its poor residents.

The ongoing influence of Christian social teachings

Hadleigh's experience with early reformed Protestantism under Henry VIII and Edward VI and with persecution under Mary apparently diminished intense religious fervour in the community. John Craig argued that by the Elizabethan period Hadleigh was in a state of religious quiescence, a 'burned over district', with no sign of the activities characteristic of 'full-blooded English Calvinism'.[79] It is true that between 1558 and 1579 43 per cent of the testaments of faith in the few surviving wills were neutral, using short, generic wordings that could have applied to either Catholic or Protestant beliefs; only 56 per cent of the wills were even mildly Protestant. As late as the final two decades of the century, only 73 per cent of the wills were mildly or definitely Protestant. Dr John Still, Hadleigh's pluralist rector from 1571 to 1593, was an amiable man active in town government. Married to the daughter of Thomas Alabaster, one of the town's most successful clothiers, he acted together with the Chief Inhabitants whenever he was in the town. But his 'religious complexion' is unclear, and there is no reason to believe that he used his pulpit to advocate religious enthusiasm or reform.[80] The ongoing performance of plays in public areas controlled by the town likewise suggests an absence of puritan concerns.

Yet that assessment ignores signs of greater religious commitment. Dr Thomas Spencer, rector from 1558 to 1571, was a reformer who had 'sat at the feet of John Knox' in Geneva during Mary's reign.[81] When Spencer died in 1571, the bishop of Norwich described him as 'the most diligent preacher in the Suffolk part of my diocese'. During Still's incumbency reformed ministers preached in at least five 'godly communities' situated within 10 miles of Hadleigh.[82] We have evidence of connections with several of those churches in the 1586 will of Julian Beamonde, a clothier and Chief Inhabitant who wrote a strongly Protestant testament of faith. Beamonde left bequests to the puritan John Holden, 'preacher of the church of Billesdon', and to two Doctors of Divinity active in the puritan 'classis' in Dedham, Essex.[83] Memory of

---

79. Craig, *Reformation*, pp. 174–5. For below, see Table 1.1.

80. A&S, *Hadleigh*, ch. 12.

81. Jones, *Hadleigh*, p. 45. For below, see *ibid.*, p. 47.

82. Craig, *Reformation*, p. 174: Bildeston, Boxford, Dedham, East Bergholt and Ipswich (see Figure Intro.1).

83. TNA PRO PROB 11/70/1. Holden was Thomas Carew's predecessor in Bildeston, a man frequently in trouble with the bishop (Patrick Collinson, 'Christian socialism in Elizabethan

Hadleigh's early Protestant preachers and Marian martyrs was kept alive through the copy of Foxe's *Actes and Monuments* available in the parish church from 1586 onwards.[84] Further, by 1598 and perhaps long before, a sermon was delivered in Hadleigh on Mondays, a day probably chosen because the market was held then. The men who delivered these addresses may well have been of more reformed nature than Hadleigh's official rector and whatever curates he named.

Moreover, even within a religiously diverse community, the social message of Christianity requiring assistance to the poor still carried weight. People who conformed to the established Protestant church, those who wanted further reform and supporters of Catholic beliefs were all reminded that one of Jesus's central teachings was that we should help the less fortunate. The Elizabethan homilies that were to be read aloud in parish churches every year included one on 'Alms deeds, and mercifulness toward the poor and needy'.[85] As well as providing familiar encouragement to help the poor, hungry and naked, thereby pleasing God, the homily pointed out in more narrowly Calvinist terms that benefactors demonstrated to others 'that they are the sons of God, and elect of him into salvation'. Dr Still, himself a charitable man who helped to oversee the town's system of poor relief, may well have promoted beneficence in others, though there is no indication that he followed Taylor in insisting that wealthy people confront the miserable lives of the poor in person and attempt to ameliorate their suffering.[86]

Religious encouragement of charity – perhaps heightened by recollection of Taylor's message, the preachers who delivered the Monday sermons and visits to neighbouring churches – was put into action in Elizabethan Hadleigh. Concern for needy people was expressed not only through the town's official network of relief but also through private charitable giving. During the first half of the queen's reign 78 per cent of the testators of the 23 surviving wills left something to the poor, an exceptionally high fraction.[87] Although the level of charitable bequests dropped to 53

Suffolk: Thomas Carew and his *Caveat for Clothiers'*, in Rawcliffe *et al.* (eds), *Counties and communities*, pp. 161–78); the Dedham men were Dr Edmund Chapman, preacher of the church, and Dr Richard Crick, Beamonde's brother-in-law, both of whom were suspended at times for their religious positions. Bildeston lay five miles NNW of Hadleigh; Dedham was six miles SSE. Beamonde came from Bildeston but described himself as from Hadleigh in his will; he had been actively engaged in the town's religious and political life, and his children were baptised there.

84. The Foxe volume, bequeathed in 1586, must have been read, for it needed to be re-covered in 1588; it was still in the church in 1607 (TNA PRO PROB 11/70/1 and HadlA 021/C/02; HadlA 004/A/01, p. 308). For below, see HadlA 004/A/01, p. 260 (the sexton was paid an extra sum for ringing the church bell on Mondays for the sermon).

85. *Certaine sermons or homilies*, eds Mary Ellen Rickey and T.B. Stroup (Gainesville, FL, 1968), pp. 154–66, esp. 161 for below.

86. Still offered in 1591 to refrain from demanding the sums due to him for burial of destitute people (HadlA 004/A/01, p. 218), and at his death in 1608 he left £50 to be used for clothing for the elderly poor (A&S, *Hadleigh*, p. 184).

87. See Table 2.2. In suburban Havering, Essex, only 28 per cent of testators left charitable bequests, 1565–90, as did 31–36 per cent of Elizabethan testators in Bishop's Stortford and Wivenhoe (McIntosh, *A community transformed*, p. 278, and her 'Poor relief in Elizabethan communities');

per cent between 1580 and 1599 (8 of 15 wills), it was still larger than in other places. In Long Melford, for example, only 29 per cent of the testators between 1558 and 1579 left anything to the poor; during the second half of Elizabeth's reign, the figure was 35 per cent.[88] In addition, nine new perpetual charities were endowed in Hadleigh between 1570 and 1601, and the willingness of busy men to accept the burdensome offices that implemented the town's system of relief may likewise have derived in part from a belief that as Christians they were obligated to help the needy.

Yet biblical texts could be used to support a rather different conception of the social message of Christianity. Around 1600 Thomas Carew, the puritan rector of the neighbouring village of Bildeston, delivered a powerful sermon that challenged the behaviour of many of Hadleigh's leading men. His vehement attack on clothiers for exploiting their workers by refusing to pay them enough to sustain their families forced its listeners to question why extensive public and private assistance to the poor was necessary. Carew, a man previously in trouble for nonconformity, had been appointed to the living of Bildeston by two reformist magnates in 1591.[89] His critique was published in 1603 as one of his *Certaine godly and necessarie sermons*, under the running title 'A Caveat for Clothiers'. Carew's strong bias in favour of the poor coupled with his surprising economic analysis led Patrick Collinson to term him a 'Christian Socialist'. In this sermon we hear echoes of the letter sent by Suffolk weavers to Thomas Cromwell in 1539 and the moral intensity of Taylor's preaching and practice.[90]

Although Carew did not say where he had originally preached this sermon, he noted that many in his audience were clothiers engaged in production of broadcloth, and his presentation assumed that those men were economically successful and prided themselves on their charitable generosity.[91] Manufacture of cloth in Bildeston was already in marked decline, raising the possibility that Carew delivered his address in Hadleigh, perhaps as one of its Monday sermons.[92] But even if he gave it

---

38 per cent of testators in Bristol, 1565–95, and 39 per cent of testators in London, 1594–7, left bequests to the poor (Ilana Krausman Ben-Amos, *The culture of giving: informal support and gift-exchange in early modern England* [Cambridge, 2008], p. 117).

88. For the Melford wills, see note 64 above. Between 1530 and 1547, 65 per cent of Melford's testators had left something to the poor, though in most cases only in association with burials or commemorative services; the figure dropped to 45 per cent during Edward's reign and to 21 per cent under Mary. For below, see A&S, *Hadleigh*, p. 99.

89. Collinson, 'Christian socialism', and his 'Puritanism and the poor', in Horrox and Jones (eds), *Pragmatic utopias* (Cambridge 2001), pp. 242–58. The first of these studies examines Carew's life, the setting in Bildeston and the contents of his sermon; the second explores its intellectual context. Bildeston, which had around 550 residents in 1603, may have decayed in part through deliberate discrimination in favour of Hadleigh's market, owing to the influence of Sir Henry Doyle (*The chorography of Suffolk*, ed. Diarmaid MacCulloch, Suffolk Records Society, vol. 19 [Ipswich, 1976], p. 30).

90. See 'Relations between clothiers and workers' and 'The impact of Rowland Taylor and opposition to him, 1544–54', above.

91. Carew, *Certaine godly and necessarie sermons* (hereafter 'Caveat'), fol. T6v.

92. Collinson, noting that Bildeston would not have contained enough clothiers in the congregation for the sermon to have had its desired impact, suggests that it and the others in the printed volume may have been delivered at one of Suffolk's 'combination lectures', perhaps at Clare

elsewhere, his assault on the clothiers and their reputation for charity would surely have become known in Hadleigh.

Carew based his 'Caveat' on the fifth chapter of the Epistle of St James. He quoted it as saying

> Goe to now yee ritch men, howle and weepe for the miseries that shall come upon you. Your riches are corrupt and your garments are moth-eaten ... . Behold the hire of the labourers which have reaped your fieldes, which is of you kept back by fraude ... . The cryes of them which have reaped are entred into the eares of the Lorde of hoastes.[93]

His central argument was direct and forceful: 'It is a thing monstrous and strange, that any should be so voyde of religion and humanity as to defraude the poore of their wages.' Carew stressed the importance of the clothmaking industry to the English economy and said he did not condemn wealth if obtained by good means, but he claimed that clothiers were in special need of his warnings, for they committed 'one of the greatest sinnes' of his era due to 'the greatnesse, variety & continuance of their opressions' and 'the multitude of those that are oppressed'.[94]

In the body of his sermon Carew began by showing that workers who made broadcloths were paid less than people in other occupations.[95] Most craftsmen and even labourers earned 8d per day if no food and drink were provided, or 4d with meals. But wages in the clothing industry were lower. With an unusual sensitivity to gender issues, Carew noted that the women who commonly prepared wool and spun yarn could not earn more than 3d or 4d per day, without food, even if they were skilled and diligent.[96] Paid by the length and quality of yarn they produced, at a rate determined by the clothiers, they were required to provide and maintain their own cards and spinning wheels. Spinners earned less than women who made hay, reaped grain, carried ale in London or were midwives, all of whom gained food and drink plus their cash wages. As a result, some women now refused to spin, instead taking other employment. Clothiers defended themselves by pointing out that women in all occupations were paid less than men, not only their spinners, but Carew responded

---

('Christian socialism', p. 175, n. 45). Intriguingly, in another of the sermons Carew refers to a hospital 'where men are whipt at their coming in and at their going out', like a Bridewell ('The reward of godlinesse', in his *Certaine godly and necessarie sermons*, fol. O6r). That description would fit Hadleigh's hospital/workhouse/house of correction, whereas Bildeston and Clare had no such institutions.

93. Carew, 'Caveat', fol. S8r. For below, see *ibid.*, fol. T3v.

94. *Ibid.*, fols T7r, T1r and T6v–7r. A similar observation but without discussion of its causes was made by Robert Reyce, author of a survey of Suffolk in 1618. Commenting that the regions in which cloth was made were wealthier than others, he pointed out at the same time that 'where the clothiers doe dwell or have dwelled, there are found the greatest number of the poor' (*Suffolk in the XVIIth century*, p. 57).

95. Carew, 'Caveat', fols T8r–V2r for this paragraph. He emphasised that he was talking only about the manufacture of broadcloths, not the newer kinds of fabrics, which offered somewhat better wages.

96. Reyce noted that those parts of Suffolk in which workers spin linen thread and practise 'other such like womens imployments' had many fewer poor people than the broadcloth areas (*Suffolk in the XVIIth century*, p. 57).

that women's labour was essential to the clothmaking process and to the clothiers' profits. A woman 'spends as much time, takes asmuch paines, and dooth as profitable worke' as a man, so why should she receive lower wages? Children were employed too, preparing wool or spinning, yet while their income was indispensable to the family's net income and to the production of sufficient yarn, they earned only 'children's wages', which were even lower than those given to women.

Weavers (who were male) were paid by the cloth, at a price again set by the clothiers.[97] Carew emphasised that most other tradesmen determined the value of their own work, but there was no negotiation between clothworkers and clothiers. Because weavers had to split their earnings with a second man who helped to operate the broad loom and a boy who made quills for it, they gained somewhere around 6d per day without meals. From that sum they had to buy and repair their loom and provide lighting. To earn even that much they had to work from 4am until 8pm, three hours longer than in most occupations. If one took their working hours into account, their earnings were similar to those of women and only half as much as workmen in other trades. Some weavers wished they had become tailors, earning 4d daily plus food and drink, while others had left their trade to become agricultural labourers or shifted over to the newer types of weaving. Those who continued to make broadcloths suffered from cold and diseases that weakened them and shortened their lives. Shermen, who finished cloth, earned somewhat higher wages, but they too worked 16 hours per day, had to pay for their own tools, were subject to theft of their cloth from the tainters (stretching units), could work only in warmer and drier weather and had to wait three to six months after delivering their finished cloth to a clothier before receiving payment.

Carew turned then to the profits gained by clothiers.[98] Arguing that 'clothiers growe more speedily and more aboundantly ritch then other men' because they pay only half as much for the work done for them, he calculated the amount they derived every day from the labour of their various employees: 2d from every adult spinner, ½–1d from every child and 3–4d from every weaver. For every cloth made they therefore gained a total of at least 10s from these underpaid wages. Some clothiers had told him they obtained twice that much. The employers derived their large incomes not from their skill in organising production and selling cloth but rather off the backs of poor people, from cheap labour, 'which is miserable gaine, as if a man should rob the spittle-house [hospital]'.

Poor workers, by contrast, lived in penury. Whereas some clothiers were worth £20,000 at the time of their death, a workman who had been employed by them for 20 years might die with nothing more than 20 groats (6s 8d).[99] A clothworking family could perhaps get by on its pooled wages if everything went well, but if they were hindered by sickness or very young children 'how shall they buy them & theirs bread, clothes, firewood, pay their house rent, and such like necessaries for their life'? Other

---

97. Carew, 'Caveat', fols V2r–4r for this paragraph.

98. *Ibid.*, fols V4v–6r for this paragraph.

99. *Ibid.*, fols V6r–7r for this paragraph. The central government had admitted in 1593 that wages for spinners and weavers were too low and that the deceits and frauds carried out by workers were the result of being underpaid (TNA PRO SP 12/244/126–9), but efforts to set new minimum wages were unsuccessful.

people in the town, moved 'partly by compulsion, and partly by compassion', were then obliged to relieve the poor. Low wages brought spiritual damage as well, for the poor 'must take the Saboth to washe their cloathes, to peece their rags, to fetch a bundle of wood, when they should have come to Church to serve God'. They were also vulnerable to the 'dangerous temptations of pilfring & stealing ..., which I feare is one woful meanes of many of the poore's living'.

Clothiers claimed that poor workers were willing to accept the wages offered, but Carew pointed out that 'Necessity hath no law, the poore must worke for little rather then sit still for nothing'.[100] To the clothiers' question of how the poor would live if they were not given work by them, he asked in turn how the clothiers would live and get their cloth made without their workers? If they kept servants in their houses to produce cloth, they would not get a tenth as much done and it would cost more than twice as much. Carew highlighted the recent substantial rise in living costs, as compared with the flat or only very slightly increased level of wages, and responded to a number of other putative defences offered by the clothiers.

Carew was especially bitter when discussing the clothiers' claim to be charitable.[101] Some prided themselves for paying poor rates of 4–6d each week or inviting their workers to a dinner at Christmas (one thinks of Walter Clerke's loaves on Christmas Eve). But if the masters paid the poor adequately for their work, they could keep their rates and their pottage. The poor could then afford to shed the moth-eaten garments off their backs and the platters bearing nothing but fat off their tables. Some clothiers bequeathed £5 or £10 to the poor at their deaths, which was better than nothing and better late than never. 'But those Clothiers that have lived in any great occupying but ten year, if when they dye they should give to the poor ten score pound [£200], in my judgment they should dye in their debt.'[102] While they 'would be ashamed to take an almes of every ritch man, they are not ashamed to take an almes of every poore man'.

He also objected to self-justifying statements that many clothiers are 'religious men and the specialest men in Townes, & such as have bin speciall instruments to further the gospell'.[103] Though the grace of God has been given to all sorts of men – to some clothiers as well as others – Carew enjoined his readers to think about how the Scriptures speak of true religion. Here he stressed the quality of mercy, returning to the Apostle James: '*Pure religion and undefiled before God* is this, to visite the fatherlesse and widowes in their adversitie.'[104] (One suspects that Carew had heard about

---

100. Carew, 'Caveat', fol. V8r.

101. *Ibid.*, fols X7v–8r. For below, see *ibid.*, fol. X8r.

102. *Ibid.*, fol. X8r. For below, see *ibid.*, fols X7v–8r.

103. *Ibid.*, fol. X8r. For below, see *ibid.*, fols X8r–Y1r.

104. In the early seventeenth century John Downame, a London puritan, said that people who went into the hovels of the poor would see for themselves 'their provision, hungrie fare, thinne cloathes and hard lodging: the children crying for hunger, and the parents out crying them because they have no food to give them; some lying in straw for want of beddes, others drinking water in stead of drinke' (*The plea of the poore*, pp. 56–60, from 1616); John Rogers of nearby Dedham, Essex insisted on the need to visit the poor in person, which he said was a long-established practice in his community (*A treatise of love*, pp. 224–5, from 1632), both as cited by Collinson, 'Puritanism and the poor', pp. 247–8.

Rowland Taylor.) Rather than following that instruction, however, clothiers not only exploited their workers, they committed usury through the way they demanded payment for the cloths they handed over to merchants for sale.

Carew thus redefined charity as individual or collective provision of assistance that would not have been necessary in a truly Christian community. We do not know how accurate his assessment was or how Hadleigh's clothiers reacted to his attack. Some of them may well have profited from their workers as Carew suggests, and perhaps their involvement in the town's system of poor relief and their unusually generous charitable bequests stemmed in part from guilt as well as from compassion. But whether Christian teachings advocated traditional forms of charity or an economic reworking of society that would obviate the need for such help, the ability of the pulpit and written texts to influence social values should not be underestimated. Preachers and religious writers wielded powerful weapons.

Hadleigh's system of poor relief grew out of the cumulative interaction of the five factors described above. They carried particular weight because of the setting within which they arose. The town was small enough that poor people could be known individually by local officials, but prosperous enough that resources were available for their relief. Further, the community's government was highly autonomous (if legally questionable), operating almost entirely without external supervision. The combination of strong motivational considerations and specific practical features led to the gradual development of what became the most extensive and complex system found in any Elizabethan town. Help for the legitimately needy was joined by mechanisms for controlling the behaviour of the poor, holding down costs and preventing unwanted outsiders from settling in the community. It must be stressed that this system emerged over the course of the half-century *before* the national legislation of 1598 and 1601 that ushered in the period known as the Old Poor Law.

Hadleigh was not alone in setting up an active programme of poor relief. Some of the five factors discussed above were present in other Elizabethan communities too, though their impact was usually of shorter duration and lacked the compounding effect seen in Hadleigh. Multifaceted systems of assistance emerged not only in other clothmaking towns in East Anglia but also in industrialised communities in the south-west of the country, market towns on main roads, ports, and county administrative centres.[105] Like Hadleigh, such places were marked by economic and demographic patterns that produced a sizeable number of poor people unable to provide for themselves, a group of wealthier people able to pay poor rates, and urban and/or parish leaders willing to use their authority to create and sustain their community's blend of help and regulation. Some but not all of their leaders held reformed Protestant attitudes towards poverty, charity and good order. Many of England's cities likewise

---

105. For distribution of active poor relief parishes by region and type of community, see McIntosh, *Poor relief in England*, pp. 131–2, 232–3, and CUP Online Appendix 9. For the rest of this paragraph, see *ibid.*, esp. chs 5.3 and 8, and McIntosh, *Controlling misbehavior*, esp. pp. 68–96 and 162–9.

initiated complex programmes of relief, but their efforts were generally hampered by the size and diversity of their poor populations, the ongoing arrival of needy immigrants and competing forms of authority. Parliamentary legislation, enforced by the church as well as the state, played a role too, for from 1552 onwards all parishes were required to gather money from more prosperous residents to assist their poor neighbours. But while some parishes ignored that requirement and others conformed only minimally, Hadleigh and a limited number of other communities went beyond the law to provide far more complete assistance and to develop creative methods of paying for aid that did not rely entirely on poor rates.

We may in conclusion glance at what happened to poor relief in Hadleigh after 1600. Although we do not have detailed information about later periods, poverty clearly worsened in the early seventeenth century. The town's economy, based on the manufacture of broadcloth, began a severe decline, magnifying need on the part of people who were poorly paid or unable to find sufficient work. Among the clothiers a new emphasis on formal education may have contributed to a lack of capital and entrepreneurial talent. Whereas most clothmakers in the mid sixteenth century had encouraged their sons to follow in their footsteps, by the end of that century and in the next clothiers and local gentlemen whose forebears had profited from cloth manufacture commonly sent their male heirs to Hadleigh's Grammar School and then on to university.[106] There they trained to become lawyers, classical scholars or churchmen, rarely returning to the town.

Sometime around 1618 Hadleigh was described as 'an ancient clothing town' filled with 'an extraordinary abundance of poverty'.[107] By then, assistance to the poor was being handled by different institutions. The Poor Laws of 1598 and 1601 had ended the option whereby towns could name and supervise Collectors for the Poor; henceforth Hadleigh's Overseers of the Poor were chosen within St Mary's parish. Appointed by the vestry (the minister, churchwardens and a small group of local leaders), the Overseers were responsible for assessing, collecting and distributing poor rates, and they operated the workhouse that continued to function in the Guildhall until the Poor Law of 1834.[108] Their accounts do not survive.

Prior to Hadleigh's incorporation in 1618 the Chief Inhabitants, some of whom were also vestrymen, continued to run the almshouses and other privately endowed charities. After receipt of the charter, responsibility for administering the charitable properties was transferred to the Corporation, which was in practice controlled by the same men. They appointed a chief collector in charge of all the charities and a subcollector who handled distributions to almshouse residents. Meanwhile, generous residents continued to endow new perpetual charities, with 15 funds for the poor established between 1601 and 1650, offering clothing, fuel and almshousing.[109] Sue

---

106. A&S, *Hadleigh*, pp. 193–7, and a personal communication from Sue Andrews.

107. A&S, *Hadleigh*, p. 151, citing a volume of notes about Hadleigh made by rector David Wilkins in 1721 (personal communication from Sue Andrews). Wilkins wrote that the quotation was from Reyce's 'Breviary of Suffolk' (1618), but it does not appear in the modern edition of the Breviary.

108. Information for this and the next paragraph comes from A&S, *Hadleigh*, pp. 112–26 and personal communications from Sue Andrews.

109. A&S, *Hadleigh*, p. 99. For below, see *ibid.*, pp. 125 and 303.

Andrews estimated that by the middle of the seventeenth century 300 people were being assisted annually through benefactions given over the past 150 years, a number that constituted about 15 per cent of the town's greatly reduced population. Hadleigh's commitment to the poor thus remained strong even after its communal wealth had declined, and a group of local leaders remained willing to devote their time and energy to operating the system.[110]

It is moving to walk through Hadleigh today and see that the residents of almshouses founded 450 to 500 years ago are still living on the original sites (though now in more modern quarters) and still receive benefits, thanks to the efforts of successive charitable trustees. Hadleigh's sixteenth-century residents and the men and women who followed them deserve ample credit for their concern for the poor, their contributions of material and human resources and their competence in managing a system that even in the twenty-first century continues to couple public and private assistance for needy people.

---

110. From the eighteenth century onwards endowments for the poor in Hadleigh have been administered separately from the market and its buildings. In the twenty-first century, the organisations that operate the projects formerly undertaken by the Chief Inhabitants are the Hadleigh Grand Feoffment Charities and the Hadleigh Market Feoffment Charity.

Appendix Intro 1

Summary accounts for the poor, 1535–1620

Year	Amt received by churchwardens for almshouses	Total amt received by the (chief) collector, largely from rents of charitable property, used for expenses such as outrents and maintenance of properties as well as poor relief	Additional amt received by subcollectors from poor rates, including arrearages, when known	Amt disbursed to the poor by the subcollectors	Total amt disbursed to poor people, the almshouses, and workhouse by the (chief) collector, the two subcollectors, and ad hoc pairs of town leaders giving out household goods
1535	7.00				
1536	7.00				
1537	7.00				
1538	7.00				
1540	9.17				
1541	6.40				
1542	10.07				
1544	8.13				
1546	7.70				
1547	17.03				
1549	9.63				
1559	9.33 ~				
1563		73.58		64.20	
1564		83.21			
1565		82.32	[33.22]^	[67.74]^	
1566			36.23	70.75	

Year	Amt received by churchwardens for almshouses	Total amt received by the (chief) collector, largely from rents of charitable property, used for expenses such as outrents and maintenance of properties as well as poor relief	Additional amt received by subcollectors from poor rates, including arrearages, when known	Amt disbursed to the poor by the subcollectors	Total amt disbursed to poor people, the almshouses, and workhouse by the (chief) collector, the two subcollectors, and ad hoc pairs of town leaders giving out household goods
1567		83.10	26.60	66.78	
1568		90.83	16.04	66.00	
1569		101.00	17.73	60.44	
1570		105.69	17.38	61.71	
1571		89.99	19.73	61.48	
1572		93.44	19.09	59.74	
1573		86.36		69.74 #	
1574		88.12		69.74 #	
1575		92.21		78.95	
1576		95.46		76.33	
1577		89.48		71.98	
1578		95.76		67.77	
1579		99.24	19.43	69.86	
1580		115.68		82.69	100.86
1581		145.86		77.23	117.03
1582		103.42	17.80	71.33	83.80
1583		98.73		66.71	80.34
1584		103.49		73.10	76.10
1585		122.70	23.65	84.60	85.37
1586		107.46		73.28	89.17
1587		110.75		80.21	101.54
1588		106.13		80.31	111.04
1589		101.08		76.32	98.66
1590		106.36	25.32	72.21	92.22
1591		130.36	25.15	74.82	102.63
1592		165.52		85.74	118.72 ^^

Year				
1593	144.70		105.26	136.46 ^^
1594	149.14	23.22	88.60	107.99
1595	146.79		101.29	129.98
1596	162.97		94.59	154.16 ^^
1597	142.92		98.34	
1598	146.55		91.99	
1599	141.60		56.58 *	
1600	160.75		58.01	
1601	157.86		57.08	
1602	141.59		57.64	
1603	162.55		59.17	
1610	151.63		68.55	
1615	162.75		71.50	
1620	167.19		77.83	

Notes: All entries in pounds.

~ Received by an unspecified 'collector', not by the churchwardens, but said to be for the almshouses.

^ An estimate derived by doubling the two recorded quarterly amounts.

The value for these two years is half of the combined accounts submitted for 1573 and 1574.

^^ The total expenditures in these years were increased by large payments to the hospital: £22.08 in 1592, £18.29 in 1593 and £44.17 in 1596.

* From 1599 onward, Hadleigh's parish church was presumably appointing Overseers of the Poor who assumed some of the duties formerly carried out by the town's subcollectors, including collection and distribution of rates and operation of the workhouse. The chief collector and single remaining subcollector focused henceforth on the almshouses and endowed charities. No detailed accounts survive from the seventeenth century.

Sources: HadIA 004/A/01, pp. 18–364, passim; HadIA 021/A/02–06, 021/B/05–09, 021/C/01–08 and 021/D/01–04.

Appendix Intro 2

Overview of information from detailed accounts about assistance to the poor, 1579–96

Year	Detailed surviving accounts of disbursements to the poor #	Assistance to individuals ##			Assistance to institutions or groups*			Total assistance recorded in detailed accounts
		Amt of recorded assistance ^	No. of individuals who received assistance with monetary value ~	No. of households in which those people lived	Almshouses	Workhouse	Poor folk: names and number unspecified	
1579	R, G, C	87.82	91	78				87.82
1580	G, C	18.17	86	67				18.17
1581	G, C	39.80	99	80				39.80
1582	R, O, G, C	82.06	149	110	1.33		0.41	83.80
1583	G, C	8.32	67	58	4.95		0.36	13.63
1584	G	3.00	39	38				3.00
1585	R, G, C	85.37	93	77				85.37
1586	G, C	15.72	108 (+ 14)	94			0.17	15.89
1587	G, C	17.93	119	91	3.46			21.39
1588	O, G, C	25.33	141 (+ 2)	97	5.40			30.73
1589	O, G, C	17.61	116	98	4.73			22.34
1590	R, G, C	85.95	101	85	5.67	0.42	0.18	92.22
1591	R, O, G, C	91.37	122	101		0.65	10.81	102.83
1592	G, C	10.00	76	65		22.08	0.90	32.98
1593	O, G, C	9.49	57	51		18.29	3.42	31.20
1594	R, O, G, C	92.58	111	91			15.41	107.99
1595	G, C	19.31	89 (+ 15)	77	8.21	0.60	0.57	28.69
1596	G, C	15.40	58	50		44.17		59.57

Notes: All values in pounds.

Types of records:

R = Regular, weekly cash payments (disbursed by subcollectors for the poor)

O = Occasional cash payments (made by chief collectors, subcollectors and/or market bailiffs)

G = Goods from private charities (distributed by chief collector or pairs of town leaders; usually recorded in separate accounts)

C = Care provided for the poor (boarding or other services, disbursed by sub- or chief collectors and/or market bailiffs)

This and all subsequent tabulations exclude the wood sold to the poor at reduced price thanks to the bequest of £10 annually left by Julian Beamonde in 1588. Analysis of the people who received the wood, for which they had to name a surety for payment, shows that nearly all were of somewhat higher economic level, not recipients of other kinds of poor relief (TNA PRO PROB 11/70/1 and HadIA 011/F/01).

* For the two institutions, expenses were mainly building repairs, firewood and – for the workhouse – supplies; for poor folk, mainly boarding, clothes, bedding, money, wood and burials.

^ The accounts did not give money values for a few distributions of cloth or clothing: 1 in 1585, 18 in 1586, 2 in 1588 and 15 in 1595.

~ The number in parentheses indicates how many additional people received only cloth or clothing for which no money value was given in the accounts.

Appendix Intro 3

Methodologies and decisions

While the overall patterns described in this book are highly likely to be accurate, at least a few of the individual entries for particular people or family groupings within the datasets may be based upon incorrect identifications or attributions. This appendix lays out where and why uncertainty arose and how such questions were handled.

Information was entered into databases and analysed using the Statistical Package for the Social Sciences (SPSS). One dataset contains entries for individual people on an annual basis, describing what sorts of assistance they received, of what monetary value and in how many payments or distributions, together with their sex, age and marital status each year and an identifying number for their household. In final form, after considerable consolidation of entries for separate weeks and months, that file includes 2,555 cases and 35 variables. A second dataset, with 603 cases and 25 variables, contains a single entry for each individual, pulling together information from the full span of 18 years. Additional files were generated for people assessed for poor rates, who worked for the town, or were paid for assisting poor people. A final set lists all legible baptisms, marriages and burials from the parish register.

In creating the databases and entering material into them, I had help from two exceptionally capable student assistants during the later 1980s. The original databases were set up by Carin Corbitt, now Bentley, in 1986–7, while she was an undergraduate at the University of Colorado at Boulder, double majoring in Computer Science and History.[1] SPSS was at that time in its formative years and difficult to use, as all commands had to be typed in by hand using the proper syntax, but she navigated the complexity with ease. I entered some of the information from the accounts and parish register into the databases. Much of the later data entry and initial preparation of mini-family trees for the recipients was done by Elspeth McIntosh, now Dusinberre, during the summers of 1987 and 1988, while she was an undergraduate at Harvard.[2] Ms Corbitt consolidated the entries within the main databases and added demographic information and material from the other files. She then did the first round of data analysis, compared Hadleigh's patterns of relief with those found in Ipswich and Norwich, and wrote up her work as her senior Honours thesis. I subsequently took notes in searchable text-based files of all relevant entries in the town book and other local records and used materials at the Suffolk Record Offices, the Essex Record Office and The National Archives (Public Record Office). Two talks about poor relief in Hadleigh that I gave at meetings were later published in

---

1. In 2012 Ms Bentley was a senior systems specialist at IBM.

2. Dr Dusinberre was an Associate Professor of Classics in 2012.

3. Marjorie K. McIntosh, 'Networks of care in Elizabethan English towns: the example of Hadleigh, Suffolk', in Horden and Smith (eds), *The locus of care*, pp. 71–89, and 'Poverty, charity, and coercion in Elizabethan England', *Journal of Interdisciplinary History*, 35 (2005), pp. 457–79.

journals or collections of essays.[3] In 2011, having just finished a general book about poor relief in England, 1350–1600, I decided that this town's system of assistance and its unusually detailed records indeed warranted a full case study. I therefore checked all entries in the databases against the original photocopies or notes, added some further information and grouped recipients into households before carrying out the quantitative analyses.

While these processes may sound relatively straightforward, the data as presented here are in fact the result of many preliminary steps and individual decisions, some of which required subjective judgments. Uncertainty could occur at various stages: (a) reading names on the original manuscripts; (b) consolidating multiple spellings of a given surname under a single spelling; (c) deciding to which person unspecific references applied; and (d) assigning individuals to households and generating demographic information.

(a) The manuscripts used for the quantitative elements of this project were written in a variety of hands and survive in diverse physical conditions. Some of the accounts were written by professional clerks, in which case the writing is quite legible and the spelling of names relatively consistent. In other cases, however, local officers apparently prepared their own accounts. Deciphering the extremely rough handwriting of the subcollectors for the poor took considerable palaeographic skill. The writing in the parish register is far more legible and consistent, but the record is not entirely complete. The pages for marriages between 1568 and 1575 are missing, and certain pages in the sections containing marriages and burials have been partially damaged, apparently by moisture, leaving the names faint or illegible. Names for about an eighth of all marriages and a quarter of the burials could not be determined.

(b) The spelling of surnames was not fixed during the sixteenth century. Educated people were generally fairly consistent in their spelling of names, but accountants with minimal schooling often attempted to reproduce in writing what they had heard orally. The spelling of subcollectors for the poor was especially variable. As we began transcribing and entering the names, we adopted a single spelling of each surname but kept a list of variant spellings. In some cases the variations were minor and fairly obvious, such as Alkocke/Awcoke or Cobbolde/Cobboll/Corboulde/Corbolle. Cadge was clearly the same family as Kadge, and Arnsby the same as Earnsby. But was the Mother Cove who received in just one year part of the same family with many recipients usually spelled Cuffe, and was the elderly couple called Willes/Welles related to the larger cluster of people spelled Wiles/Wyles? To resolve such problems we looked at the types of relief given, the years in which relief was awarded and dates of death.

(c) We needed also to decide to which person an imprecise reference applied (e.g., old Gedge, Father Skrevner or Ryvett's girl). When lists of distributed goods record two people with the same surname but different attributes in the same year, they were presumably different people: e.g., blind widow Wolf and Mother Wolf, or Father Cromer of the almshouse and Robert Cromer. But when shoes were given to 'Bartholemew's 3 children', and we know from the parish register that there were four children in the household at the time, we had to make an arbitrary assignment. In doing so, we drew upon information from more clearly designated records. In this example, we knew that shoes were normally given to older children, aged 5–9, often as they were leaving their natal families to take up positions as informal servants in another household. Since the youngest of the Bartholemew children was at that time only three years old, we attributed the shoes to the three older children. Another question derived from the way in which a very few children or young people were described. Whereas most wordings make family relationships clear, phrases like 'the wench at Smith's' or 'the lad at Merydall's' may have referred not to biological children but to servants or other youngsters living in the household. Since, however, we could not make that distinction, we treated those references as children of the family. Nearly all imprecise references could be assigned, but when the information was impossibly minimal (e.g., a few pence given to 'the widow by the pump' or 'the dumb boy', when no other records mention a pump or a dumb boy), we created artificial people called 'unknown' plus an identification number. For those 16 people we entered information about what they received and anything known about their age and marital status but did not assign them to family or household groupings. The detailed analyses of individual people pertain only to the 587 for whom we have more secure information.

(d) Many of the family and household relationships described in this study are based upon probable identifications and links between people, not absolutely definite information. Once the mini-family trees of immediate relatives had been checked, I divided the recipients into household units. In some cases this resulted in as many as three or four separate households of recipients with the same surname. Demographic material was derived in part from the poor relief records and parish register and in part from the family trees and household groupings. We had to decide which people were married couples, how many children they had (Hadleigh's parish register rarely gives the name of the father or mother of babies) and whether the parents were alive at the time a child received relief. The number of children living within the household at the time of receipt of aid refers to those aged 0–12 years who are mentioned in the accounts or parish register, thus providing minimum values: there may have been other children about whom we did not find information, and the children of most of the older recipients had already left home. It was particularly difficult to spot adults who had never married, though one might have expected to see a number of unmarried women in an English clothmaking town of this period. We could only identify these when a woman was consistently described in her own first and last name, never as wife of a named man, widow or mother of children. That created an *a priori* assumption – which we then explored further – that she was single. (The label 'Mother' referred to age, not to marital or procreative status.[4]) Because women whose spouse had died were often called widows, while men in the same position were rarely termed widowers, we have less information about the marital status of men than women.

---

4. Of 14 women termed 'Mother' whose marital status is definitely known, 9 (64 per cent) were widows when they were first described that way, 4 (29 per cent) were currently married, and 1 (7 per cent) had apparently never married. Of 9 men called 'Father', 2 (22 per cent) were widowers when that designation was first used; 7 (78 per cent) were currently married. For the ages of Mothers and Fathers, see Chapter 3, note 4.

Some distributions of goods – canvas, other kinds of cloth, wood and clothing or shoes – did not give a money value for each item. In nearly all cases I was able to establish a value, either from the total given on the account (e.g., 40 ells of canvas worth 40s in sum) or by putting together individual expenses in preparing the distribution (e.g., the amount paid for cutting, bundling and carrying wood from outside the town to people's homes, the almshouses or workhouse). Those totals were then divided by the number of units to generate a value per unit. For a few distributions I used the value per unit for the same item from the previous year. No amounts at all were given in the accounts for distributions of cloth or clothing to one person in 1585, eighteen in 1586 and two in 1595. Those people were included in the analyses of recipients but the value of the items received was excluded from analysis of the total amount expended.

Appendix 1.1

Population information based on Hadleigh's parish register, 1560–99

	1560–64	1565–9	1570–74 #	1575–9	1580–84	1585–9	1590–94	1595–9
Average no. of								
– baptisms	86.6	87.6	89.4	104.2	112.6	106.6	90.6	86.4
– marriages	25.8	20.0	—	25.4	23.2	21.4	22.2	21.2
– burials	59.8	52.8	62.0	48.0	71.8	58.8	71.6	62.0
Estimated total population								
– from baptisms	2,497	2,356	2,723	3,083	3,279	3,253	2,778	2,769
– from marriages	2,113	2,064	—	2,490	2,432	2,208	2,308	2,468
Ratios								
– baptisms/marriages	3.36	4.38	—	4.1	4.85	4.98	4.08	4.08
% of national ratio	100%	133%	—	120%	140%	144%	115%	115%
– baptisms/burials	1.45	1.66	1.44	2.17	1.57	1.81	1.27	1.39
% of national ratio	113%	112%	1.07	141%	99%	137%	103%	112%
Years of exceptionally high mortality			1572		1582–3		1592	

Notes: For each quinquennium, the average number of baptisms and marriages was calculated from the parish register. That number was used in conjunction with the quinquennial crude birth and marriage rates from Table A3.1 of Wrigley and Schofield, *Population history of England*, to obtain a total estimated population. Decadal ratios for baptisms/marriages and quinquennial ratios for baptisms/burials at the national level come from *ibid.*, Tables 6.13 and 6.8.
Hadleigh's marriage register for 1570–74 is defective.

Appendix 1.2

Distribution of wealth, 1524 subsidy, Hadleigh and comparable communities

	Hadleigh (urban plus rural)	16 country towns in Bucks., Rutl., and Sussex	Romford, Essex (a suburban market town), plus its agricultural hinterland
*Level and type of assessment**			
under £2, on wages	114 = 38%	40%	28%
£2, on wages, goods or land	79 = 26%	26%	23%
£3–19, on goods or land	76 = 25%	29%	41%
£20–49, on goods or land	24 = 8%		4%
		} 6% {	
£50 or more, on goods or land	11 = 4%		3%
No. of people assessed	304	average of 136 per town	218

Notes:
* Descriptors of occupational level/status in the comparable places:
  <£2 lesser labourers and servants; lesser cottagers
  £2 prosperous labourers and servants; small craftsmen; prosperous cottagers and lesser husbandmen
  £3–9 lesser/middling tradesmen and craftsmen; middling husbandmen
  £10–19 middling/richer tradesmen and craftsmen; prosperous husbandmen and lesser yeomen
  £20+ prosperous tradesmen and craftsmen; merchants; prosperous yeomen; gentlemen

Sources: *Suffolk in 1524*, pp. 153–7; Cornwall, 'English country towns'; TNA PRO E 179/108/150; and McIntosh, *A community transformed*, pp. 165–9.

Appendix 1.3

Occupations mentioned in Hadleigh records, 1540–99

Occupations	Largest no. of people mentioned per decade	Decade with most people mentioned
A. Woollen cloth and clothing, manufacture and sale		
Clothier/clothmaker (some also merchant or broker)	19	1550s
Weaver/occasionally webster	15	1590s
Draper/mercer	4	1540s
Cardmaker/cardboard maker	3	1540s
Sherman	3	1570s
Fuller/farmer of fulling mill	3	1580s
Dyer/woadsetter	2	1540s
Tailor	2	1580s
Wringer (presumably of wet cloths)	2	1580s–90s
Stainer/painter (probl. of cloth, not wood)	1	1550s/1580s
Currier (of cloth)	1	1570s–90s
Burler (= cloth finisher, removing burls)	1	1580s–90s
Hatter/haberdasher	1	1580s
Wiredrawer (probl. used for making cards)	1	1590s
Total	58	
B. Agriculture and status designations		
Gentleman/esquire/Master/knight	28	1580s
Yeoman	5	1540s
Husbandman	3	1550s
Total	36	
C. Food, drink, and candles		
Butcher	6	1550s
Alehouse or inn keeper/vintner	3	1570s
Miller/farmer of wind mill (for grain)	3	1580s
Baker	1	1550s–60s
Brewer	1	1550s/1580s
(Tallow) chandler	1	1570s
Fishmonger	1	1570s
Fowler	1	1590s
Total	17	
D. Retailers (other than specialised goods)		
Rented a shop or stall of unspecified nature	15	1580s
Merchant (see also clothier + merchant)	1	1540s–1570s
Broker/dealer (see also clothier + broker)	1	1550s
Total	17	

Occupations	Largest no. of people mentioned per decade	Decade with most people mentioned
E. Health, education and writing		
Surgeon	2	1580s
Notary public	2	1580s
Barber	2	1590s
Apothecary	1	1580s
Curer	1	1580s
Total	13	
F. Leather workers		
Cobbler/shoemaker/cordwainer	5	1590s
Glover	3	1540s
Tanner	2	1590s
Collar maker	1	1550s
Total	11	
G. Metal and glass workers		
(Black) smith/iron worker	3	1570s
Plumber	1	1540s
Wheelwright	1	1560s–90s
Bell worker	1	1560s–90s
Glazier/glass worker	1	1590s
Total	7	
H. Wood and building workers		
Cooper	2	1580s
Carpenter	1	1540s–90s
Thatcher	1	1580s
Dauber	1	1590s
Total	5	
I. Clergymen		
Dr of Theology, Divinity, or Law/rector of Hadleigh	4	1590s
Minister/chaplain/vicar	1	1580s–90s
Curate	3	1550s
Total	8	
J. Other		
(Common) carrier/carter	4	1590s
Labourer	3	1580s
Sexton/grave digger	2	1550s
Gardener	1	1550s
Gelder	1	1580s
Total	11	
Total no. of occupations and agriculture/status designations in the largest decades combined	56	
Total no. of people in the largest decades combined	183	

Appendix 2.1

Did grain prices, seasonality and high mortality affect poor relief?

One finds little relationship between grain prices and the level of poor relief in Hadleigh. During six years between 1579 and 1596, Hadleigh's total outlay for charitable assistance was unusually high (£108 or more, excluding expenses for the workhouse), but only three of those years saw unusually high prices for grain (an indexed level of 600 or more).[1] In three other years of high expenditures in Hadleigh, grain prices did not rise above an indexed level of 434, whereas in two other years of exceptionally costly grain, Hadleigh's expenses were no more than £92.

At best a weak correlation is seen between seasonality and the amount of assistance provided. Analysis of weekly or monthly 'benevolence' payments to the poor for the three years in which the accounts are broken down at that level provides no clear indication that assistance increased during the winter and early spring months.[2] In 1579 and 1585 payments did not increase in those seasons, but there may have been some impact in 1594. The highest weekly averages in the latter year came in January and February and then dropped between March and July. The average rose slightly in the late summer and autumn before rising a little further in late November and December. While that pattern might suggest hardship in the colder months, there was no increase in the number of burials during the winter that year.[3] Moreover, the situation in 1594 was complicated by apparent concern on the part of the town's officials with the mounting cost of relief. In late April the size of all regular payments given directly to the poor was reduced. The total for the previous weeks, around 36s 4d, dropped to 31s 6d in the week of 28April, though the number of people assisted did not change. The weekly amount then remained at a somewhat lower level for the rest of the year.

Burials of poor people at the town's expense may have been related at least in part to the total level of mortality in the town as affected by weather and the presence of epidemics. The average number of total burials per month in Hadleigh was higher than national figures in January, February and November (suggesting illnesses associated with cold weather), but lower than national levels in the late summer and early autumn (suggesting a lower incidence of plague and other hot-weather diseases).[4] The

`1. High expenditures for the poor in Hadleigh and high grain prices in 1594, 1595 and 1596; high expenditures in Hadleigh but not high grain prices in 1581, 1588 and 1593; high prices for grain but not high expenditures in Hadleigh in 1586 and 1590 (App. Intro.1 and Thirsk, *Chapters from the agrarian history*, pp. 150–51).

2. For 1579, 1585 and 1594 (HadlA 021/A/02, 021/C/01 and 021/D/02).

3. SRO-I FB 81/D1/1.

4. National indexed figures are from Wrigley and Schofield, *Population history of England*, Table 8.3.

unusually large number of payments for the burial of destitute poor people in a few years may have resulted from mortality during plague epidemics. Of 153 payments for winding sheets or burials of the poor, 48 were scattered over the course of 12 years. In three years, however, many more public burials were provided. In 1582, the town paid for the burial of 24 poor people and in 1592 for 41.The parish register indicates that 1582–3 and 1592 were years of exceptionally high mortality, almost certainly due to the plague.[5] But in 1591, 40 poor were buried by the town, and that was not a year of unusually high mortality. Burials of the poor, which numbered nearly 8 times above normal, included 38 people described merely as 'poor folk', without individual names. If mortality had been severe, one might have thought that these were people whom the collectors had been unable to identify before burial, but that was evidently not the case. Nor was the price of grain and other agricultural products high in that year.[6] A more likely explanation is that in 1591 the collectors were experimenting with housing some of the sick poor together, paying people to provide simple care for them as well as food and healing. The town may therefore have felt responsible for burying those people whom it had taken into care even if they did not record their individual names.

---

5. During the last four months of 1582, 71 burials were recorded for the parish as a whole, with another 28 the following January and February. The 12-month total for September 1582 to August 1583 was 130 burials, 145% higher than the average of 53 for the previous nine years. During the calendar year 1592, 118 burials were recorded, 97% higher than the average of 60 for the 7 previous years. In 1591, below, 63 burials were recorded, barely above the eight-year average of 6 and with no month above the normal range of deaths.

6. Thirsk, *Chapters from the agrarian history*, p. 121. For below, see Chapter 5, 'Care for people who were ill or disabled', below.

Appendix 2.2

Occasional goods or services given to individual poor people

| | No. of items distributed or services rendered | For household goods | | Total value of goods and services distributed over the full span (in pounds) | Recipients of goods or services | | | |
| | | | | | No. of distributions or services to: | | | |
		Total no. of units distributed over full span	Aver. amt distributed annually per person		Adult women	Adult men	Children/ teenagers	No info.
Household goods								
Canvas (in ells) #	714	1,063 ells	67 inches	55.04	387	252	70	5
Various kinds of woollen cloth (including broad blanket and narrow twill, usually in yards)	361	504 yards	52 inches	51.33	140	79	141	1
Wood for fuel (in loads)	240	304 loads	1.3 loads	30.73	115	119	5	1
Clothing (coats, waistcoats, petticoats, stockings, hose, smocks, shirts and other)	208			c.43.0	47	54	105	2
Shoes: making or mending	90			4.73	5	32	51	2
Winding sheets or burials ^	167			c. 14.5	33	44	32	58
Services other than boarding and burial (sewing = 25; healing = 16; washing = 4) ~	45			16.6	16	12	15	2

Notes: Household goods were usually distributed once per year, while clothing and services were awarded as needed throughout the year.

Ells were calculated here as 45 inches in length, yards as 36 inches.

^ Includes sheets or burials for unnamed poor folk: an unspecified number in 1590 (entered as 4 here based on the size of the payment); 38 in 1591; and an unspecified number in 1592 (entered as 12, based on the size of the payment). Most people received only a sheet or burial, but eight were given both.

~ For boarding, see Chapter 3, 'Individual recipients of assistance', below.

Appendix 2.3

Bequests to the poor by religious testament, Hadleigh wills, 1500–99

| Nature of religious testament | Wills with bequests to the poor | | | | Wills with no bequests to the poor | Total |
	Only at burial/obit	Outright only	Burial and outright	Total		
Traditional/Catholic	2 = 10% of traditional wills	2 = 10%	0	4 = 20%	16 = 80%	20 = 21% of all wills
Neutral/none/mixed*	4* = 11%	16* = 42%	3 = 8%	23 = 61%	15** = 39%	38 = 40%
Mildly/probably reformist	1 = 6%	10 = 56%	0	11 = 61%	7 = 39%	18 = 19%
Definitely Protestant	0	15 = 75%	3 = 15%	18 = 90%	2 = 10%	20 = 21%
Total	7 = 7% of all wills	43 = 45%	6 = 6%	56 = 58%	40 = 42%	96

Notes: For which testators are included, see Table 1.1, first note; for the distinction between distributions at burials/obits and outright assistance, see Table 2.2, note #. I did not count residual bequests (property or money that would go to the poor only if the immediate beneficiaries died without heir).
* Each asterisk designates a mixed testament of faith, containing both traditional and Protestant elements.

Total amount bequeathed to Hadleigh's poor in surviving wills, by period

| Periods | Amount bequeathed (in pounds) | | | | | Total, cash value given | Average amount with cash value bequeathed per year |
| | By local people | | | By outsiders | | | |
	No. of wills with bequests to poor	Cash value given	No cash value given	No. of wills with bequests to poor	Cash value given		
1500–33, Catholic	4	10.10	wheat and malt to be sold at low price to poor	0		10.10	0.30
1534–47, early reformed influences in Hadleigh	7	37.33		0		37.33	2.87
1547–53, Edward VI	15	176.58	cloth to be sold, profits to poor; 2 parcels of land, profits to poor in perpetuity	0		176.58	27.17
1553–8, Mary	4	298.97^		0		298.97^	54.36^
1558–79, early Elizabethan	18	386.25	wheat; a tenement, income for poor in perpetuity towards building a Bridewell; cloth and wood; 6 bushels of wheat	2	16.67	404.92	19.28
1580–99, late Elizabethan #	8	188.80	2 tenements, income for clothing in perpetuity	4	73.33	262.13	13.11
Total	56	1100.03		6	93.33	1193.36	

Notes: Bequests to be distributed over a designated period of years or in perpetuity, if they had a cash value, have been counted within periods, starting in the year after the will was proved. Thus, a bequest of £10 per year for 10 years left in 1551 would be counted as a total of £20 in Edward's reign, £50 in Mary's reign and £30 in the early Elizabethan period.

^ These values are distorted by two large bequests from the John Ravens, father and son, towards new almshouses.

This table excludes a gift by Alice Parking in 1590 of two tenements whose income was to be used towards establishing a

Appendix 3.1

Named people buried at the town's expense

A. Age and sex of individual recipients of winding sheet or burial

	Children/teenagers	20–49 yrs	50+ yrs	Age unknown	Total
Females	12	9	18	2	41 = 41%
Males	15	13	19	9	56 = 57%
Total individuals	29* = 29%	22 = 22%	37 = 37%	11 = 11%	99*

B. Number of recipients per household

	No. of households	No. of individuals
1 person buried	61 = 78%	61 = 63%
2 people buried		
Husband and wife (5 of them elderly)	7	14
Mother and child	3	6
Father and child	2	4
Sibling children	4	8
Total	16 = 21%	32 = 33%
4 people buried		
Father and 3 children	1 = 1%	4 = 4%
Total	78 #	97 #

Notes:
* Includes two children of unknown sex.
# Excludes two people who could not be assigned to a household.

Appendix 3.2

Recipients of poor relief in Hadleigh and Norwich in the 1570s

| | Hadleigh, 1579 | | | | | Norwich, 1570 | | | | |
| | Females | | Males | | | Females | | Males | | |
	Number	Aver. amt recd/wk (in pence)	Number	Aver. amt recd/wk (in pence)	Total number	Number	Aver. amt recd/wk (in pence)	No. and %	Aver. amt recd/wk (in pence)	Total number
Children and teens	7 = 8%	7.5	5 = 5%	2.0	13 # = 14%	0		0		0
Younger adults (probl. or def. aged 20–49 yrs)										
Married	4 = 4%	1.8	10 = 11%	2.5	14 = 15%	2 = 1%	2.5	23 = 14%	2.5	25 = 15%
Widow(er)	3 = 3%	5.0	0	0	3 = 3%	21* = 13%	1.7	0	0	21* = 13%
Marital status unknown	1 = 1%	0.2	4 = 4%	1.6	5 = 5%	2 = 1%	2.0	0	0	2 = 1%
(Disabled or sick)	(1 = 1%)	10.6	(2 = 2%)	2.1	(3 = 3%)	(3 = 2%)	2.7	(2 = 1%)	2.0	(5 = 3%)
Total	8 = 9%	2.8	14 = 15%	2.2	22 = 24%	25 = 15%	1.7	23 = 14%	2.5	48 = 29%
Older adults (probl. or def. aged 50+ yrs)										
Married	11 = 12%	4.1	8 = 9%	7.7	19 = 21%	1 = 1%	2.0	32 = 19%	3.6	33 = 20%
Widow(er)	5 = 5%	3.1	1 = 1%	12.4	6 = 7%	49* = 30%	2.5	0		49* = 30%
Marital status unknown	13 = 14%	6.8	7 = 8%	4.5	20 = 22%	31 = 19%	3.0	3 = 2%	3.8	34 = 21%
(Disabled or sick)	(1 = 1%)	1.7	(2 = 2%)	7.5	(3 = 3%)	(20 = 12%)	2.9	(11 = 7%)	4.0	(31 = 19%)
Total	29 = 32%	5.1	16 = 18%	6.6	45 = 49%	81 = 49%	2.7	35 = 21%	3.6	116 = 70%
Adult, age unknown	6 = 7%	3.8	5 = 5%	1.1	11 = 12%	1 = 1%	2.5	0	0	1 = 1%
Total	50 = 55%	4.9	40 = 44%	3.8	91 #	107 = 65%	2.5	58 = 35%	3.2	165

Notes: I am grateful to Carin Corbett (Bentley), who prepared the Norwich figures for this table from *Norwich census of the poor*. Disabled or sick people were counted under their marital status but noted separately as well, in parentheses.

\# Includes one child of unknown sex and age.

Appendix 3.3

Recipients of poor relief in Hadleigh and Ipswich in the 1590s

| | Hadleigh, 1594 | | | | | Ipswich, 1597 | | | | |
| | Females | | Males | | | Females | | Males | | |
	Number	Aver. amt recd/wk (in pence)	Number	Aver. amt recd/wk (in pence)	Total number	Number	Aver. amt recd/wk (in pence)	No. and %	Aver. amt recd/wk (in pence)	Total number
Younger adults (probl. or def. aged 20–49 yrs)										
Single	1 = 1%	4.0	0	0	1 = 1%	0	0	0	0	0
Married	3 = 3%	6.1	9 = 8%	2.4	12 = 11%	0	0	2 = 4%	9.0	2 = 4%
Widow(er)	8 = 7%	1.8	1 = 1%	7.4	9 = 8%	5 = 11%	5.2	0		5 = 11%
Marital status unknown	0	0	3 = 3%	1.7	3 = 3%	2 = 4%	5.9	1 = 2%	7.0	3 = 7%
(Disabled or sick)	(0)	0	(0)	0	(0)	(0)		(3 = 6%)	8.0	(3 = 7%)
Total	12 = 11%	3.0	13 = 12%	2.6	25 = 23%	7 = 15%	5.4	3 = 6%	8.3	10 = 22%
Older adults (probl. or def. aged 50+ yrs)										
Single	2 = 2%	6.6	0		2 = 2%	0	0	0	0	0
Married	10 = 9%	6.4	5 = 5%	7.6	15 = 14%	0	0	14 = 30%	8.2	14 = 30%
Widow(er)	26 = 23%	4.5	4 = 4%	5.8	30 = 27%	14 = 30%	7.2	0		14 = 30%
Marital status unknown	3 = 3%	4.7	6 = 5%	5.1	9 = 8%	5 = 11%	6.9	2 = 4%	5.8	7 = 15%
(Disabled or sick)	(2 = 2%)	3.7	(3 = 3%)	4.5	(5 = 5%)	(5 = 11%)	8.8	(7 = 15%)	10.0	(12 = 26%)
Total	41 = 37%	5.0	15 = 14%	6.1	56 = 50%	19 = 41%	7.1	16 = 35%	7.9	35 = 76%
Adult, age unknown	9 = 8%	3.3	4 = 4%	0.7	13 = 12%	1 = 2%	6.6	0	0	1 = 2%
Total	66 = 59%	4.3	44 = 40%	3.2	111 #	27 = 59%	6.6	19 = 41%	7.9	46

Notes: I am grateful to Carin Corbett (Bentley), who prepared the Ipswich figures for this table from *Poor relief in Elizabethan Ipswich*. Disabled or sick people were counted under their marital status but noted separately as well, in parentheses.
\# Includes 1 child of unknown sex and age.

Appendix 3.4

Types of relief received by individuals in 1582, by sex and age

Ages	Females	Males	Sex unknown and institutions	Category total
0–4 years	(N = 2)	(N = 8)	(N = 0)	(N = 10)
Hhg only		3		
Clothes/shoes only	1	1		
Occasional money only	1			
Occasional money + burial		1		
Burial only		1		
Total, occasional only	2	6		8
Regular money + burial		1		
Boarding + clothes/shoes		1		
Total, regular money or boarding	0	2		2
5–9 years	(N = 5)	(N = 6)	(N = 0)	(N = 11)
Hhg only		2		
Clothes/shoes only	2	1		
Hhg + clothes/shoes		1		
Clothes/shoes + burial		1		
Total, occasional only	2	5		7
Regular money + burial	1			
Boarding	1			
Boarding + clothes/shoes + occasional money	1	1		
Total, regular money or boarding	3	1		4
Child, age unknown	(N = 2)	(N = 10)	(N = 4)	(N = 16)
Hhg only	1	2	1	
Clothes/shoes only		1	1	
Hhg + clothes/shoes		1		
Burial only		2	2	
Total, occasional only	1	6	4	11
Boarding	1	3		
Boarding + Hhg + clothes/shoes		1		
Total, regular money or boarding	1	4		5
Age 10–19 (N = 0)	(N = 1)	(N = 0)	(N = 1)	
Burial only		1		
Total, occasional only		1		1

Ages	Females	Males	Sex unknown and institutions	Category total
Age 20–49	(N = 14)	(N = 21)	(N = 0)	(N = 35)
Hhg only	10	4		
Clothes/shoes only		3		
Occasional money only	1	8		
Occasional money + clothes/shoes		1		
Occasional money + burial		1		
Burial only	1			
Total, occasional only	12	17		29
Regular money		3		
Regular money + Hhg	1			
Regular money + clothes/shoes		1		
Boarding	1			
Total, regular money or boarding	2	4		6
Age 50+	(N = 33)	(N = 30)	(N = 0)	(N = 63)
Hhg only	7	8		
Occasional money only	7	5		
Occasional money + Hhg		2		
Occasional money + burial	2	1		
Burial only	2	1		
Total, occasional only	18	17		35
Regular money	11	2		
Regular money + Hhg	3	5		
Regular money + clothes/shoes		1		
Regular money + Hhg + clothes/shoes		1		
Regular money + Hhg + burial	1			
Boarding		1		
Boarding + Hhg		1		
Boarding + Hhg + occasional money		1		
Boarding + regular money + Hhg + clothes/shoes		1		
Total, regular money or boarding	15	13		28
Adult, age unknown	(N = 7)	(N = 5)	(N = 0)	(N = 12)
Hhg only	3	2		
Clothes/shoes+ burial	1			
Occasional money only	2	1		
Occasional money + burial		1		
Total, occasional only	6	4		10
Regular money	1			
Regular money + clothes/shoes + burial		1		
Total, regular money or boarding	1	1		2

Ages		Females	Males	Sex unknown and institutions	Category total
No information about age		(N = 1)	(N = 1)		
	Boarding			1	1
Other	Almshouses: firewood only			1 entry	1 entry
	Poor people (unspecified): clothes only			1 entry	1 entry
Total		63 = 42% of total	81 = 54%	5 indivs = 3%	149 indivs + 2 other entries
Summary by type of assistance					
	Occasional assistance only	41 = 65%	56 = 69%	4 indivs = 80% + 2 other entries	101 indivs + 2 other entries
	Regular money or boarding (with or without occasional assistance as well)	22 = 34%	25 = 31%	1 indiv. = 20%	48 indivs = 32%

Notes:
Hhg = Household goods = lengths of canvas and/or lengths of woollen cloth and/or loads of firewood, given once in the year.
Clothes/shoes = either or both items, given as needed.
Occasional money = no more than nine payments in the year.
Regular money = 10 or more payments in the year.

Appendix 5.1

Mini-biographies of twelve residents of Hadleigh's almshouses, 1582–1602

Biographical information has been assembled from the list of almshouse residents in 1594, those who received payments there in 1602, poor relief accounts from 1579 to 1596, the parish registers, 1558–1602, and other town records.[1] The sketches below constitute the most likely individual histories given the information available.

Ann or Agnes Berdwell, for whom there is no record of a marriage prior to 1595, was aged 68 in 1594.[2] Five years earlier she had started to receive canvas or occasional money, and it was only recently that she had moved into the Benton Street almshouse. Her weekly stipend in 1594 was just 7d, suggesting that she was still able to earn some money. Among her neighbours in the house at that time were John and Katherine Cromer (see below). After Katherine's death in 1595, John married Ann, who was then 70. John died two years later, but Ann remained in the almshouse through 1602, when she received 8d per week, now aged 76.

John and Joan Bough were married in 1559 and had a family of children born in the following 15 years. John paid poor rates in 1579 and 1582, while the family was living in Biggen – later Angel – Street. His assessments were at the fairly low level of 3d or 4d per quarter. The Boughs continued to be economically self-sufficient through at least 1596, receiving no poor relief, but by 1602 they were in an almshouse, each one receiving 8d per week. At that time they would probably have been in their 70s.

Widow **Elizabeth Bull** was aged 68 in 1594. In 1568, when she was 42, she had married Steven Bull, a labourer, in what was probably not her initial marriage. During the early 1580s Steven did odd jobs for the town, but by 1587 he was dead and Elizabeth began to receive annual grants of wood or canvas. She may have moved into Pykenham's almshouse in 1590, when she was aged 64, for she received regular payments of 6d per week in the next few years; she was certainly there in 1594, when she was given 7d weekly. By 1602, when she was 76, she received at the exceptionally high level of 10d for the entire 52 weeks.

The oldest almshouse resident in 1594 was **John Cromer**, aged 90, who was then married to **Katherine**, aged 63. They lived in the Benton Street houses. John and Katherine had married in 1565, when he was 61 and she was 34, probably not the first marriage for him and perhaps not for her. Between 1580 and 1594 the couple received occasional grants of blanketing, canvas and clothing while still living at home. They

---

1. HadlA 037/G/01 and 022/A/04; 021/A/02–06, 021/B/05–09, 021/C/01–18 and 021/D/01–04; 004/A/01; and SRO-I FB 81/D1/1.

2. In the list of residents in 1594, this surname was written as Berdolf, a name that does not appear in any other Hadleigh records; it was presumably a variant of Berdall (or Berdwell/Bardwell), a common local name.

apparently moved into the almshouse in 1585, when he was 81 and she was 54; at first they received 6d weekly, but the sum had risen to 9d by 1594. Katherine died in April 1595 at the age of 64. After fourteen months of solitary living, John, then 92, married his neighbour in the almshouse, Ann Berdwell (see above). John died in 1598 at the age of 94.

Living in Pykenham's almshouse in 1594, **Katherine Debenham** (or Debnam, as it was pronounced and usually written locally) was a widow aged 72 years. She had married William Debnam by 1550, when she was aged 28, and various children were born over the following 16 years. William died in 1584, when Katherine was 62, and the following year she received regular payments at 5d per week. In 1588 she was given some canvas while living in the Swynburne household, though the town was not paying to board her there. By 1590, at the age of 68, she had moved into the almshouse, where she received 6d per week at first, then 9d. She died in 1597, aged 75.

Father **John Gedge** was a resident of one of the almshouses in 1582. The Gedges were the most extensive poor relief family in Hadleigh, with nine recipients spread among three separate households and over three generations. John was already in an almshouse by 1579, when he was given the exceptionally large sum of 1s per week throughout the year in addition to the canvas, cloth and clothes he continued to receive for the next four years. In 1582 he was boarded temporarily with another poor relief family, probably due to illness or an injury; he died two years later.

Simon Merydall (occasionally written as Meridaye), a widower living in Pykenham's almshouse, was aged 64 in 1594. He and Alice Cooe, part of a local family with many members who received relief, had married in 1575, when he was aged 45. This was probably a second marriage for him, and over the next decade he and Alice had five children. Simon was given health care and some money during an illness in 1579, but he and his family were then self-sufficient for the next six years. In 1586 his daughters Anne, Emily and Marjorie – aged 5, 7 and 8 years – were given clothing, probably when they went into service. Between 1587 and 1591 Simon received fuel, canvas, cloth and occasional cash, and Alice was given money during the illness that led to her death in November 1591. In that same year, at the age of 61, Simon began receiving regular weekly payments and by 1594 he was in the almshouse. He died in 1598 at the age of 68.

John Mychell was aged 74 in 1594 and his wife **Joann** (called **Ann** on the 1594 list) was 63. John had married Marian Trascam, probably a second wife, in 1565, when he was 45. Between 1579 and 1585, while living in Benton Street, he paid poor rates at the very low level of 2d per quarter. In October 1593, after Marian's death, the 73-year-old John married Joann Pryor, a widow aged 62 whose previous husband had died five years before. Neither John nor Joann received any assistance from the town until they moved into Pykenham's almshouse in 1594 and began getting weekly payments. In 1602, John, then aged 82, lived in the almshouse for nine weeks before his death, while Joann – aged 71 – remained for the full year, receiving the normal 8d per week.

Joan Wolf was a widow aged 71 years in 1594. In 1579, when she was 56, she was described as Mother Wolf and received cash assistance twelve times during the year; her husband John, 'old Father Wolf', received regular weekly payments. Both of them were given canvas and occasional additional money during the next few years, and in 1585, at the age of 64, Joan began to receive ongoing payments. The couple may have moved into Pykenham's almshouse then. John died in 1589, and by 1594 Joan was said to be blind. In 1602 she received the unusually large stipend of 12d per week throughout the year. She died in February 1603, when she was 80 years old.

References

Manuscripts in the Hadleigh Archive (HadlA), Guildhall–Town Hall complex

The list below shows two references for each document: the first is the current reference, used in this study, while the one noted as (ex-) is the form cited in W.A.B. Jones's *Hadleigh through the ages* and in the essays I have previously published about Hadleigh.

001/A/01 (ex-1/A/1). Inspeximus charter confirming grant of weekly market and fair, 1432

001/B/01 (ex-1/B/1). Conveyance of market and rights, including Cherchecrofte, 1438

001/C/01 (ex-1/C/1). Nineteenth-century summary of grant by Edward VI to Archbishop Cranmer, freedom from toll for men of Hadleigh

001/C/02 (ex-1/C/2). Nineteenth-century abstract of confirmation of existing liberties and privileges by Elizabeth I

001/C/03 (ex-1/C/3). Nineteenth-century abstract of exemplification by Elizabeth I confirming letters patent from time of Edward the Confessor, giving privileges to tenants of Dean and Chapter of Canterbury at Hadleigh

004/A/01 (ex-4/1). Book of town accounts, memoranda and other records, 1534–1619

011/F/01 (ex-11/F/1). Account book, Julian Beamont's charity, 1588 ff.

011/N/01 (ex-11/A/2). Account book, Alice Parkin's charity, 1580 ff.

021/A/01 (ex-21/01). Accounts, market bailiffs and churchwardens, 1547–9

021/A/02 (ex-21/07). Accounts, collector, market bailiffs, churchwardens, subcollectors, 1579

021/A/03 (ex-21/11). Accounts, subcollectors, churchwardens, market bailiffs, chief collector, 1582

021/A/04 (ex-21/27). Accounts, hospital, 1595

021/A/05 (ex-21/28). Accounts, chief collector, 1596

021/A/06 (ex-21/29). Accounts, chief collector, including charges for hospital, 1598

021/B/01 (ex-21/03). Accounts, collector, 1569

021/B/02 (ex-21/04). Accounts, collector, 1570

021/B/03 (ex-21/05). Accounts, collector, 1571

021/B/04 (ex-21/06). Accounts, collector, 1572

021/B/05 (ex-21/09). Accounts, chief collector, 1580

021/B/06 (ex-21/10). Accounts, chief collector, 1581

021/B/07 (ex-21/12). Accounts, chief collector, 1583

021/B/08 (ex-21/15). Accounts, chief collector, 1587

021/B/09 (ex-21/18). Accounts, (chief) collector for the poor, including hospital, 1589

021/C/01 (ex-21/13). Accounts, subcollectors, 1585

021/C/02 (ex-21/16). Accounts, chief collector, 1588

021/C/03 (ex-21/17). Accounts, chief collector, 1589

021/C/04 (ex-21/19). Accounts, subcollectors, 1590

021/C/05 (ex-21/20). Accounts, subcollectors, 1591

021/C/06 (ex-21/21). Accounts, chief collector, 1591

021/C/07 (ex-21/22). Accounts, chief collector, 1592

021/C/08 (ex-21/23). Accounts, chief collector, 1593

021/C/09 (ex-21/30). Accounts, chief collector, 1599

021/D/01 (ex-21/14). Accounts, chief collector, 1586

021/D/02 (ex-21/24). Accounts, subcollectors, 1594

021/D/03 (ex-21/25). Accounts, chief collector, 1594

021/D/04 (ex-21/26). Accounts, chief collector, 1595

021/E/01 (ex-21/02). Accounts, collector, 1564

022/A/04 (ex-22/04). Accounts, undercollector for the almshouses, 1602

025/A/01 (ex-25/09). Will of John Brownsmith, 1485

025/B/04 (ex-25/03). Extract from will of Thomas Alabaster, 1591

025/B/05 (ex-25/04). Extract from will of Olivor Aylerde, 1592

025/C/01 (ex-25/11). Extract from will of Edward Clarke, 1583

025/D/05 (ex-25/24). Extract from will of Thomas Orson, 1569

025/D/08 (ex-25/26). Extract from will of Edmund Painter, 1572

025/D/09 (ex-25/27). Extract from will of Alicia Parkins, 1580

025/E/01 (ex-25/29). Will of Dr Pykenham, 1497

025/G/02 (ex-25/36). Extract from will of John Raven, 1555

025/G/04 (ex-25/38). Extract from will of John Raven, 1555

025/I/03 (ex-25/53). Will of John Daniel, 1507

026/C/06 (ex-26/26). Bond, John Hoper *et al.* to Henry Doyle *et al.*, £10 for Gild of St John, 1542

026/C/07 (ex-26/27). Bond, William Gleson *et al.* to Henry Doyle *et al.* for £12 for Gild of Jesus, 1542

026/C/08 (ex-26/28). Bond, Robert Hood *et al.* to Henry Doyle *et al.* for 5 marks for Gild of St John, 1542

026/D/04 (ex-26/32). Bond, James Walter *et al.* to Robert Veysye *et al.* for £20, concerning a gild, 1544

026/D/05 (ex-26/33). Bond, Henry Boole *et al.* to Henry Doyle *et al.* for £10 for Gild of St John, 1545

026/E/02 (ex-26/42). Bond, Richard Smyth to William Forth *et al.*, £6, re taking orphaned children, 1581

026/E/05 (ex-26/45). Bond, Thomas Corbold to Edmund Doyle *et al.*, £10, concerning taking girl as servant, 1588

026/G/02 (ex-26/46). Bond, George Wylde to Edward Doyly *et al.*, £20, concerning poor newcomers, 1588

026/G/03 (ex-26/47). Bond, John Holbard to William Forth *et al.*, £10, concerning expulsion of girl from the town, 1590

026/G/04 (ex-26/48). Bond, Edward Doyly of Layham to John Still *et al.*, £10, concerning a woman taken vagrant and sent to workhouse, 1590

026/G/05 (ex-26/50). Bond, Nicholas Spincke to Henry Doylye *et al.*, £10, concerning taking an orphan boy, 1592

026/H/05 (ex-26/44). Translation of bond, Thomas Corbold to Edmund Doyley *et al.*, £10, concerning taking boy as servant, 1588

037/G/01 (ex-11/A/3). Report of visitors, undated but 1594

Printed primary sources

Accounts of the feoffees of the town lands of Bury St Edmunds, 1569–1622, ed. Margaret Statham, Suffolk Records Society, vol. 46 (Woodbridge, 2003).

Acts of the Privy Council of England, 1542–1604, ed. J.R. Dasent, 32 vols (London, 1890–1907).

An index of indentures of Norwich apprentices enrolled with the Norwich assembly, Henry VII–George II, eds W.M. Rising and P. Millican, Norfolk Record Society, vol. 29 (Norwich, 1959).

Calendar of letters and papers, foreign and domestic, of the reign of Henry VIII, 22 vols in 37 parts (London, 1864–1932).

Carew, Thomas, 'A caveat for craftesmen and clothiers' and 'The reward of godlinesse', in his *Certaine godly and necessarie sermons* (London, 1603).

Certaine sermons or homilies, eds Mary Ellen Rickey and T.B. Stroup (Gainesville, FL, 1968).

The chorography of Suffolk, ed. Diarmaid MacCulloch, Suffolk Records Society, vol. 19 (Ipswich, 1976).

Cranmer, Thomas, *Miscellaneous writings and letters of Thomas Cranmer*, vol. ii, ed. J.E. Cox, Parker Society (Cambridge, 1846).

Deloney, Thomas, *The novels of Thomas Deloney*, ed. Merritt E. Lawlis (Bloomington, IN, 1961).

Foxe, John, *Actes and monuments of matters most special and memorable, happenyng in the church* (London, 1563 and later editions).

Hall, Edward, *Hall's chronicle* (London, 1809).

The Norwich census of the poor, 1570, ed. John F. Pound, Norfolk Record Society, vol. 40 (Norwich, 1971).

Poor relief in Elizabethan Ipswich, ed. John Webb, Suffolk Records Society, vol. 9 (Ipswich, 1966).

Reyce, Robert, *Suffolk in the XVIIth century: the breviary of Suffolk*, ed. Francis Hervey (London, 1902).

Statutes of the realm, 12 vols (London, 1810–28).

Suffolk in 1524: subsidy returns, Suffolk Green Books 10 (Woodbridge, 1910).

Suffolk in 1568: subsidy returns, Suffolk Green Books 12 (Bury St Edmunds, 1909).

Taylor, John, *Carriers cosmographie* (London, 1637).

Visitation articles and injunctions of the period of the Reformation, vol. ii, eds Walter H. Frere and W.M. Kennedy (London, 1910).

Wriothesley, Charles, *A chronicle of England during the reigns of the Tudors*, vol. i, ed. W.D. Hamilton, Camden Society, new series (London, 1875).

Secondary studies

Andrews, Sue, 'The charitable response to poverty during the late medieval and early modern periods in the local context of Hadleigh, Suffolk', MA thesis (University of Essex, 2000).

— and Springall, Tony, *Hadleigh and the Alabaster family: the story of a Suffolk town during the Tudor and Stuart periods* (privately printed, Bildeston, Suffolk, 2005).

Anon., 'Changing names in the High Street', *The Hadleigh Historian*, 4 (2011), p. 19.

—, 'Hadleigh on the map VII: medieval town planning', *The Hadleigh Historian*, 7 (2011–12), pp. 15–17.

—, 'This is not the Guildhall!', *The Hadleigh Historian*, 5 (2011), pp. 4–7.

—, 'Women of Hadleigh V: Alice Parkins', *The Hadleigh Historian*, 5 (2011), pp. 12–14.

—, 'Women of Hadleigh VII: Mathilda Groome', *The Hadleigh Historian*, 7 (2011–12), p. 20.

Archer, Ian, 'Hospitals in sixteenth- and seventeenth-century England', in Scheutz *et al.* (eds), *Europaeisches spitalwesen*, pp. 53–74.

Bailey, Mark, *Medieval Suffolk: an economic and social history, 1200–1500* (Woodbridge, 2007).

Beier, A.L., 'The social problems of an Elizabethan country town: Warwick, 1580–90', in Clark (ed.), *Country towns in pre-industrial England*, pp. 46–85.

—, 'Poverty and progress in early modern England', in Beier, Cannadine and Rosenheim (eds), *The first modern society*, pp. 201–39.

—, Cannadine, David and Rosenheim, James M. (eds), *The first modern society: essays in honour of Lawrence Stone* (Cambridge, 1989).

Ben-Amos, Ilana Krausman, *The culture of giving: informal support and gift-exchange in early modern England* (Cambridge, 2008).

Botelho, Lynn A., *Old age and the English poor law, 1500–1700* (Woodbridge, 2004).

Brown, W. Newman, 'The receipt of poor relief and family situation', in Smith (ed.), *Land, kinship and life-cycle*, pp. 405–22.

Clark, Peter (ed.), *Country towns in pre-industrial England* (Leicester, 1981).

Collinson, Patrick, 'Christian socialism in Elizabethan Suffolk: Thomas Carew and his *Caveat for Clothiers*', in Rawcliffe *et al.* (eds), *Counties and communities*, pp. 161–78.

—, 'Puritanism and the poor', in Horrox and Jones (eds), *Pragmatic utopias*, pp. 242–58.

Cornwall, Julian, 'English country towns in the fifteen twenties', *Economic History Review*, 2nd ser., 15 (1962), pp. 54–69.

Craig, John, *Reformation, politics and polemics* (Aldershot, 2001).

Dymond, David and Paine, Clive, *The spoil of Melford church: the reformation in a Suffolk parish* (Ipswich, 1992).

Hampson, E.M., *The treatment of poverty in Cambridgeshire, 1597–1834* (Cambridge, 1934).

Hindle, Steve, *On the parish? The micro-politics of poor relief in rural England, c. 1550–1750* (Oxford, 2004).

Horden, Peregrine, and Smith, Richard (eds), *The locus of care* (London, 1998).

Horrox, Rosemary, and Rees Jones, Sarah (eds), *Pragmatic utopias* (Cambridge, 2001).

Jones, W.A.B., 'Hadleigh, a Viking royal town', typescript published in reduced form as *Hadleigh through the ages*.

—, *Hadleigh through the ages* (Ipswich, 1977).

Kennell, Roger, *Hadleigh Deanery Tower through six centuries* (Hadleigh, 2011).

MacCulloch, Diarmaid, 'Kett's rebellion in context', in Slack (ed.), *Rebellion, popular protest and the social order*, pp. 39–62.

—, *Suffolk and the Tudors* (Oxford, 1986).

—, *Thomas Cranmer: a life* (New Haven, CT, 1996).

McIntosh, Marjorie Keniston, 'Servants and the household unit in an Elizabethan English community', *Journal of Family History*, 9 (1984), pp. 3–23.

—, *A community transformed: the manor and Liberty of Havering, 1500–1620* (Cambridge, 1991).

—, *Controlling misbehavior in England, 1370–1600* (Cambridge, 1998).

—, 'Networks of care in Elizabethan English towns: the example of Hadleigh, Suffolk', in Horden and Smith (eds), *The locus of care*, pp. 71–89.

—, 'Poverty, charity, and coercion in Elizabethan England', *Journal of Interdisciplinary History*, 35 (2005), pp. 457–79.

—, *Working women in English society, 1300–1620* (Cambridge, 2005).

—, *Poor relief in England, 1350–1600* (Cambridge, 2012).

—, 'Poor relief in Elizabethan communities: an analysis of collectors' accounts', forthcoming.

Ottaway, Susannah R., *The decline of life: old age in eighteenth-century England* (Cambridge, 2004).

Pilgrim, John E., 'The cloth industry in Essex and Suffolk, 1558–1640', MA thesis (University of London, 1940).

Rawcliffe, Carole, Virgoe, Roger, and Wilson, R.G. (eds), *Counties and communities: essays on East Anglian history presented to Hassell Smith* (Norwich, 1996).

Scheutz, Martin, Sommerlechner, A., Weigl, H., and Weiss, A.S. (eds), *Europaeisches spitalwesen. institutionelle fuersorge in mittelalter und frueher neuzeit* (Munich, 2008).

Slack, Paul (ed.), *Rebellion, popular protest and the social order in early modern England* (Cambridge, 1984).

Slack, Paul, *Poverty and policy in Tudor and Stuart England* (London, 1988).

Smith, Richard M. (ed.), *Land, kinship and life-cycle* (Cambridge, 1984).

Sokoll, Thomas, *Household and family among the poor: the case of two Essex communities in the late eighteenth and early nineteenth centuries* (Bochum, 1993).

Statham, Margaret, *Jankyn Smyth and the Guildhall feoffees*, Guildhall Feoffment Trust (Bury St Edmunds, 1981).

Thirsk, Joan (ed.), *Chapters from the agrarian history of England and Wales, 1500–1750*, vol. i, Economic change: prices, wages, profits and rents 1500–1750, ed. Peter J. Bowden (Cambridge, 1990).

Thornton, Gladys A., *A history of Clare, Suffolk* (Cambridge, 1928).

Unwin, George, *Studies in economic history: the collected papers of George Unwin*, ed. R.H. Tawney (1927; London, 1958).

VCH Suffolk [Victoria county history of Suffolk], vol. ii (London, 1907).

Wales, Tim, 'Poverty, poor relief and the life cycle', in Smith (ed.), *Land, kinship and life-cycle*, pp. 351–404.

Wigmore, Elizabeth, *Holy Trinity hospital, Long Melford: a 16th-century almshouse* (Long Melford, 1995).

Williams, Samantha, *Poverty, gender and life-cycle under the English poor law, 1760–1834* (Woodbridge, 2011).

Wood, Andy, *The 1549 rebellions and the making of early modern England* (Cambridge, 2007).

—, *Riot, rebellion and popular politics in early modern England* (Basingstoke, 2002).

Wrigley, E.A., Davies, R.S., Oeppen, J.E., and Schofield, R.S., *English population history from family reconstitution, 1580–1837* (Cambridge, 1997).

Wrigley, E.A. and Schofield, R.S., *The population history of England, 1541–1871* (London, 1981).

Index